WITHDRAWN
UTSA LIBRARIES

D0783073

Streamlining Library Services

**What We Do,
How Much Time It Takes,
What It Costs,
How We Can Do It Better.**

Richard M. Dougherty

Scarecrow Press, Inc.
Lanham, Maryland • Toronto • Plymouth, UK
2008

SCARECROW PRESS, INC.

Published in the United States of America
by Scarecrow Press, Inc.
A wholly owned subsidiary of
The Rowman & Littlefield Publishing Group, Inc.
4501 Forbes Boulevard, Suite 200, Lanham, Maryland 20706
www.scarecrowpress.com

Estover Road
Plymouth PL6 7PY
United Kingdom

Library
University of Texas
at San Antonio

Copyright © 2008 by Richard M. Dougherty

All rights reserved. No part of this publication may be reproduced, stored in a
retrieval system, or transmitted in any form or by any means, electronic,
mechanical, photocopying, recording, or otherwise, without the prior
permission of the publisher.

British Library Cataloguing in Publication Information Available

Library of Congress Cataloging-in-Publication Data
Dougherty, Richard M.
  Streamlining library services : what we do, how much time it takes, what it
costs, and how we can do it better / Richard M. Dougherty.
    p. cm.
  Rev. ed. of: Scientific management of library operations. 2nd ed. 1982.
  Includes bibliographical references and index.
  ISBN-13: 978-0-8108-5198-6 (pbk. : alk. paper)
  ISBN-10: 0-8108-5198-9 (pbk. : alk. paper)
  1.   Library administration. I. Dougherty, Richard M. Scientific management
of library operations. II. Title.
  Z678.D6 2008
  025.1–dc22   2007040288

⊖™ The paper used in this publication meets the minimum requirements of
American National Standard for Information Sciences—Permanence of Paper
for Printed Library Materials, ANSI/NISO Z39.48-1992.
Manufactured in the United States of America.

Contents

Section Four: How Much Time It Takes

Section Five: How Much It Costs

Section Six: Post-Study Activities

Figures

Preamble

Recent years have been characterized by enormous tumult in our society—9/11, the war on terrorism, the threat of global warming, escalating health care costs, and the energy crunch have impacted all facets of our society. In the world of technology, the spectacular rise and equally spectacular fall of the dot.coms also symbolize the turbulence of recent years.

Until Google announced that it intended to digitize millions of volumes at a group of university libraries, it was safe to say that change in libraries hadn't grabbed many headlines, but that doesn't mean that changes in libraries haven't been dramatic. The explosive growth in the number and power of search engines coupled with the proliferation of full-text databases and networks illustrate the constant change with which libraries must now routinely deal.

Library administrators have been faced with many difficult and painful choices in recent years as budgets have remained persistently tight, and society and governments demand greater accountability among social institutions such as libraries. And even when and if the budget pendulum swings back, there will never be "enough" money. One way to free up staff time and dollar resources is to streamline processes and procedures, or better yet, get rid of existing operations that are redundant or unnecessary. I was particularly taken with a recent comment attributed to a Hewlett Packard official who observed: "If a thing is not worth doing, it is not worth doing well."[1]

While the demands for greater accountability and the lack of funds are strong incentives for finding ways to save time and money, there is also another compelling reason: the constant stream of new technological tools and the organizational changes these new tools spark that currently overwhelm so many library staff members. It seems like only yesterday that reference librarians were working with giant database vendors such as BRS and ORBIT, but today those companies are only a memory as staff routinely exploit full-text Web resources, and struggle to keep up with new advances in software and hardware. Was there ever a better time to step back and examine what staff are doing, and explore ways to improve operational efficiency and effectiveness in order to improve library services? Even a cursory examination is likely to reveal operations, and even policies, that are no longer valid or necessary. In a nutshell, saving the time and conserving the energy of busy library staff so that their attention can be focused on priority services and activities is what this new edition of *Scientific Management of Library Operations* (SMLO), now entitled *Streamlining Library Services* (SLS) is all about.

Note

1. Carol J. Loomis, "Why Carly's Big Bet Is Failing," *Fortune* 151, no. 3 (February 7, 2005): 55. The article was referring to part of HP's hardware operations. The hardware operations were barely making a profit. This raised the question of whether or not HP should continue that part of their business, or if they should spin it off.

Preface

I've learned over the years that very few librarians have traditionally placed a high priority on process analysis or in increasing the efficiency of operations. That does not mean that individual library staffs don't apply good old-fashioned common sense and adopt shortcuts to achieve efficiencies whenever possible. But librarianship is a service profession, not a bottom-line oriented business, and as such, librarians don't normally assign a high priority to efficiency of operations. The underlying theme of this book is that opportunities to improve daily jobs and enhance services are being overlooked every day.

While attitudes toward work simplification haven't changed a great deal since the second edition of this book appeared in 1982, the work environment has changed dramatically. In fact, it has been transformed. Advances in technology now drive change at a rapid pace, and keeping up is both expensive and time consuming. Tight budgets have made keeping up with technology especially difficult. And while some activities in libraries such as in-person ready reference and circulation of books and journals have declined, many libraries continue to report increases in the demand for services and resources. The rapid transformation from paper to digital documents is also driving changes in libraries. And who is to say what lies ahead? What developments will be the new drivers of change? We only know that the tide of change is not likely to recede any time soon.

I don't believe I'm overstating the situation when I say that the work environment has become very stressful. Many staff workers have mentioned to me that they feel almost overwhelmed by the unrelenting pace of change in all aspects of library operations. How many times does one hear plaints such as "How can I keep doing more and more with less and less? The stress is getting to me!"

Today the incentive for examining and streamlining library workflows and the processes and procedures that comprise them should be compelling, but that doesn't seem to be the case for many librarians. I remain convinced, however, that the streamlining of workflows will reduce stress in the workplace by eliminating unnecessary work and freeing human and dollar resources so that they can be used to improve library services. Yes, to my mind, analysis and streamlining of workflows make a great deal of sense.

Purpose of the Book

My objective in preparing this thoroughly revised edition is to present library managers and staff with the tools necessary to analyze and streamline library services. There are no magic bullets, but there are a variety of tools and techniques that can be applied to improve library operations. My purpose is to assist library staff in their efforts to identify what work is done, how much time it takes, and what it costs. I also want to provide information that can be used to analyze and interpret data, streamline library processes, and where appropriate, help to free dollar resources to initiate or enhance services that merit higher priority. Finally I offer tips on how to implement new activities and services, and how to manage the resultant organizational changes.

Intended Audience

I envision a broad audience for *Streamlining Library Services* (SLS). The message is equally relevant to librarians and staff in all types of libraries. There should be no exceptions. Those who administrate, conduct, or participate in studies should all find SLS useful. Moreover, staff whose work is analyzed will want to understand what is happening, and how they can benefit from the experience. I have intentionally tried to keep SLS straightforward and practical. The tools and ideas presented aren't difficult to apply.

How to Use the Book

I hope that readers will consult SLS whenever they discover that an activity, i.e., a system, service, process, or a procedure, doesn't seem to be working as intended. SLS is intended to serve as a guide to those who seek to improve library activities in order to introduce new services and manage change.

The topic of workflow analysis has become incredibly complex. While most of the tools and techniques featured in the second edition were drawn directly from the field of industrial management, today's process analysis also draws on social science and engineering specialties such as organizational psychology, management, organizational change, human computer interfaces (HCI), and innovation diffusion. What I have tried to do is to provide the basic information that will satisfy the needs of most library studies. I've also included a variety of leads to print and Web-based resources. As the reader will quickly grasp, there is a wealth of resources available to those who need to dig deeper into a specific topic or tool.

Basic Definitions

I've already used the terms workflow, process, procedure, and systems several times. Other terms that will be frequently used are "task," "operation," and "activities." While not complex terms, they do have specific meanings in the context of SLS:

- **Task**—in the context of work analysis describes a series of work steps that collectively comprise a procedure, e.g., adhering the label to the spine of a book. In some instances "operation" is used as a synonym.

- **Procedure**—a series of well-defined actions followed in a regular definite order, e.g., book labeling or shelf listing.

- **Process**—a series of related procedures. A process is almost always comprised of more than one well-defined procedure, e.g., cataloging process is comprised of a series of procedures, such as descriptive and subject cataloging, copy cataloging, shelf listing, etc.

- **System**—a combination of related processes and procedures organized into a complex whole, e.g., technical processes system.

- **Workflow**—a general way to describe a series of tasks, procedures, and processes; also denotes the flow of work performed.

- **Activities**—another generic term used to describe a series of processes such as reference services, book selection procedures, etc.

- **Efficient**—able to function well or achieve a desired result without waste.

- **Effective**—causing a result, especially the desired or intended result; one can be efficient and still be ineffective, e.g., reference questions may be answered quickly, but if the answers are wrong or incomplete, the service isn't effective.

Roots of the Book

The first two editions of *Scientific Management of Library Operations* were greatly influenced by the work of a small group of industrial management pioneers, and an even smaller group of librarians who successfully applied the tools and principles of scientific management to library operations and procedures in the years immediately preceding and following World War II. Notable among this group were Ralph R. Shaw, Joseph Wheeler, and Jewel Hardkopf who used the tools to analyze, simplify, and improve work methods in public, government, and academic libraries.[1]

As fate would have it, Ralph Shaw was Dean of the Rutgers School of Library Service when Fred Heinritz, my co-author of the first two editions, and I arrived on campus. Shaw's interest in "working smart" had already made an impact on the school. Shaw taught a course on scientific management for a while, but eventually one of his graduate students, Ted Hines, assumed the mantle from Shaw. Fred and I learned the basics of scientific management from Professor Hines. One assignment in the course was to conduct an actual time and motion study. Since I was working in the Linden Public Library as an intern, I asked permission to study the library's circulation system. The system in question was already pretty slick, and I didn't expect to find much to improve. What surprised me was how many improvements I was able to identify and recommend. It was this experience that hooked me on the potential of scientific management techniques and tools to improve library processes.

As luck would have it, Fred and I both accepted positions at the University of North Carolina, Chapel Hill, after our doctoral research had been completed. Fred joined the faculty in the library school, and I became head of the acquisitions department in the library system.

I found that many of the existing processes and procedures, while well defined, seemed circuitous and cumbersome. I quickly realized that here was a superb opportunity to test how well the tools of scientific management might contribute to improving the department's operations. A thorough analysis using flow charts, workflow diagrams, flow process charts, and several time analyses revealed a variety of ways the existing labyrinth of processes and procedures could be streamlined and simplified. Over the next few months, with the assistance of many full- and part-time staff in the department, new procedures and processes were gradually introduced. Productivity was greatly increased, and this was accomplished without staff working harder—they just worked smarter.

I also learned an important lesson that I've never forgotten: all levels of staff members, whether student assistants, support staff, or experienced professionals, have creative ideas to contribute on how to improve workflows. I also learned that more and more staff members were willing to volunteer their thoughts as they began to believe this "new guy with the spanking brand-new PhD" was really willing to listen, and more importantly, even accept their ideas. What the staff didn't fully appreciate was how much I needed their help. What I knew about acquisitions work in the beginning is hardly worth mentioning; I really needed their advice and suggestions as well as their cooperation. When I think back on those early days, I'm still impressed at the gains in productivity we were able to achieve working together. For example, bibliographic searching and order form processing and handling increased by over 40 percent with fewer staff involved in the actual work.

This experience convinced me that scientific management techniques and tools could be applied to a wide variety of library processes and procedures. Fred and I began talking about whether we could combine what we had learned at Rutgers with my on-the-job experience and his special interest in statistics and statistical methods. Since there was no existing library text on the subject, we contacted Ralph Shaw who was also president of Scarecrow Press about our idea. Would Scarecrow be interested in a book on scientific management in libraries? Even though we weren't particularly experienced, Shaw encouraged us and we were off and running.

The first edition of SMLO was published in 1966. SMLO, in library terms, proved to be a best seller, and in fact, a number of library schools began to use SMLO as a text. For a brief period Fred and I thought SMLO was going to make a meaningful impact on library operations, but that was not to be for a couple of reasons.

Scientific management, as an approach to management, had gone out of favor in the 1930s, and many people unfortunately continued to associate the philosophy of scientific management with the tools of analysis the pioneers of scientific management had developed.

Second, the late 1960s coincided with the dawning of the era of library automation. Library systems analysis was the term most often used to describe library processes and procedures. In retrospect Fred and I probably would have been smart to have entitled the book *Systems Analysis of Library Operations*. I believe the library world's fascination with the potential of computers and automated procedures contributed to the decline in interest of scientific management techniques and work simplification that occurred. Automation became the favored way to address problems dealing with processes and procedures. Managers seemed to assume that they could simply automate inefficiencies out of their processes. Computers processed data so much faster than their manual counterparts. It didn't seem to occur to managers that inefficiencies in manual processes and procedures were often simply perpetuated as inefficient automated processes and procedures. This phenomenon became known as "garbage in, garbage out." Fred and I thought it was a mistake, but the reality was that interest in scientific management faded as automation took hold.

At about the same time automation was being introduced to libraries, librarians, particularly front-line professionals in academic libraries, became increasingly interested in what became known as "participatory management." The younger generation of librarians, the boomers, wanted more say about how they were managed, and how decisions that affected them and library services were made. These librarians were chaffing from what they viewed as overly restrictive autocratic managers. We all know that enormous changes in the way libraries are managed have occurred since the beginning of the participative management movement of the 1970s.

Throughout the 1970s and 1980s many librarians continued to confuse the tools of scientific management with the philosophy associated with this school of management. I suppose this shouldn't have been surprising since most management writers of that period unanimously dismissed scientific management as an obsolete philosophy. Of course it was obsolete, but were the tools that the scientific management pioneers developed also obsolete? This failure to distinguish between the tools and the underlying philosophy used to frustrate the dickens out of Fred and me. My response then as now is the same: "tools are tools, not a philosophy." The tools of scientific management can be applied in any kind of organizational setting whether participatory, democratic, or autocratic. As is pointed out in the first chapter, it was the work of Edward Deming and his TQM movement that revived interest, and lent a patina of respectability to tools that had been developed over a half-century ago.

The second edition of SMLO, which appeared in 1982, added material on how to design a new system and organize systems projects. There was also greater recognition of ergonomics. But the tools of analysis remained largely the same, e.g., flow process and flow diagrams, etc. What had changed markedly between the first and second editions was the influence of automation.

Computer technology then as now was changing very rapidly. Online catalogs were already beginning to dot the library landscape. The mini-computer had replaced large central processors for some library applications, and microcomputers were beginning to make an impact. We suggested that more library operations would certainly be computerized in the 1980s. Boy, was that an understatement!

After the second edition of SMLO appeared, Fred and I developed a new set of interests, but because changes were occurring so dramatically, we decided not to undertake another writing project. Technological developments had overtaken interest in the tools of scientific management. Integrated library systems, networks, the Internet and the Web were dramatically transforming the library's work environment.

But while the environment had changed dramatically, I also discovered that many libraries continued to struggle with work processes and procedures. Paper didn't always disappear; in fact, there were complaints that paperwork had actually proliferated. Automated systems, while powerful and fast, occasionally had cumbersome inefficiencies built into their software. Changes were taking place so quickly, there wasn't always time to step back, reflect, and ask simple questions such as: "Do we still need to be doing this work, or, can we simplify this process?"

The New Edition

This third edition is written from a slightly different perspective than were the earlier editions. The first two editions assumed that process and procedural analyses were responsibilities that professional librarians should routinely embrace. This new edition doesn't make that assumption. While I continue to believe that efficiency and effectiveness of operations should always be everyone's professional priority, this edition assumes that most studies are undertaken only after a specific problem emerges. In a sense, I've taken more of a "point-of-need" approach in this new edition.

I've also intentionally placed more emphasis on how achieving greater operational efficiency and effectiveness can help enhance existing services or launch new, innovative services. That is really the reason why I changed the title of this edition to *Streamlining Library Services*. Previously the focus was on improving operations, now the key is improving operations in order to enhance services.

SLS has been tailored to address today's needs, and help readers to make important choices on how to streamline workflows, processes, and procedures. New to this edition is a chapter on managing organizational change. This material was added not only to assist managers who are implementing systems, but also to assist those who are responsible for introducing new services and who must navigate the effort through the staff turbulence that the changes often spawn. SLS is intended to be a practical guide—and hopefully an enjoyable read.

Note

1. Richard Logsden, who himself was an early advocate of applying time and motion techniques to library operations, published an informative account of how time and motion techniques were applied by librarians in the years immediately following World War II. Time and motion techniques were more popular among librarians than most people realize. Moreover, these techniques were used to study a wide variety of library processes and procedures. See Richard Logsden, "Time and Motion Studies in Libraries," *Library Trends* 2 (1954): 401-9.

Acknowledgements

The most difficult challenge I faced in preparing this new edition was to describe a work environment in libraries that has been almost totally transformed since the last edition appeared. This dramatic transformation got underway about the time I stepped down as Director of Libraries at the University of Michigan, and really gained momentum after I retired from the School of Information at the University. Even though I was actively consulting and conducting workshops, one painful fact of life I learned very quickly was how rapidly a retiree's knowledge base becomes obsolete.

Scarecrow encouraged Fred Heinritz and me to update *Scientific Management* on a number of occasions, but each time we made the attempt, we got bogged down. Finally, Fred told me he was packing it in, and was going to enjoy his retirement. He also suggested that I too turn my attention to other interests as in "Why don't you get a new life!"

I would have taken Fred's advice if it hadn't been for an invitation from Bernie Fradkin, then director of the College of DuPage Library, to organize a teleconference on virtual reference, a hot topic at the time. After some hesitation I finally agreed, but not without a great deal of trepidation. In addition to knowing very little about organizing a teleconference, I knew next to nothing about virtual reference.

The first program was an absorbing, nerve-wracking experience. It brought together three fascinating professionals who knew a great deal about virtual reference and its likely implications for libraries and reference service. Subsequent programs also brought together many terrific, and often opinionated, professional leaders who were, and still are, on the cutting edge of change. Over time these experts painted for me a vivid picture of the work environment in libraries. For me, gaining a clearer picture was key because the principles and techniques underlying the tools of analysis had largely remained the same. I was sufficiently encouraged to begin writing again, and once underway, it actually became fun because it afforded me an opportunity to dredge up stories, illustrations, and anecdotes that I had accumulated over the years.

Yes, I owe Bernie and all of the teleconference guests who have contributed to my education, a big "thank you." There are simply too many to acknowledge individually, but you know who you are. Thanks.

Many friends and former colleagues have filled in details when I discovered gaps in my knowledge. From the University of Michigan: Anne Beaubien, Bonnie Dede, Joan Gatewood, Bill Gosling, Brenda Johnson, Jean Loup, Barbara MacAdam, Lynn Marko, John Wilkin, and Shannon Zachary. I also received helpful advice and suggestions from Steven Bell (Temple University), Ed Rivenburgh (SUNY, Geneseo), Mary Ann Hodel (Orlando Public Library), Carol Ann Hughes (UC Irvine), Deborah Barreau (Catholic University), Buff Hirko (formerly head of the Virtual Library Network in Washington State), and Josie Parker and Eli Neuburger, both of the Ann Arbor District Library.

I want to extend a special thanks to the staff of 747-FAST, the document delivery service at the University of Michigan Library. Leif Bachman and his staff were wonderful. They tracked down a number of items that I couldn't easily locate. Their assistance was particularly appreciated because I quickly learned that databases are neither seamlessly linked, nor comprehensive. The problems I encountered were probably due to my own inadequacies, but clearly I could not have navigated the world of publications without the assistance of Leif and his staff.

There might be a temptation for readers to attribute some of my stories to developments at the University of Michigan, but that would be a mistake—I assiduously avoided drawing illustrations from my UM experiences. UM is a great library with a wonderful staff.

I also need to thank several people from Scarecrow Press. Former presidents Al Daub and Norman Horrocks kept encouraging me to make the effort. Shirley Lambert was particularly helpful in helping me get started, and more recently, Sue Eason and Martin Dillon have provided guidance and suggestions.

Emily Dougherty, my daughter, and an aspiring pastry chef, is also a gifted photographer. She is responsible for many of photos that appear in the book. Emily also filmed several procedures that I later analyzed frame by frame. Thank you sweetie for helping out your old man.

My heartiest thanks are extended to Laura Maki who is responsible for laying out the book and its many figures. This proved to be no trivial challenge even with the various software packages that are currently available.

Last but not least, my wife, Ann Dougherty, whose editing talents are absolutely essential. In fact, for the past thirty years she has torn apart (not always very gently) and put back together everything I have written in a more concise and cohesive fashion. This book wouldn't have reached final form without her.

If I've forgotten people who I should have thanked, I'm sorry. I've done the best my faulty memory permits.

—R.M.D.

Section One
Looking Backward, Looking Forward

Chapter One

The Roots of Scientific Management

Scope note: This chapter traces the development of the tools that served as the basis for the scientific management movement, discusses the reasons why the scientific management philosophy gradually went out of favor, and summarizes the contributions of W. Edward Deming. It was the work and influence of Deming that rekindled interest in process and work analysis, and the use of the tools and techniques originally developed by Frederick Taylor, Frank Gilbreth, and other pioneers of the scientific management movement. This chapter discusses how Deming's TQM philosophy and techniques were embraced by a number of libraries, but also presents several reasons why management techniques such as TQM seem to have a limited organizational life span.

Frederick Taylor (1856-1915), an engineer, is often referred to as the Father of the Scientific Management movement. Taylor studied the physical rather than the psychological aspects of work. This was true with the other pioneers as well. They were all chiefly interested in analyzing what was done; they were much less concerned about the psychological aspects of work—how workers were affected by the jobs they performed. Since many of the pioneers realized that workers were also humans and not machines, some advocates like Henry Gantt began to speak out against such a narrow approach to the study of work.

The immediate tangible gains achieved by applying scientific management principles were impressive, but unfortunately there were also reported incidents of abuse. Some managers employed scientific management techniques to increase efficiency, and once successful, subsequently increased worker production requirements. Such tactics proved to be extremely short-sighted because they sowed the seeds that created a generation of cynics toward scientific management.

Management scientists also felt that scientific management techniques were an overly mechanistic approach to solving work-related problems. But it was not until the labor movement gained momentum, and until research and experience increased the general understanding of the relationships among the physical, psychological, and sociological aspects of work, that the human side of management began to assume greater importance. It is safe to conclude that the rise of unionism, and the decline in interest in scientific management as a management philosophy are related.

A series of experiments conducted at the Hawthorne plant of the Western Electric Company between 1927 and 1932 helped to explode the myth that the workers were concerned only with the size of their pay checks.[1] The Hawthorne experiments revealed that the motivations of individuals or groups of workers are complex, and that there are many factors—physical, psychological, and social—that influence productivity. Money was only one of several factors.

Many of Taylor's closest associates made noteworthy contributions to the movement. Among them were Carl Barth, Horace Hathaway, Morris Cooke, and Henry Gantt.[2] Gantt is best known for the development of techniques for planning and scheduling work; organizational planners still use the principles of Gantt's charting techniques in planning and organizing projects. And, as just mentioned, Gantt was one of the earliest management scientists to focus his attention on the concerns of the worker.

Frank (1868-1924) and Lillian Gilbreth (1878-1972), who achieved a sort of accidental immortality via the best-selling book *Cheaper by the Dozen*, rank with Taylor as contributors to the development of scientific management philosophy and techniques. Early in their careers the Gilbreths became interested in the elimination of nonproductive motions. In order to perform their studies they devised and perfected the flow process chart. Frank Gilbreth always tried to achieve what he termed as the "one best method of doing a job." The Gilbreths' contributions resulted in improvements in many industries, and led to the development and refinement of such techniques as micromotion and the use of motion pictures to study work.

The tools that were developed by the pioneers didn't disappear. They became part of basic courses in industrial engineering where time and motion study is still regularly taught. I took such a course at Purdue as an undergraduate. I suppose this was one reason why the subject so intrigued me when I entered library school and came under the influence of Ralph Shaw.

It was the work and influence of W. Edward Deming that rekindled interest in process and work analysis, although his approach to process improvement was embedded in his philosophy of better quality control. His techniques came to be known as Total Quality Management (TQM).[3] At its core, TQM techniques strive to create a work environment that respects the contributions of staff, and acknowledges that most problems stem from faulty procedures and policies rather than uncaring or incompetent employees. In his *Out of Crisis*, Deming articulated his philosophy that became widely known as Deming's Fourteen Points.

Deming tried to convince America's top managers in the 1970s that quality control was important, but his ideas mostly fell on deaf ears. Japanese managers, however, were much more receptive to his ideas, and it wasn't too long before Japanese products began to replace their American counterparts on the shelves of department stores and in the showrooms of auto dealers. I'm sure that Deming never envisioned how his assistance to the Japanese auto industry would contribute to the demise of the U.S. auto industry years later. Not surprisingly, Deming became a management icon to the Japanese.

The more one learns about complex organizations, the clearer it becomes why the rules of a bureaucracy can so often stifle staff enthusiasm and cause staff talents to be underutilized. Take a look at the plight of many of today's public school teachers who want to try new teaching methodologies to bring innovation to the classroom. They are constantly precluded from doing so by rules and regulations—some imposed by administrations and some by restrictive labor contracts. It doesn't take long to realize what it means to struggle against the rigidity of organizations.

What Deming did, and did so masterfully, was to bring together a philosophy that emphasized staff involvement, and quality of product using many of the tools that had their roots in the work of Gilbreth, Taylor, and others. Deming clearly showed that the tools developed by the pioneers of scientific management could be employed in many types of work environments.

Quite a few libraries undertook TQM projects, and a number of success stories were reported in the literature. Scientific management tools worked well in analyzing work done in the context of TQM. But TQM, like zero-based budgeting and other so-called "management panaceas," was also a bit faddish and interest flourished for a short time and then died out. In part the problem was that too many organizations that had eagerly embraced TQM techniques soon found themselves bogged down during the implementation stages. I'm familiar with a couple of universities that made large investments in TQM programs, but achieved only marginal successes because too many faculty and staff hadn't bought into the objectives of the program.[4]

Some managers may have dismissed TQM when the influence of the Internet and Web resources became so pervasive. TQM produces organizational change incrementally, and while there is nothing inherently wrong with incremental change, organizations, including libraries, are now changing, or facing the prospect of change, at a pace that is much more dynamic than what can be expected from incremental changes. But ironically, the tools of TQM are as applicable today as when Deming first introduced TQM.

One of my objectives is to persuade readers that tools of analysis can be used to great advantage regardless of the organization's approach to management. The tools and techniques presented in SLS can be used to learn more about what we do in libraries, what the activities cost, and how much time is involved. Librarians can then follow up such analyses with programs and projects that will increase productivity, efficiency and effectiveness of what they do, and accomplish all this in ways that improve the day-to-day work life of library staff.

Notes

1. F. J. Roethlisberger and W. J. Dickson, *Management and the Worker* (Cambridge: Harvard University Press, 1939).

2. There is a large body of literature recounting the contributions of pioneers such as Taylor, the Gilbreths, Gantt, Barth, and others. One useful source for background information is Daniel A. Wren, *The Evolution of Management Thought,* 2nd ed. (New York: Wiley, 1979). One can also find biographic sketches of the pioneers at http://www.wikipedia.com (17 May 2007).

3. There is an extensive body of literature on the subject of TQM. Deming himself wrote one of the most influential treatises on the topic. *See* W. Edward Deming, *Out of the Crisis* (Cambridge: MIT Center for Advanced Engineering Study, 1985).

4. Those interested in TQM might wish to consult a collection of essays that appeared while TQM was at its height of popularity among librarians. *See* Rosanna M. O'Neil, *Total Quality Management in Libraries: A Sourcebook* (Englewood, Colo.: Libraries Unlimited, 1994).

Chapter Two

The Impact of Technology: Environments, Productivity, and Staff Roles

Scope note: Technology has served as the driving force behind significant changes in library systems and services. This chapter points out how technology has made possible noteworthy increases in library productivity, how technology and changes in student behavior have prompted libraries to adopt a more open approach to organizing library services, and how these changes are leading to more changes in jobs and the roles library staff play. In such a dynamic environment it is especially important for libraries to examine workflows and activities.

The impact of technology has gone a long way toward transforming the physical environment in which libraries operate and the services they offer. The changing nature of these processes and services all underscore the importance and potential benefit of analyzing library workflows and policies.

Technology and Library Environments

It wasn't too many years ago that libraries possessed a sort of quasi-monopoly on information. If a student or other information seeker needed information he/she had little choice but to visit a library. However, the growing availability of electronic resources, virtual reference services, laptop computers, and wireless communication networks have bestowed information seekers with enormous freedoms. One might say that the patrons are now in control of their information world.

Since information seekers can shop the Web for the information and services they need, there is less incentive to trek to the library. The wide availability of wireless connections in classrooms, dorms, student centers, and in local Starbucks, Barnes & Noble, Borders, or cyber cafes further lessens the need for students to visit their libraries.

These and other developments have prompted librarians to thoroughly rethink how their library service areas are physically organized. This rethinking led many libraries to adopt a new service model commonly known as an "information or library commons."[1] A commons area can be described as a mixed-use space that easily accommodates those who wish to collaborate, seek introspection and quiet, or wish to use a range of technological tools. Among the services that are typically offered are face-to-face peer-learning consultants, course-specific workshops, writing support, and programs to teach information and technology literacy. All of these services are designed to help students learn the process of information inquiry.

The overall objective of a commons area is to accommodate a variety of needs and tastes and to make patrons comfortable, thus the huge influx of café facilities in libraries. In the long run libraries are striving to create spaces that will gain favor with the multitasking millennial student. This is true of academic libraries as well as public libraries.

Not only have service offerings been expanded, there are numerous examples of libraries providing expanded access to new tools such as OCLC's Fiction Finder Project, RLG's RedLightGreen, ProQuest's Smart Search, Elsevier's Scopus, Talis's Whisper, and Endeca's ProFind.[2] These discovery tools have greatly enhanced the accessibility and availability of information.

Other examples of how libraries have responded to advances in technology are growth in virtual reference services; collaboration with faculty to teach information literacy; more involvement in choosing resources and managing licenses; programs to collect and digitize archival materials; and finally, creating and maintaining digital repositories. The Google Book Search project that strives to digitize all or parts of the collections of major university and research libraries is also a significant effort that could have far-ranging implications for publishers, scholars, and librarians.

Now a new technological revolution is unfolding. Some characterize this new era as Web 2.0. The Web 2.0 environment features a range of new tools and services such as MySpace, Flickr, wikis, and del.icio.us; students especially are flocking to them. These new tools and services allow students to socialize and collaborate very easily. But the Web 2.0 era also refers to the need for librarians to seek input from students and to be more responsive to their changing needs and preferences.[3]

Dempsey Lorcan of OCLC suggests that this new era makes it especially important that librarians focus on how students work, and how librarians can save students time. He characterizes this need as the library "getting in the flow" of the user.[4]

Keeping in mind that libraries must now compete for the business of those seeking information and materials, this imperative for me raises the issue of customer service.[5] Providing open and inviting environments and enhancing services aren't necessarily sufficient if service quality leaves patrons frustrated or angry. Unfortunately too many librarians still don't fully appreciate how poor customer service can negatively affect a library's image among patrons.[6]

The point to keep in mind is that excellence in customer service is more than projecting a responsive attitude; it also involves doing whatever is possible to eliminate red tape and unnecessary procedures and policies. The imperative of excellent customer service is just another reason why librarians need to review and analyze all processes and procedures that affect the quality of public service.

Technology and Productivity

Now we need to turn our attention to how technology has increased and continues to increase the productivity of librarians and how it impacts the roles of library staff.

The early versions of some automated modules, i.e., serials, circulation, acquisitions, etc., didn't always lead to significantly greater productivity. For example, some of the automated procedures supported by early versions of NOTIS weren't particularly efficient.[7] I recall analyzing some of the NOTIS serials procedures at a local library, and marveling at how cumbersome some of the subroutines seemed to be. The former manual system was quicker and easier to operate, but the accuracy and availability of statistics had been vastly improved, and over time the automated procedures were streamlined.

I also recall studying procedures at a library that had recently adopted an early version of OCLC's interlibrary lending system. The availability of OCLC's immense database and supporting procedures certainly added to the capabilities of ILL, but in this instance, use of the system had added to the library's operational complexity. In part, the problem stemmed from the library's failure to integrate properly its local procedures with those of OCLC's system. When the anticipated increases in productivity didn't occur, management was greatly disappointed. At first the unit head blamed deficiencies in the OCLC system, but a careful analysis clearly revealed that the culprit was a home-grown MIS tracking system that was being used, and which was the pride of the unit head. This MIS tracking system was very slow and cumbersome; its inferior performance was in effect negating many of the advantages of using OCLC. Changes were made and productivity improved almost immediately.

While some of the earliest automated system modules were cumbersome, there is no doubt that even the earliest of automated circulation systems permitted easy check out and discharge of materials, and production of overdue notices, which led to significant increases in productivity and patron services. But I believe the real breakthrough in productivity occurred when shared cataloging gained traction among librarians. Moreover, the shift from card to online catalogs enabled a whole range of cataloging operations to be automated and this made a significant difference. These changes made it possible to decrease the number of professional catalogers a library needed, to increase the roles of support staff in the creation of bibliographic records, to eliminate many varieties of manual card filing and checking operations, and perhaps most important, to share authority records.

The newer integrated library systems have further streamlined aspects of cataloging, acquisitions, and authority work. Furthermore, public services have been enhanced and extended by the availability of chat software, federated searching systems, and the rapidly expanding availability of digital resources.

Other enhancements include circulation modules that permit patrons to reserve and renew books online from their homes; RFID tags that permit a level of inventorying collections that heretofore was impractical; and ILL software that enables libraries to eliminate most, if not all, their paper records.

These improvements are but a sampling of how technology has increased productivity in libraries. Productivity increases have helped library administrators grapple with the tight budgets of recent years. For example, increased productivity in technical services has made it possible for libraries to migrate staff gradually and steadily from technical service units into public service activities where demands for service are increasing at a time when additional staff can't be appointed.

I believe the adoption of technology by librarians has been quite a remarkable accomplishment, especially by a profession with a conservative, risk-adverse reputation. I've worked with many librarians, particularly those who were mid-career and beyond, who didn't choose librarianship because it was technologically oriented, but because it was service based and oriented toward literature and learning. For some, librarianship has changed almost beyond recognition in recent years. No wonder so many librarians have expressed to me their feelings of being organizationally disoriented. But in spite of our conservative nature as a profession, we need to pat ourselves on the back because librarians have always been one of the early adapters of emerging technologies all the way back to microfilm, punch-card supported systems in circulation and technical services, and later photocopiers, fax machines, and wireless technology.

Technology and Staff Roles

As already noted technological advances coupled with new public service concepts has led to significant changes in many jobs and the roles that staff play. Using the media to help students to become information literate, and working with students and faculty to navigate the Web, are excellent examples of activities in which library staff are now routinely engaged. Additionally, as more and more routine library work is automated, the lines of responsibility between professionals and support staff have become further blurred. The shifting of roles and responsibilities from professionals to support staff is certainly not a new trend; for example, copy catalogers and reference assistants have gradually assumed more and more tasks that were previously strictly "professional." It's true, however, that technology has greatly accelerated this trend.

The roles of library staff are also being impacted by the greater complexity of library systems and the growing need for collaboration within or among libraries. Resource sharing, preserving, and digitizing collections are three examples. In such instances support staff frequently find themselves working side by side with professional librarians. The bottom line is that the pervasive role of technology only underscores the importance of analyzing workflows, processes, and jobs.

Notes

1. Garten and Williams have succinctly described how libraries are responding to new patron needs and demands. Their piece discusses how use of space is changing to meet new needs. *See*

Edward D. Garten and Delmus E. Williams, "Repurposing Older Libraries for New Times: Creating New Learning Space," *Library Issues* 27, no. 2 (March 2006). Another very useful report presents an overview that compares the approaches that several libraries have taken in creating information commons. Libraries in both the United States and Canada are profiled. The author explores their missions, features, and strengths and weaknesses. *See* Laurie A. MacWhinnie, "The Information Commons: The Academic Library of the Future," *Portal: Libraries and the Academy* 3, no. 2 (April 2003): 241-57. Another article dealing with information commons reports on the use of focus groups to collect data regarding patrons' needs and interests in the library. This information was used to design new physical spaces in the library. *See* Britt Anna Fagerheim and Sandra J. Weingart, "Using Focus Groups to Assess Student Needs," *Library Review* 54, no. 9 (2005): 524-30.

2. North Carolina State University Library recently announced its new catalog based on a technology developed by the Endeca Corporation. More information about this development can be found at: http://www.lib.ncsu.edu/news/libraries.php?p=1998&more=1 (17 May 2007). By the time SLS appears in print it is very likely that other libraries will have adopted this new approach to providing information about local collections. The latest information can be found at http://www.lib.ncsu.edu/endeca/ (6 December 2007). While it is risky to cite specific products because the list is likely to become quickly dated, it's important to remember that librarians have been and will continue to provide new tools and services as they become available.

3. One article describes a Web 2.0 service as "Any service, physical or virtual, that successfully reaches users, is evaluated frequently, and makes use of customer input..." And libraries offering Web 2.0 type services qualify as Library 2.0. *See* Michael E. Casey and Laura C. Savastinuk, "Library 2.0: Service for the Next-Generation Library," *Library Journal* 131, no. 14 (1 September 2006): 40-42. I couldn't agree more with the authors about the need to obtain input from patrons, but the authors are in effect putting old wine in new bottles. The need to obtain input and adjust to new patron needs has long been advocated by market researchers and advocates of the Learning Organization. Maybe this new nomenclature will be more successful in communicating with New Generation librarians.

4. Dempsey Lorcan has offered some provocative and insightful observations about the changing behaviors of students. See http://www.ariadne.ac.uk/issue46/dempsey (17 May 2007).

5. I prefer to use the terms "patron" or "user" to describe those who use and benefit from library resources and services, but when referring to the specific topic of customer service, I use the term "customer" for patron because customer is the term normally used by market researchers.

6. I realize mentioning the issue of customer service can raise the hackles of public service librarians who believe they are already offering first-rate services. They don't like being told that there is a need to improve customer service, and some especially bridle at being told that they might have to attend a customer-service training program. Regardless of reactions, excellence in service is absolutely essential if academic and public librarians are going to continue to attract young people as patrons.

7. NOTIS was one of the pioneer integrated library systems developed by the systems staff at Northwestern University Library for use by the library's staff. NOTIS was eventually spun off and marketed to other libraries.

Section Two
Diagnosing Problems and Preparing for a Study

Chapter Three

Identifying Targets of Opportunity

Scope note: The automation of library operations coupled with the wide-spread use of integrated library systems has led some librarians to conclude that automation has obviated the need to examine existing activities. This is an incorrect conclusion. This chapter presents briefly a variety of activities that should be viewed as possible candidates for review and analysis, particularly when the library spends significant resources to support that activity. Numerous candidates ranging from reference, cataloging, acquisitions, and ILL to preservation and digitization projects are cited.

Identifying targets of opportunity for analysis in libraries is easy because so many library services and activities are based on a labyrinth of processes, procedures, and policies. While we would like it to be otherwise, many existing processes and procedures are carried out inefficiently in terms of costs and effort expended. Even worse, there is work that could be entirely eliminated if we were more willing to question why the activity is needed at all. This is true even in this era of the integrated library system.

Integrated library systems have certainly transformed most library workflows. Most of the changes represent advances but not always. Lots of files and forms have been combined and/or eliminated through the use of multi-purpose databases. But as I noted in the previous chapter, there are occasionally automated processes and procedures that appear to be less efficient than their manual counterparts. One reason often cited is that it is difficult for a local library to alter a procedure that is embedded in a packaged integrated library system. A recent form of recognition that automated procedures and manual operations don't necessarily dovetail smoothly has been the establishment of an engineering specialty known as Human Computer Interface (HCI). These specialists strive to create smoother interactions between workers and computer-based systems. We will mention the work of HCI specialists in greater detail in Chapter 8.

Working in collaborative environments has also grown in significance. Shared cataloging, resource sharing, and preservation are traditional examples, whereas joint purchase agreements involving licenses, and digitization projects are more recent additions to the list of collaborative activities. The common factor of these activities is that they are either too complex and/or too costly for libraries to take on individually. Libraries must work together in order to succeed. And if libraries are working together, they will require new workflows, processes, procedures, and policies in order to create the necessary infrastructures. It just makes good common sense to examine closely the activities that undergird cooperative and collaborative projects.

Today most activities are heavily dependent on the use of technology and software products. They are almost always complex; none of them should be newly introduced or revamped without careful planning and thought. They include:

- creating new reference structures that effectively accommodate both Web-based information resources and traditional reference services;

- providing access to a proliferation of electronic products while maintaining a level of access to print resources that is acceptable to local patrons;

- acquiring electronic products and providing access to electronic publications that require the negotiation of licenses;

- gearing up to support distant education-related information services and information literacy programs;

- judging the appropriateness of outsourcing activity;

- reengineering work flows and jobs and adjusting job assignments in order to create efficient and effective interfaces between outsourced activities and local procedures;

- striving to find an effective balance between commercial document delivery services and traditional interlibrary loan lending and borrowing;

- providing ongoing training for staff and patrons to use new and upgraded software and electronic products;

- implementing new integrated systems which require extensive retraining and adjustment; and

- creating, maintaining, and supporting networks of wireless PCs.

In the last few years I've conducted numerous workshops on how to analyze and streamline processes and procedures. I've been impressed by the number of activities participants have been able to identify as candidates for analysis and improvement. Let's briefly examine some of the other activities that are often cited as contenders for analysis.

Reference-Related Activities

Web-based resources and the technologies that support various forms of digital reference are causing libraries to rethink how their information services are provided. New operating environments are changing the way support activities are organized and work is performed. More librarians are involved in various forms of information literacy programs. Lots of questions are being asked: Who uses reference and for what purposes? Are there differences in how reference is used by in-person information seekers and those who are remote from the desk? What time of the day is information sought? What obstacles to use does a patron encounter? What activities do individual staff members perform on a day-to-day basis? What duties require professional competencies? How have the underlying processes and procedures changed?

Reference/Information Desk Organization and Staffing

What activities actually occur at the reference desk? How do staff members spend their time while at the desk? Are professional librarians spending too much time answering questions that might be classified as directional or ready reference? Is it the philosophy of the library that a professional handle all questions? How much time is consumed in support of different activities? There are many other relevant questions that could have been posed.

Evaluating New Services

As more and more staff and dollar resources are committed to innovative forms of reference such as chat and virtual reference, the pressures to assess and evaluate these new services will increase.

Document Delivery Activities

The use of databases and the retrieval and delivery of documents, either at the desk or via the Web, fax, or mail requires a variety of handling procedures. What are the copyright handling policies? How is compliance assured? Must forms be processed? Are they well designed? Have document-handling procedures been well thought out? Are they efficient? Is every procedure *really necessary?* Who is doing the actual work? Are staff members being used effectively?

Layout of Work Areas

Is the workspace organized so that a reference specialist is able to work effectively with a patron who has requested information? How does one accommodate the needs of patrons who approach the desk, and those who are remote from it? How can work areas be designed to minimize the movement of staff and patrons?

Use of Library's Web Site

Who uses the Web site? For what purposes are they using it? What problems do patrons encounter? How can the use of the library's Web page be enhanced?

Processing of Documents

Are there still paper documents that must be processed? For example, updates to loose-leaf services, handbooks, and directories? How is this done? Who does it? Can this work be streamlined or eliminated entirely?

Other Activities Related to Reference

Scheduling at the reference desk; making appointments for personalized reference; special check out of reference materials; collecting meaningful reference statistics; database use statistics; dealing with printer malfunctions; photocopy jams or refilling printers that run out of paper; locating microfilm materials; conducting trials of new databases.

Cataloging

Beginning with the appearance of OCLC in the 1970s, cataloging operations have been in a constant state of flux. OCLC copy cataloging prompted libraries to analyze their cataloging procedures. Many libraries soon reorganized routines, such as the creation of copy cataloging units. During this period we began to hear more and more about catalogers doing only original work. We also became more conscious about the real costs of original cataloging. A more recent trend is outsourcing cataloging work to a third party vendor in order to reduce costs, to improve processing turn-around times, and to serve as a catalyst for organizational change, e.g., reassigning catalogers to other duties.

Copy Cataloging

Cataloging with copy is designed to speed the flow of new acquisitions through technical services and onto the shelves. This work can involve both professional and support staff. How the jobs and procedures are organized can have a major impact on costs and performance. This is an activity that merits careful study.

Outsourcing of Cataloging

When does outsourcing make sense for a library? Would outsourcing be attractive, if existing in-house procedures were efficiently organized? As Deming always asserted, inefficient activities are more often due to inefficient procedures and policies than to non-performing staff.

Cataloging of Digital Data

What is involved in such activities? What can be done to ensure their economic viability? What existing procedures need to be modified? Who should perform which tasks? No library can afford to do all that it would like to do in the digital realm; how can work be better organized; should the library be collaborating with others?

Activities Related to Cataloging

Database maintenance, shelf listing, CD-ROM preparation, new book preparation, cataloging materials in a shared database—these are all activities that can consume considerable time and attention; moreover, most of them involve processes and procedures that lend themselves to analysis.

ILB and ILL

Budgetary constraints have forced libraries to rely more heavily on the resources of other libraries. Since ILB/ILL processes and procedures can be quite complicated, these activities should be prime targets for analysis.[1] Documenting how forms and materials are handled and the distances traveled by staff can produce some startling results. Since there are software packages available, such as ILLiad, OCLC's interlibrary management software package, libraries, particularly those that maintain active ILB/ILL services, ought to be able to eliminate most if not all of their paper files.

Interface Between Paper and Electronic Files

How does one interface digital files with paper-based files? Ideally there shouldn't be many paper-based files still in use, but that is not always the case. It is worthwhile checking to see that unnecessary paper-based files haven't lingered beyond their useful life.

Accounting and Bookkeeping Procedures

ILL accounting and bookkeeping is often complicated because of adherence to institutional policies. I've known libraries to spend $10 for every $5 it collects. Obviously this is a false economy. Handling of invoices and related documents cannot only be time consuming but also nonproductive. Are records necessary; who maintains the files; can paper files be eliminated entirely?

ILL/ILB Tracking Systems

It is often advantageous to introduce an ILL/ILB tracking system to track the status of a transaction at any given time. Such capabilities have long been a staple for such companies as UPS and Fed-Ex. A few years ago some libraries created their own local versions of tracking systems, but these weren't always efficient; some even led to delays in handling transactions. Fortunately, today ILL modules in most integrated systems allow for automatic updates. Tracking systems can also be used to monitor workloads and performance, e.g., the average time required to transmit a borrowing request via U.S. mail or e-mail, or the time required to acquire a requested book. Since existing library ILL software packages now offer tracking capabilities, homegrown MIS tracking systems should be a thing of the past. If one still exists in your library, consider that a red flag.

Reciprocal Borrowing Arrangements

Groups of libraries or even entire states are adopting various programs to allow expanding the sharing of resources. It is important to make certain that such arrangements don't inject unnecessary rules and regulations. Hopefully the paperwork can be avoided through the use of shared or networked integrated systems.

Selection and Acquisition of Print and Electronic Resources

The acquisition of print monographs and serial publications including periodicals and continuations often involves complicated procedures and considerable materials handling. These procedures can offer opportunities to streamline operations. For example, each branch in a decentralized public library system selects titles independent of other branches; as a result, orders are placed and received at different times. This practice makes it very difficult for the library to enjoy the economies of scale in cataloging and processing items without delaying some of the submitted orders. This illustration also highlights how the actions of one unit can unintentionally impact the performance of another unit.

Approval Plans

The handling of approval plans shouldn't be taken for granted. Poorly developed profiles or the excessive use of approval slips can lead to wasteful activities. Or, the use of approval plans from multiple vendors, if not carefully coordinated, can result in either overlap or gaps among the plans and lead to staff confusion.

Ordering New Materials

Fortunately most integrated library systems allow for online ordering of new materials. But even with automated systems, print materials must be moved from workstation to workstation once they are received. Decisions also have to be made about how material is acquired, and how it will be handled once received. When and whether blanket orders, approval plans, or individual orders be utilized? The handling procedures for approval plans and title-by-title purchases are quite different, e.g., payment routines. Moreover, the way the workflows are organized can materially affect throughput. For example, some libraries hold up books when an invoicing problem is discovered. Others let problem books flow into cataloging and on to patrons without incurring any further delay. This last example also underscores how a single policy can influence overall operational performance.

Electronic Resources

So far I have focused attention on print publications, but we all know that the growth in popularity of electronic publications and online resources has been remarkable. There are now many academic libraries that spend sizeable portions of their serials budget on electronic formats. The growing popularity of digital subscriptions raises a new set of issues. What are the interfaces between the print and digital versions; what are the local handling procedures; how is selection coordinated among units; what are the relations between the local library and its vendors; how are payments, claims, etc. handled; is there a policy regarding canceling print editions when a digital version is available? As libraries become less print oriented, there will be a variety of processes and policies that need to be carefully analyzed and reviewed.

Licensing

Dealing with licenses and licensing has become an important and very intricate activity. Some libraries have created special units; others have assigned the work to reference or acquisitions staff. Dealing with licenses is a specialty that can require considerable knowledge about contracts, contract law, copyrights, etc. Persons responsible for licenses need to be sensitive to how an individual license might impact public services or the operation of a local network. Processing a license isn't the same as ordering a new book or journal subscription. Drastically different handling procedures are needed. Here also is an example of a set of issues that suggests a multi-unit line of attack to decision making may be the appropriate approach.

Preservation and Scanning

Even when preservation was limited to microfilming only, the necessary handling processes could be complicated and time consuming, and often costly. Now that a growing number of libraries are actively involved with digitizing materials for purposes of preservation or creating digital collections, the amount of time devoted to these activities has greatly increased. Are the handling procedures efficient? Is the selection process rational? Since inspections can be frequent, are all of them necessary? Once again, there may be plenty of opportunities to streamline workflows.

Weeding and Withdrawals

More and more libraries are either weeding or withdrawing volumes from active collections as space is exhausted. Like preservation and scanning itself, the selection and review processes can become expensive activities. Withdrawals or transfers also require one-time record maintenance.

The increased availability of texts in electronic formats also raises retention issues. Once an electronic version is available, should the print copy be retained, sent to remote storage, or even discarded? The course of action selected will affect record keeping, and will also have space implications. Of course, before any decisions are made questions of copyright may need to be resolved. This is another illustration of how policy and resultant workflows are intertwined; workflows should always reflect carefully crafted policies. The bottom line is that all types of weeding and withdrawal processes should be carefully planned.

Gift Acceptance and Handling

Here is another activity that involves not only workflow analysis but also policy analysis. Many libraries traditionally accepted gifts of marginal value in order to maintain good relations between themselves and their donors, but as costs of processing and retention have increased, these libraries have begun to ask objectively "Is the item worth the cost of adding it to the collection?" This is an important question because gift acceptance and handling are time consuming and costly.

Circulation

There are myriad procedures that comprise an automated circulation system. The introduction of RFID technology offers new opportunities to speed up charge-outs and check-ins. There are also numerous ancillary procedures that may require handling of books or processing forms, e.g., registration of patrons, processing fines, placing reserves and holds. Other circulation activities that consume time, dollars, and energy are reshelving books, locating and removing books from the shelf, shelf-reading, conducting inventories, placing and returning reserves, etc. Again, RFID technology may offer opportunities that heretofore were not available. Since circulation often represents the "face of the library to the public" and so much time and money is involved with circulation activities, it makes sense to review how procedures are working, how well they interface with automated procedures, and whether or not existing policies are in harmony with the library's public service objectives.

Administrative

There is an almost endless list of administrative activities that might qualify as candidates for review and analysis.

Accounting and Bookkeeping

Keeping records for all types of purchases; handling time and pay records for students and hourly staff.

Hiring Process and Procedures

Many people mention the delays that occur in the hiring of new staff, regardless of the category of staff involved, e.g., student assistants, library assistants, professionals, specialists, etc. Since such procedures may be complex and involve lots of paper, a review of what happens during a hiring process can reap real benefits.

Performance Appraisals

There is frequently considerable paper handling associated with staff performance appraisals. There is also the added requirement of maintaining confidentiality of records. This is often a process that is worth reviewing.

Training

All sorts of training programs are necessary; e.g., new staff, faculty, and students in how to use new systems, software packages, and databases. There is also a need to keep current staff up to date with new developments. Specialized training programs such as tours and instruction for ESL students are needed. A lot of work is required in planning and executing training programs. There are numerous ways to get bogged in procedures and paperwork.

Email and Blogs

Special mention needs to be given to the use of email communication and the creation of blogs. With regard to email there are really two issues. First, the volume of email has become enormous. Staff members need to be encouraged, if not given specific instructions, on how to handle email efficiently. Second, there is also the policy issue of what is an appropriate or inappropriate use of email.[2] This matter can sometimes get sticky if a library's administration appears to be too strict. The important point is that there needs to be clear policy.

Don't let blogs get out of hand. Blogs are easy to create, but they can gradually begin to consume a great deal of staff time and attention. What is the situation in the library? Have blogs become common? Is the time spent maintaining blogs commensurate with the benefits they derive?

Other Administrative Support Activities

Scheduling meeting room use; planning staff meetings; building maintenance procedures; emergency procedures; patron satisfaction measures; mail delivery and processing; getting travel requests funded; designing an efficient voice mail system; ordering supplies for entire library; use of paper-based forms and computer templates. These are all important support activities that can absorb a surprising amount of time and money.

Notes

1. A group of libraries that decides to undertake a formal ILL/ILB resource-sharing arrangement would be wise to examine relevant workflows at all of the participating libraries before new workflows and processes are introduced.

2. The potential for streamlining email routines is enormous if staff members are instructed on how to use email effectively. One site I found particularly useful was: Pace Productivity, Inc., *How to Use E-mail Effectively*, http://www.getmoredone.com/tips5.html (17 May 2007).

Chapter Four

Identifying the Problem: Diagnostic Tools

Scope note: It is essential to secure agreement on the causes of a problem before undertaking any study. It is very easy to focus on symptoms rather than the root causes. This chapter presents a series of tools and techniques that are designed to pinpoint problems.

When workflow-related problems arise it is very important to identify the root cause(s). It is very easy to fall into the trap of confusing a symptom with the real cause. Several years ago I misdiagnosed the cause of a problem, and if my mistake hadn't been discovered, we would have pursued the wrong course of action. Even though this incident occurred some time ago, it is still relevant, and illustrates the importance of making every effort to identify the real cause of a problem before acting.

My story has to do with an acquisitions department. We had been receiving lots of complaints from faculty that RUSH orders were not being handled expeditiously. Unfortunately this situation was causing faculty who actually ordered books to openly criticize the library. Initially they applied pressure on the acquisitions librarian who in turn put more pressure on the ordering staff. Luckily one staff member, a student assistant no less, did some investigating on his own. He discovered that quite a few of the titles requested RUSH weren't being picked up at the circulation desk. He contacted a few faculty acquaintances, and inquired why they hadn't picked up the titles after they had received notifications that they had arrived. What he learned was that these faculty were ordering titles RUSH because they were so dissatisfied with the handling time for routine orders. They thought that by ordering RUSH they would get their books quicker even if they didn't need them as RUSH items. In fact what they were doing unintentionally was bogging down the entire system. What was needed was not to speed up the handling of RUSH orders, but to improve the procedures for handling routine orders so that credibility with faculty could be restored. In time faculty learned that they didn't need to order books RUSH in order to beat the system.

Bringing library staff and faculty together to discuss the situation might have been another way to identify the real issue. Organized focus-group sessions would have probably brought to light why so many books were being ordered RUSH. Faculty would have had an opportunity to register their complaints, and it wouldn't have surprised me if one of the faculty participants even bragged about how he had gotten around his frustrations.

Focus Groups

Focus groups are designed to explore peoples' perceptions, feelings, and views about different products and services. Focus groups elicit beliefs, emotions, and ideas that are difficult to glean from survey data. Focus groups rely on open-ended questions to generate discussion. The questions used in focus-group sessions are usually predetermined and carefully sequenced. A typical focus-group session may include between 12 and 23 people. A typical session will last for two hours. Most studies that rely on focus groups should include 3 to 10 groups to ensure that the full range of views and opinions are put on the table. It is important to invite participants who are knowledgeable about the product or service to be explored. A skilled moderator should conduct each focus group.

In libraries there has been a tendency to cut corners in order to save money. Saving money is a laudable objective, but in the case of focus groups, cutting corners invites skewed or shallow results. For example, if a member of the staff conducts the interviews, or sits in the room to observe the proceedings first hand, the tone of the conversations will be affected. There will be a greater tendency for subjects to say what he/she believes the library wants to hear rather than being candid.

The literature on how to organize and conduct focus group is rich.[1] The Web also serves as a rich resource for information; I was able to locate very quickly the names of several organizations that conduct focus groups as well as a variety of free resources.

Finally, focus groups can be used for a variety of purposes in addition to problem identification. For example, several libraries used student focus groups to gain a better sense of student preferences and needs as part of their planning for information commons.[2]

Brainstorming

This technique was developed by Alexander F. Osborn, a principal of the New York advertising agency Batten, Barton, Durstine and Osborn.[3] Osborn coined the term to mean using the brain to creatively storm a problem. Brainstorming remains one of the most effective techniques for identifying problems and creating resourceful alternatives.[4]

The sole concern of brainstorming is idea generation, not idea evaluation. A group of 6 to 8 staff members can be presented with a problem and asked to identify as many potential solutions as possible.[5] When assembling a group, make every effort to avoid supervisor and supervisee relationships; in fact, try to avoid any relationship in which one person might intentionally or unintentionally intimidate another. This is important because brainstorming is based on the premise that when people interact in an unrestrained setting, creative ideas are generated, and as one person generates an idea, it serves to stimulate the thinking of others that in turn stimulate still more ideas. Such exchanges are often contagious, creating an atmosphere of free discussion and spontaneous thought. The objective is to generate as many ideas as possible in the belief that the greater the number of ideas, the greater the likelihood of generating a course of action that will be helpful or even innovative. The four rules governing brainstorming sessions are:

- Criticism is prohibited. Judgment of ideas must be withheld until all ideas have been generated. Experience shows that criticism inhibits the free flow of ideas and group creativity.
- "Freewheeling" is welcome. The wilder and further out the ideas the better. It is easier to "tame down" ideas than to "think them up."
- Quantity is desired. The greater the number of ideas generated, the greater the likelihood of an outstanding solution.
- Combination and improvements are sought. In addition to contributing ideas of their own, members are encouraged to suggest how the ideas of others can be improved, or how two or more ideas can be combined into still another idea.

Brainstorming sessions usually last from 30 minutes to an hour. Group members should be given a one-page summary of the problem a couple of days in advance of the session. The advance notice gives staff an opportunity to think about the subject of the session on their own. The summary should include some background information and examples of the kinds of ideas desired. Even a 30-minute session is likely to generate over 50 ideas. Most ideas will prove to be impractical or off-target, but almost always a few will merit serious consideration.

I've personally benefited from ideas generated from groups of staff and students. I still vividly recall a series of brainstorms with groups of students. We wanted students to speak frankly about what they liked and disliked about our services, and about how we could improve our service offerings. We found that there were a lot of things we were doing right, but we also learned that many students assiduously avoided the library, coming only "when they had to." This attitude was not welcome news because we knew the library was beginning to compete with other campus agencies for the attention of students. Two immediate actions stemmed from the sessions: First, we expanded group study areas. Second, we introduced a much more permissive food and drink policy.

Providing participants with some key headings before beginning a brainstorming session often helps a group to think more systematically about a problem. This approach can be especially helpful when asking the group to think about next steps.[6] A sample set of headings are:

Data	Diagnosis	Direction	Do Next
(Symptoms) Causes	Possible approaches	Possible steps	Next

Nominal Group Technique (NGT)

The nominal group technique was developed by André Delbecq and Andrew Van de Ven.[7] The NGT is a structured small-group process for generating ideas. This technique differs from brainstorming in two important ways: first, it doesn't rely on the free association of ideas, and second, it purposely attempts to restrict verbal interaction.[8]

This technique is particularly useful in situations where not only individual ideas need to be tapped, but also when a group consensus is desired. It generally follows a highly structured procedure involving five steps.

- **Step 1:** Seven to ten individuals of varying backgrounds and training are brought together as a group and familiarized with a problem such as, "How can we speed the flow of books through technical services?"

- **Step 2:** Working silently and alone, each group member is asked to prepare a list of ideas in response to the problem.

- **Step 3:** After a period of 10 to 15 minutes, each member of the group shares his/her ideas with the others, one at a time, in a round-robin fashion. A facilitator records the ideas on a flip chart for all to see. The round-robin process continues until all ideas are presented and recorded.

- **Step 4:** A period of structured interaction follows in which group members openly discuss and evaluate each of the generated ideas. During this process, ideas may be reworded, combined, deleted, or added.

- **Step 5:** Each member of the group is asked to rank the ideas in order of assessed importance. This vote is done privately. Following a brief discussion of the vote's outcome, a final secret ballot is conducted. The group's preference is the arithmetic total of the ranked votes. This concludes the meeting.

I recall using the NGT technique with a group of librarians who were members of a regional consortium. The objective of the exercise was to identify priority projects about which a consensus among members might exist. Each person was given an opportunity to contribute ideas, and the process was conducted in a way that maximized the likelihood that the outcome would be acceptable to all those in attendance, even though the final decision might not represent the original preference of some who attended the meeting.

The results of the session were successful, but the agreed upon priority was a surprise to many in attendance. Initially there was an unspoken assumption among certain members that the most important consortium activity was to expand the existing resource-sharing programs, and that the consortium would play a leadership role in launching a reciprocal borrowing program. But as the exercise progressed, discussions revealed that some members held strenuous objections to reciprocal borrowing. It soon became obvious that no consensus was achievable. But a consensus did emerge when members agreed that they wanted the consortium to become more proactive in providing training and staff development programs. We also learned that most members were willing to pay extra for such activities. This was a real surprise.

Even though the effort to involve the consortium in reciprocal borrowing failed, the discussions still proved to be helpful. Getting member objections out on the table in a formal setting helped consortium leaders begin the process of responding to expressed objections. The objections stemmed, not surprisingly, from the "have" libraries that were surrounded by the "have not" libraries from communities that didn't adequately support their own libraries. Eventually a voluntary reciprocal borrowing program was initiated. Not perfect but a start.

Pareto Chart

The Pareto chart is named for an Italian economist who found that 20 percent of the families in Italy controlled 80 percent of the country's wealth. In librarianship one well-known example of this phenomenon is that 20 percent of the titles in a library's collection normally account for 80 percent of its total circulation. In point of fact many similar relationships can be identified in librarianship. Today many people are familiar with the 80-20 rule.[9]

A Pareto chart is a special form of a vertical bar graph that is organized to highlight which among a series of problems are truly the most important. With this information in hand it is a great deal easier to decide the order in which problems ought to be tackled. The length of the bar represents the frequency of occurrence, and the bars are arranged in order from the longest on the left to the shortest on the right. (See Figure 4-1.)

The results of an actual study will nicely illustrate the value of a Pareto chart. A library was experiencing what it judged to be an unacceptably high rate of failures in searching ILL requests, but they didn't know what was causing the failures. Moreover, there are a variety of reasons why an ILL requested item might not be located during the search. The causes for failure include: inadequate training of staff in how to read and interpret L.C. classification numbers, misshelfed books, books shelved in special locations not known to the searcher, incorrect or inadequate citations, etc. An analysis was undertaken. Figure 4-1 summarizes the results of the analysis of 500 "Not on Shelf" interlibrary lending transactions. The first three causes accounted for 81 percent of the failures. After reviewing these data, the ILL supervisor decided to overhaul the unit's training procedures. She also recommended to the circulation department that it needed to pay more attention to the training of its shelving staff.

It is possible that a simple brainstorming session with staff might have also identified the root causes of the failures, but not in this case. The circulation supervisor had been adamant that shelving problems weren't a major cause for the failures, but the analysis showed otherwise. While there may be many occasions when staff agree on the causes of a problem, there may be other times when there

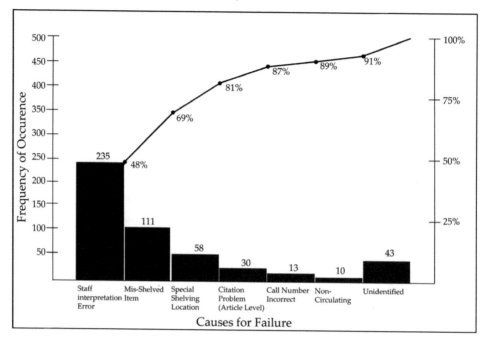

Figure 4-1 Pareto Chart: Analysis of 500 "Not on Shelf" lending transactions (item not in circulation).

will no agreement as to either the identity or the importance of possible causes. When disagreements occur, a Pareto-type data-gathering exercise can help clarify the problem. Data necessary to construct a Pareto chart is often based on simple data collection techniques such as check lists. Data can also be collected employing more sophisticated sampling techniques, but I have encountered no instances in libraries where statistical precision is worth the effort.

Constructing a Pareto Chart

- Decide what categories you will use to group items.

- Decide what measurement is most suitable, e.g., cost, time, activity, or frequency.

- Select the time period to be studied, e.g., last two weeks or last two months, etc.

- Gather necessary data on each category, e.g., book in its proper location but overlooked by staff.

- Calculate the subtotals for each category.

- Compare the frequency or cost of each category relative to all other categories, i.e., which are the causes for failure that occur most frequently or whose occurrences cost the most?

- List the categories from left to right on the horizontal axis in order of decreasing frequency or cost. The categories containing the fewest items can be combined into an "other" category. A graph line is created as follows: Calculate and describe cumulative sums. This is done by adding the sub-totals for the first and second categories, and placing a dot above the second bar and indicating that sum. To that sum add the subtotal for the third category. Continue the process for all of the bars until 100 percent is reached on the right-hand scale. (See Figure 4-1.)

In our ILL illustration, it quickly became clear that the most frequent cause for failing to find requested items was staff problems related to interpreting the LC classification numbers. In these instances the book requested was actually available for circulation. Since student assistants conducted most of the searches, the action taken was to strengthen the library's training program.

Illustrative Applications

Pareto analyses can be applied to many library-oriented situations. My illustration focused on why books couldn't be located on the shelves, but I could have used this tool for many other purposes. For example:

- Why turn-around times for new orders seem excessively long.
- Why it takes so long to get a new periodical subscription processed.
- What type of errors are most likely to be made by bibliographical searchers.
- Why the operating costs of the accounting unit are so high.
- What are the most important complaints voiced by patrons.

Cause-and-Effect Diagram (Fishbone)

A cause-and-effect diagram is a tool that is also designed to identify the root cause of problems as distinguished from less important aspects.[10] Earlier in the chapter I illustrated the danger of mistaking symptoms for root causes when I described the problem with RUSH books. Here is another illustration that derives from the realm of hotel management.

A friend of mine who works as a Change Management expert was assisting the Marriott Corporation. She was helping the company to adopt a TQM-like form of internal analysis. Early in the engagement, the client had cited the rising cost of wine as a growing concern (Marriott buys lots of wine). The client confirmed that management had already begun to respond by buying cheaper wine in order to bring the costs back into line. Later, one of the TQM teams uncovered the real reason why wine costs had been escalating. The cause of the problem had nothing to do with the costs of wine. The team discovered that a significant amount of complimentary wine was being distributed to appease guests who had experienced problems with reservations, check-in, or other basic hotel services. The corrective action was not to buy cheaper wine, but to take actions that would improve basic hotel services.

Constructing a Cause-and-Effect Diagram
The effect of the problem is stated on the right side of the chart:

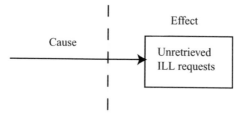

The influences or "causes" are listed to the left. For every effect there are likely to be several major categories of causes. Major causes can be grouped under general categories; for example, in industry, categories commonly include methods, materials, people, equipment, and environment. In organizations such as libraries, the categories often include: policies, procedures, and people. Don't be limited by these suggestions; use whatever categories that help you and your team to think creatively.

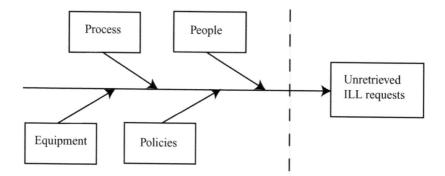

The possible root causes—little fish bones—are attached to the major categories in a logical order. From the list of causes, the objective is to identify and select the most probable root causes that merit further examination. Push the causes as close to the "roots" as possible and practical. Again, the goal is to focus on the root cause and not get distracted by the less important causes.

In our previous library illustration using a Pareto chart, the problem posed was that books supposedly on the shelf couldn't be located. (See Figure 4-1.) This analysis revealed that almost one-half of the failures were due to staff misinterpretations of the data on the request form. New staff had trouble with LC class numbers, which was partially caused by carelessness, but most importantly because of inadequate training. Had we dug a little deeper, we would have also discovered that clearly spelled out procedural manuals didn't exist. (See Figure 4-2.)

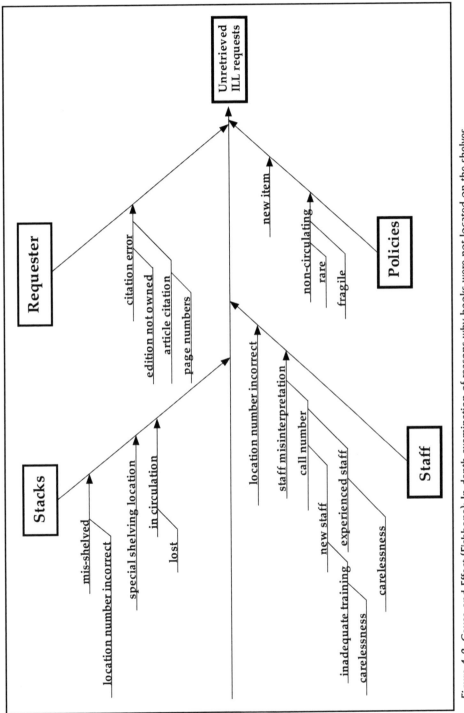

Figure 4-2 Cause-and-Effect (Fishbone): In-depth examination of reasons why books were not located on the shelves.

The absence of these manuals had a major impact on the quality of training. Each trainer took her own approach, and as a consequence, student assistants didn't receive uniform training. Some were carefully trained; others weren't trained as well.

Illustrative Applications

- What are the reasons why the cost of collecting fees for books lent is often considerable?

- Why do hiring procedures require so much time before a hiring decision is made?

- What are the causes for reference questions not being answered correctly?

- Why aren't reserve books on the shelves or why aren't data inserted into the database in a timely manner?

Final Thoughts

Clearly there are a variety of ways to diagnose a problem. An important point to remember is to not get into debates about root causes of a problem, and not to get distracted with what are only symptoms of the problem. I've always found that bringing together involved and knowledgeable staff in a focus group-like setting, and engaging them in a brainstorming session, to be an effective and relatively simple way of gaining an overview of the situation. Once there is agreement on the cause(s) of a problem, it is time to begin developing a methodology to study it.

Notes

1. Thomas L. Greenbaum, *Moderating Focus Groups: A Practical Guide for Group Facilitation* (Thousand Oaks, Calif.: Sage Publications, 2000).

2. The authors queried students' attitudes to assess their needs in the library's new information commons. The report summarizes both the methodology and the findings. *See* Britt Anna Fagerheim and Sandra J. Weingart, "Using Focus Groups to Assess Student Needs," *Library Review* 54, no. 9 (2005): 524-30.

3. Alexander F. Osborn, *Applied Imagination: Principles and Procedures for Creative Problem-solving*, 3rd ed. (New York: Scribner, 1963).

4. There are many approaches to creative thinking. I've personally attended a number of creative thinking workshops. While I found them interesting, I decided that they weren't any more effective than brainstorming to stimulate staff ideas. For more on creative thinking *see* Michael Michalko, *A Handbook of Creative Thinking Techniques* (Berkeley, Calif.: Ten Speed Press, 1991).

5. Mind mapping is another technique that facilitates the generation of ideas. This method is designed to emulate the way the brain works. Related topics radiate from the central idea like the spokes of a wheel. Mind mapping is a technique developed by Tony Buzan and is a registered trademark. I've never used this method although I have observed a mind mapping session. More information about mind mapping can be found at http://www.mind-mapping.co.uk/ (16 November 2006). Mind mapping™ is also briefly described by Mayo and Goodrich. *See* Diane Mayo and Jeanne Goodrich, *Staffing for Results: A Guide to Working Smarter* (Chicago and London: American Library Association, 2002), 33-34.

6. Roger Fisher, Alan Sharp, and John Richardson, *Getting it Done: How to Lead when You're not in Charge* (New York: Harper, 1998), 109.

7. André L. Delbecq, Andrew H. Van de Ven, and David H. Gustafson, *Group Techniques for Program Planning: A Guide to Nominal Group and Delphi Processes* (Middleton, Wisc.: Green Briar Press, 1986).

8. Management texts frequently devote space to discussions such as Brainstorming, Nominal Group Techniques, Pareto Charts, and Cause and Effect Diagrams. I found the following two sources to be particularly useful: *See* James M. Higgins, *101 Creative Problem Solving Techniques: The Handbook of New Ideas for Business* (New York: New Management Publishing, 1994). *See also* Nancy R. Tague, *The Quality Toolbox,* 2nd ed. (Milwaukee, Wisc.: ASQ Quality Press, 2005).

9. Higgins, *101 Creative Problem Solving Techniques: The Handbook of New Ideas for Business*, 150-53.

10. Higgins, *101 Creative Problem Solving Techniques: The Handbook of New Ideas for Business*, 44-48.

Chapter Five

Preparing for a Study

Scope note: There may be considerable pressure to get on with a study, but before launching any study, it is wise to run through a pre-study checklist. This chapter discusses activities that should precede the actual study. How should the study be organized? What will be studied and why? Who will conduct the study? What data will be collected? What tools will be used to collect the data? Have staff members been informed? Has the project been thoroughly thought through? These are all important considerations.

What's at Issue

I suspect that many readers will disagree with the following statement: almost any library process could be improved if one were only willing to conduct a thorough study. Based on my experience, however, I'll stand behind that observation. But having made that assertion, I will also concede that most library studies are undertaken in reaction to an immediate problem; for example, a process or a service that isn't working as expected or isn't working at all. Here are a few illustrations:

- Books aren't getting reshelved in a timely manner; new books are waiting to be cataloged; interlibrary borrowing requests languish in the ILB unit.

- Patrons are complaining that new books aren't getting to them quickly enough. They ask: "Why can't the library go down to Borders or Barnes & Noble and buy new titles and get them on the shelves in a few hours?"

- Staff members are complaining about being stressed and overworked.

- Lots of questions are being raised about what is really happening in reference. Management doesn't seem to appreciate all of the changes that are occurring in this key service area.

Symptoms such as patron complaints and backlogs of work can quickly signal to library staff that something isn't working well. If such problems are not remedied in a timely manner, the library's service credibility could be damaged. When staff and patron complaints are associated with a specific workflow or process, these activities should become immediate candidates for review and analysis.

Why wait for a problem to become disruptive? Why not assume that all existing processes and workflows could be improved if one only made the effort to

37

improve them? I believe there are some enormous potential benefits to be reaped by libraries that create organizational cultures that place a priority on process and procedural excellence. If one is willing to accept the assumption that we can do better, where should we begin? For a start, workflows and processes that are complicated, and routinely consume significant resources are likely candidates for improvement, e.g., reference desk activities and activities that have undergone lots of recent changes. As a matter of fact, many of the activities briefly described in Chapter 3 meet these criteria.

What to Look for

Let's examine some of the characteristics of processes and procedures that are most likely to cause operational inefficiencies.

Frequently Performed Operations

Charging and discharging materials at a circulation desk, shelving materials, and preparing new items for the shelves are all examples of frequently performed procedures. Other routine and repetitious procedures include handling reserves, checking in new periodicals, and processing new borrower registrations, holds, and reserves. If efficiencies in any of these frequently performed operations can be achieved, then dollar savings or improvements in service could be significant.

There are also frequently performed operations that are part of complicated processes, for example, cataloging of paper or digital materials. Cataloging normally involves updating and maintaining large databases as well as processing the physical or digital items. Other complicated processes that are frequently performed include selection and handling of books for preservation or digital scanning, or selection of titles for purchase in a decentralized environment. In large library systems, document delivery and interlibrary borrowing and lending are also frequently performed activities.

Activities That Involve Movement of Staff or Materials

Handling of new books in technical services is a prime example of a complicated process that involves significant movement of staff and materials. Other important library workflows that can involve significant movement are preservation and digitization, interlibrary lending and borrowing, and circulation reshelving activities. It is probably worth mentioning that movement is not necessarily limited to movement between two distant points. Short distances multiplied by high frequency equal long distances. The layout of a reference area can involve short distances that are frequently traveled. I've found that it is easy to underestimate the amount of time that can be consumed in moving from one place to another.

Activities That Have Experienced Considerable Change

While I could cite a variety of examples, reference service is hard to overlook. What happens behind the reference desk has changed dramatically in recent years, and possibly more important, the prospects for continued change are very likely. Many of the changes in reference have impacted traditional procedures, so it makes a great deal of sense to ask whether the work procedures that supported reference in the past are still needed today. Similar questions about technical service operations are also appropriate.

Activities That Involve Paperwork

While automated systems have enabled libraries to eliminate many forms and files, there are still libraries that use paper forms. There are also numerous activities associated with administrative and personnel work that require paperwork. Procedures such as staff evaluations, hiring new student assistants or staff members, processing of bills, or organizing staff training are among the candidates that immediately come to mind. It is surprising how often administrative procedures are found to be overly cumbersome.

Activities That Are Costly

Most library staff members are more interested in the service aspects of an activity than they are in how much it costs to provide the services, but costs are something that management should not ignore; therefore, activities that consume lots of dollars merit special attention. But again, costs alone shouldn't be a sufficient reason for elimination or necessarily even partial curtailment. Judgment needs to be exercised. A story that is probably apocryphal in origin is one of my favorites. "Cuts by the Score" is a classic story of a time-study expert run amuck. While I hope it provokes a chuckle or two, its message is undeniable.

Cuts by the Score[1]

For considerable periods the four oboe players have nothing to do. Their numbers should be reduced, and the work spread more evenly over the whole of the concert, thus eliminating peak loads of activity.

All twelve first violins were playing the identical notes. This seems unnecessary duplication. The staff of this section should be drastically cut. If a large volume of sound is required, it could be obtained by means of electronic amplifier apparatus.

Much effort was absorbed in the playing of demi-semi-quavers. This is an excessive refinement. It is recommended that all notes be rounded up to the nearest semiquaver. If this were done, it would be possible to use trainees and lower grade operatives more extensively.

There seems to be too much repetition of some musical passages. Scores should be drastically pruned. No useful purpose is served by repeating on the horns a passage which has already been handled by the strings. It is estimated that if all redundant passages were eliminated, the whole concert time of two hours could be reduced to twenty minutes, and there wouldn't be any need for an interval.

The conductor agreed generally with these recommendations but registered the opinion that there might be some falling-off in box office receipts. In that unlikely event it should be possible to close sections of the auditorium entirely, with a consequential savings of overhead expenses—lighting, attendance, etc.

If worse came to worse, the whole thing could be abandoned, and the public could go to Albert Hall instead.

S. Tone Deaf

To illustrate the point, let's return to reference services. We know that reference services are expensive, but for most libraries reference has long been a core activity. While no library wants to waste money, I don't believe any professional library would want to curtail a core service simply because it was expensive. Even though the Google generation of library patrons is forcing a rethinking of traditional reference services, I believe most librarians want to reconfigure digital information services so that they continue to be responsive to the needs of this generation of patrons. The challenge is to use available resources as effectively as possible. I don't think I've ever heard anyone suggest that reference service be eliminated simply because it was costly.

Nonetheless, there is no reason why one shouldn't seek ways to reduce the costs of expensive activities, particularly if the savings can be made without reductions in the quality of service, or in the case of technical services, the quality of products produced.

When Patron Service Is Critical

There was a time when the library was the only source of books unless one was willing to purchase a title. This type of monopoly was particularly evident on campuses. But as already noted, with the emergence of Web resources, the library's monopoly disappeared. Now libraries must compete for the loyalty of potential patrons as well as retain the attention of current patrons. In the commercial sector, it is often said that "poor customer service affects the bottom line." Equally relevant for libraries is the belief that "dissatisfied customers are likely to tell five to seven times as many people about their bad experience than will satisfied customers," and "for every customer who complains about a minor problem, fifty remain silent." Or finally, "it costs approximately five times as much to attract one new customer than it does to retain an existing one." All of these simple truisms suggest to me that processes involving patrons merit special attention. There should be a special incentive to eliminate unnecessary policies and needless irksome procedures.

Organizing a Study: Overview

A study might be a relatively straightforward examination of a set of procedures that are well defined, e.g., circulation desk routines. Or it could involve a

complicated network of workflows consisting of numerous processes and procedures, e.g., the selection, ordering, and cataloging of new books in a decentralized
public library system. In general the preparation steps one takes to organize a study
are very similar regardless of the study's complexity.

Agreeing on What Needs to Be Studied

The first step is to define the problem and to identify what is to be studied. Usually
this question is fairly obvious because something has gone wrong and needs to be fixed.

For example, the library begins to incur complaints from the public about a
seeming failure to get new books on the shelf in a timely manner. The cause could
be due to a variety of reasons: slowness of selection, failure of the acquisitions
department to issue orders promptly, poor vendor performance, cataloging blockages, or a combination of these factors. It is also possible that an agency outside
the library is the real culprit, e.g., a county mandate that books can be ordered
only once a month. When the subject of what needs to be included in a study is
not clear, it is best to spend some additional time diagnosing a problem rather than
rushing to action. Several tools that can help to diagnose problems were discussed
in Chapter 4.

This leads me to ask: Is a study always necessary? What if the problem is
caused by factors not related to existing workflows? When new books don't reach
the shelves in a timely manner one might be tempted to jump to the conclusion that
the cause is due to faulty workflows. In many libraries that would probably be an
accurate assessment, but it wouldn't necessarily always be the correct conclusion.
For example, a library prides itself on being able to get new books into the hands
of patrons soon after they are displayed at Borders or Barnes & Noble. This desire
is prominently displayed in the library's strategic plan, but an existing community
policy prevents the library from achieving this service priority. Local authorities
insist that the library always receive the largest discount possible, and yes, this
policy limits the selection of vendors, which slows down the delivery of new acquisitions. In this case, launching a study of workflows would have been a costly
mistake and would not have solved the problem. What is really needed is a strategy
that will convince local authorities that an exception to the discount rule is necessary for the library to be responsive to its patrons—who are also voters.

Staying on Target

There is also the related problem of distinguishing between symptoms and
the real problem. It is easy to get distracted or sidetracked. To illustrate this point,
consider how people from different levels of an organization might view the same
problem from vastly different perspectives. Here are examples:

- The Head of Technical Services believes that the workflows in the cataloging
  department are uneven and that the staff are poorly utilized so there is a need
  to redesign jobs.

- The Head of Cataloging believes that the staff simply don't work at the same speed; some are very fast while others barely work up to a minimum level. These staff members are not carrying their share of the load.

- Individual catalogers believe that some co-workers simply do not care. One staff member is even more specific and singles out a specific person. All was going well until Joe started cutting out. You know, Joe doesn't give a damn about the rest of us.

Or, a similar situation:

- The Head of Technical Services feels that the Acquisitions Department is not as productive as one has a right to expect. She wonders, "Has a procedural bottleneck developed somewhere within the unit?"

- The Head of the Acquisitions Department feels that some staff are not taking enough time to verify the accuracy of their own work, so as a result, he has to recheck their work.

- Staff members grumble among themselves that the department head has a compulsion to check their work. It is their view that the head of the unit is a real #*^%*#! The staff strongly feel that they are all fast, careful workers.

The above illustrations clearly point out the importance of not getting sidetracked by peripheral issues. Lots of problems could be at play. Poor supervision, inadequate training of staff, and/or inadequate communications are but a few of the possibilities. It is just good common sense to get a handle on the real problem(s) before plunging ahead with a study.

Objectives and Scope of the Study

Once the problem(s) is identified, it is necessary to spell out the objectives and boundaries of the study; that is, what will and will not be included in the study, and how the activities to be studied relate to other activities. Figure 5-1 depicts the network of procedures that would be included in this study of a circulation system. One would want to include all the activities that are involved with the circulation of materials.

The boundaries selected can have a significant impact on the findings of a study. For example, if one studied the costs of digitizing books, but didn't include the costs of selecting or preparing the books for digitization; or, if a time and cost study of acquiring and cataloging a new book were conducted, but the reported results didn't include administrative overhead costs, the reported results of these two studies might be accurate but would they be realistic? The answer could be yes if the limitations were understood by all involved, but no, if those who conducted the study simply failed to include relevant activities or information.

Once the study team is in agreement about the objectives, and the boundaries of the study are identified, it is important to see that this information is clearly communicated to responsible managers. It is equally important that these same managers buy into the study objectives and scope.

What Will Be Studied?

This point might seem obvious, but it is not always so. For example, if we plan to study the new book selection process in a decentralized public library system, will we study the staff members who are involved with the selection process, or will we study what happens to the information that is generated during the selection process. This distinction could make a big difference. What staff members do and the decisions they make in a selection process will look considerably different if one studies what happens to the information that the process generates. It might be necessary to study both what staff do and what happens with the information that is involved in the process.

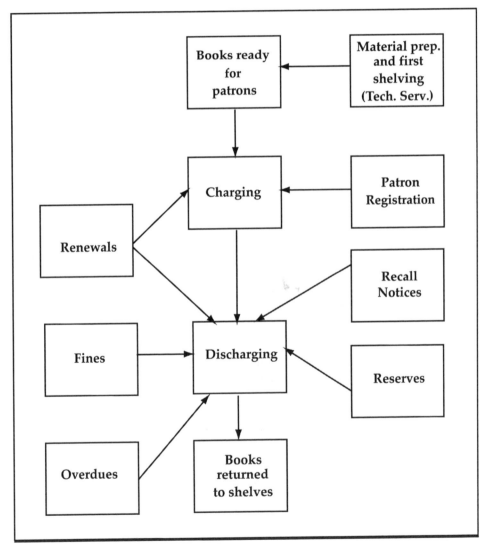

Figure 5-1 Block Diagram: Typical circulation system.

Who Conducts the Study?

There should be no reason why a team of staff working together couldn't successfully undertake most studies of processes and workflows, even those consisting of multiple complicated procedures.

Some libraries continue to contract with large consulting firms from the corporate sector. I've never been fond of this option even though consultants from such firms are usually competent in the use of analytical tools. The problem is that they often lack a thorough understanding or appreciation of professional values and service objectives. Although such consultants may work to assure everyone that they are quite aware of our values, when their reports are issued, too often one discovers that in spite of their assurances, the report still focuses primarily on costs and productivity—just the type of assessment one would expect in an industrial setting. Somehow the values and service objectives got lost, misunderstood, or worse, ignored. I've examined reports that reminded me of our time-study analyst who ran amuck in the orchestra pit—efficiency for the sake of efficiency. I'm still biased against hiring consulting firms who employ analysts to audit library activities when the analysts don't understand what is important in libraries and for librarians.

Another option to assigning all responsibilities to a work team is to arrange for the team to work with a person on the staff who already possesses the requisite analytical skills. This could be the in-house systems person or a working librarian, e.g., reference librarian or a cataloger who possesses analytical skills, or an outside librarian consultant. Any of these approaches can be successful.

There are both advantages and disadvantages to bringing in an outside librarian consultant. One advantage of using an outsider is that the on-site staff members can harbor personal biases or be so caught up in internal politics that their objectivity is compromised. Another advantage is that the outside consultant can speak more candidly on controversial issues since the consultant will leave the scene once the project is completed.

One advantage of using on-site staff is that they will be available to assist in the implementation of a study's recommendations after the outsider has departed. Being able to follow through is of vital importance. As is discussed later in the book, my experiences have convinced me that most failures in process analysis and organizational change occur during the implementation phase.

My personal preference is to involve a staff team directly in the study process, or if not actually conducting the study, involve a staff team in an advisory capacity working with the outside consultant. While I favor the use of staff teams, a team approach to problem solving is no panacea. One needs to exercise care and judgment in appointing a team. First, one needs to make every effort to include a mix of the right people, e.g., staff who are intimately familiar with the activity, staff who possess the requisite analytical skills, staff who have demonstrated their commitment to the study, and staff who are skilled at working on teams. Second, once the study begins, if it is found that a specific expertise is missing, the team and responsible managers need to be willing to take steps to add the necessary expertise.

It is also essential that members of a team become adept in using group problem-solving techniques, and become familiar with the basic principles of group dynamics. These skills include understanding the different roles people play in a group, how individuals interact while working in a group, and how to act not only as the leader but also simply as a member of the group. One must also learn how to deal with disruptive behavior, e.g., personality clashes, the rambler, and the inarticulate speaker.

The literature of group development is quite extensive. The life cycle of groups, for example, has been given considerable attention. B. W. Tuckman identifies four stages of group development: forming, norming, storming, and performing.[2] M.A.C Jensen adds a fifth stage, adjourning.[3] The important point to remember is that staff who are appointed to study teams need to know how to function in a group. Simply appointing a team and setting them loose is really asking for trouble.[4]

The Need for Data

Ever find yourself sitting in committee meeting or during a coffee break talking about a problem or an issue, and the group seems to spin its wheels while reaching no resolution? For instance, a reference staff member claims that books aren't getting back to the shelves quickly enough, but a circulation assistant vehemently denies this is the case. Almost instantly an interlibrary loan assistant and another reference assistant chime in and challenge the circulation assistant's denial. Who is right?

Another hot button issue for some librarians is the outsourcing of part or all of cataloging. Management announces that it plans to outsource original cataloging. This could make a great deal of sense, but not always. What might make more sense is to analyze existing cataloging procedures in order to ensure that they are as efficient and effective as possible. A study might reveal that in-house procedures are faster, more responsive to patron needs, and more economical than outsourcing, but one is not likely to know for sure without collecting data and conducting an analysis of existing work processes and procedures. A study might also uncover opportunities to further improve existing operations, so much so that the improvements would make outsourcing a poor choice. Without data the decision cannot proceed beyond an emotional level.

Another emotional issue concerns the future of reference services. In recent years, many questions have been raised about reference work because of the introduction of digital and chat reference services. Consider for a moment the following scenario: Management concludes that there is a need for a general information desk with no professional staffing. What led management to this conclusion? Was the decision based on actual data? Management further asserts that fewer professionally trained librarians are needed at the reference desk. They argue that the vast majority of questions being asked don't require professional expertise. How does management know this? Will others necessarily agree? Or let us pursue this illustration further: A general information desk is established, but does it result in more or fewer complex questions at the reference desk? How should the reference desk be staffed? An un-intended effect of a triage type organization is that this arrangement may discourage some people from seeking help beyond the general information desk.

I don't presume to know the answers to these questions, but I am willing to assert that better decisions will be made if they are backed up with objective data. Fortunately there are tools, such as work sampling that can help answer these and other questions.

What Kinds of Data Can be Collected?

Different data can be collected with different tools. SLS presents a variety of tools and techniques for analyzing a variety of library services, processes, and procedures. The tools of process and procedural analysis are powerful, simple, and versatile. All of the tools and techniques listed below are presented in the chapters that follow.

- Flow-process charts and flow charts enable one to dissect simple or compli-cated processes and procedures that involve yes-or-no decisions.

- Work-flow diagrams can track handling procedures that involve significant movement of staff, forms, or materials.

- Tracking tools can help determine how much time is required to complete each stage of a complicated workflow. Tracking tools can help to spot where delays occur in a process, e.g., tracking an interlibrary request or a new book order.

- Time-study techniques help to establish how much time is required to perform a particular series of actions. Several techniques are presented for determining how much time is spent performing each step in a process or a procedure.

- Work sampling is a special purpose time-study technique that allows one to study what actions occur in a specified work area, e.g., a circulation desk or a reference desk.

- Cost analyses determine how much an activity costs. The study techniques employed will depend on the level of accuracy that is desired.

Gathering the Data

Once the study is organized, and the individual(s) or team charged to conduct the study has been identified, a first step is to decide what data will need to be collected. The data, once collected, organized, and analyzed, will provide helpful guidance to those responsible for developing an improved activity.

What usually vexes analysts is not a scarcity, but rather an overabundance of data that must be sifted through, evaluated, and arranged. Often the crucial task is to develop a methodology that discriminates between useful and unnecessary data. There is a limit to how much information can be derived from a given body of data, and one should resist the temptation to generalize beyond its usefulness. One must also consider the costs in time and effort to collect data in comparison to the potential benefits. It is important to exercise judgment and avoid overkill. The need for exercising judgments will become clearer as we begin focusing on costs and times. Before undertaking a study, it is common sense to contemplate the following possible implications.

- *Time*—how much time is available to complete the study?
- *Money*—what is the size of the budget available for the study?
- *Current record*—what data are already available?
- *Potential payoff*—what is the potential payoff to the organization?
- *Precision*—how precise does the data need to be?

When an activity under review involves complex operations and involves a significant number of staff, there are more opportunities to discover ways to make improvements; under such circumstances it is easier to justify conducting a more thorough study.

Chapters 6 through 14 present a series of tools and techniques that can be employed to collect a variety of data. These tools are designed to chart either what is done, how much time it takes, or how much the activity costs. Again, the choice of tools and techniques will depend on the specific circumstances.

Other Considerations
Errors and Precision
Before the actual data-gathering phase begins, it is essential to consider how accurate the collected data need to be. What level of precision do we need? Most people, in any profession, would likely respond "the results of the study need to be accurate." That statement implies there is no room for errors. We are conditioned to seek perfection, but achieving perfection is fanciful at best, and certainly not attainable in the real world; fortunately perfection is not required in library studies. For example, does it really matter whether it takes 2 or 3 seconds to check out a book, 20 or 23 seconds to label a new book, 59 or 62 minutes to scan the average monograph, or 14 or 15 minutes to answer the average chat reference question? Precise sampling techniques are available, but the question remains: Is a high degree of precision necessarily required, or will a technique less rigorous produce satisfactory results? Those analyzing activities will gradually learn from experience to judge what level of precision is required. Sampling issues are discussed in greater detail in Chapter 12, and errors and acceptable level of errors are discussed in greater detail in Chapter 17.

Getting the Staff on Board
Before embarking on any study, it is essential to talk with staff, and if at all possible, seek their approval and support. If staff members aren't informed about

the purposes of a study, opposition is almost guaranteed later. You can be sure that some staff members are going to feel threatened because they are afraid their deficiencies will come to light, or that their jobs are in jeopardy. Losing one's job is an extreme outcome, but it is very possible that staff roles and jobs will change as an outcome of the study.

Securing staff agreement isn't always easy to achieve. When managers began to urge a rethinking of traditional reference services because use statistics were reflecting sharp declines, many reference librarians raised some strenuous objections. Even though face-to-face reference had been significantly undercut by the impact of the Web, some reference librarians felt strongly that the need for change had been grossly overstated. As a listener to countless arguments about the need for change, I actually began to build a list of reasons why agreement often proved elusive.

- Reference librarians and their administrators had no common vision about reference service in the future that bound them together.

- Reference staff were comfortable with what they were doing. They weren't dissatisfied and felt no pressure to change.

- Reference staff felt overextended and since they weren't getting the additional dollar support they were requesting, felt underappreciated and maybe a little resentful.

- Reference staff were too close to their day-to-day activities and were not able to appreciate the "big picture" impact technology was having on reference and information services.

In such situations every effort should be made by managers to achieve the support and agreement of staff, but if agreement can't be achieved and the study proceeds anyway, staff members still need to understand why the study is necessary and what might be the possible outcomes. The bottom line is: don't rush ahead without informing staff.

Final Thoughts

A useful way to conclude the preparation stage is to review the project in the context of what is known as Deming's P.D.C.A. cycle. (See Figure 5-2.) In the Planning Stage make sure that the plan clarifies the issues, objectives, strategies, and actions that will be required. During the Do stage make sure that those responsible for conducting the study are well prepared, and once

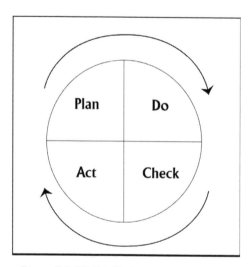

Figure 5-2 P.D.C.A. Cycle.

they are prepared, be ready to launch forward with the study. In the Check phase make sure that study results are consistent with what had been planned. If satisfied with the quality of the results, be ready to act and develop an improved solution. Engaging in this process throughout the study is likely to reveal further improvements and refinements that might be introduced. It is this process of continuous review and examination that formed the basis of what Deming and others called continuous improvement. Adopting the P.D.C.A. cycle as a guide can serve as an effective way of organizing and executing an effective plan.

Notes

1. The following excerpts are from a report by O & M after a visit to the Royal Festival Hall. From the British Ministry of Transport Bulletin. "Cuts by the score" [Parody of civil service rationalization applied to an orchestra] by S. Tone Deaf, State Librarian 3 no. 1 (February 1953): 2.

2. Bruce W. Tuckman, "Developmental Sequence in Small Groups," *Psychological Bulletin* 63 (November 1965): 384-99.

3. Mary Ann C. Jensen, "Stages of Small-Group Development Revisited," *Group & Organization Studies* 2 (December 1977): 419-27.

4. Daniel Levi's book on group dynamics is one source that I've found useful. The author provides an in-depth, scholarly treatment about how teams work. Levi also provides extensive information on how teams operate and how teamwork skills are developed. *See* Daniel Levi, *Group Dynamics for Teams,* 2nd ed. (Thousand Oaks, Calif.: Sage Publications, 2001). Sage Publications has published numerous monographs on the subject of teamwork and group dynamics. Its URL is http://www.sagepub.com/home.nav (17 May 2007). Those who prefer treatments that are library related may want to consult Barbara Dewey & Sheila Creth, *Team Power: Making Library Meetings Work* (Chicago: American Library Association, 1993).

Section Three
What We Do: The Tools

Chapter Six

Block Diagram

Scope note: The block diagram provides an overview of an activity. It is particularly helpful in determining what activities need to be included in a study. The most common application of a block diagram is the organization chart that depicts the relationships in a hierarchical organization.

A block diagram provides a pictorial overview of a system, process, or procedure. Too often neglected, this initial step can serve as a valuable aid in helping to gain an overview of the activities that are to be analyzed. Lacking an overview, a study team may structure the boundaries of a study too narrowly or too broadly. The block diagram provides a level of detail that allows one to examine the basic relationships among the elements of a workflow, and its related processes and procedures. It helps to identify what activities should be included and excluded.

Figure 6-1 provides an overview of an ILL borrowing process. This diagram clearly reveals that multiple sources of requests would need to be included in any study of this process, such as email, OPAC requests, Web-based forms, and in-person submitted forms. And as shown in Figure 6-1 a block diagram can also be designed to show the direction of the flow as activity progresses through a process.

Block diagrams can be used in a variety of ways. The typical organization chart is probably the most common application of a block diagram. The diagram shown in Figure 6-2 depicts the hierarchical and lateral authority relationships among units of a typical library organization. The tool thus provides an overview of the "chain of command." A block diagram can also be used to organize and highlight the elements of a cost study. (See Figure 14-1, page 171.) This block diagram identifies the cost centers associated with a group of reference activities.

Constructing a block diagram is not difficult. The symbols used are a combination of boxes and connecting lines that denote the direction in which a system flows. Other shapes may be used if they seem more applicable to a given situation. A single line with an arrow at each end denotes a two-way flow as shown in Figure 6-1.

A typical library circulation system was shown in Figure 5-1, page 43 in the last chapter. From the diagram one can easily determine that the system consists of several interrelated procedures: patron registration, renewals, fines, overdue

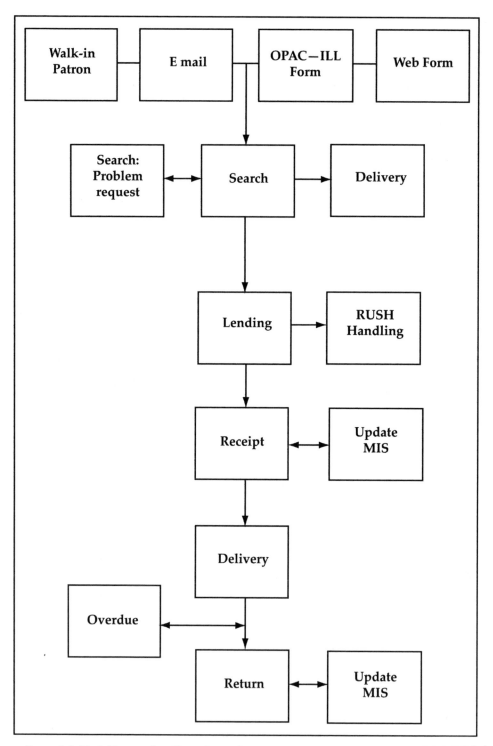

Figure 6-1 Block Diagram: Interlibrary borrowing process.

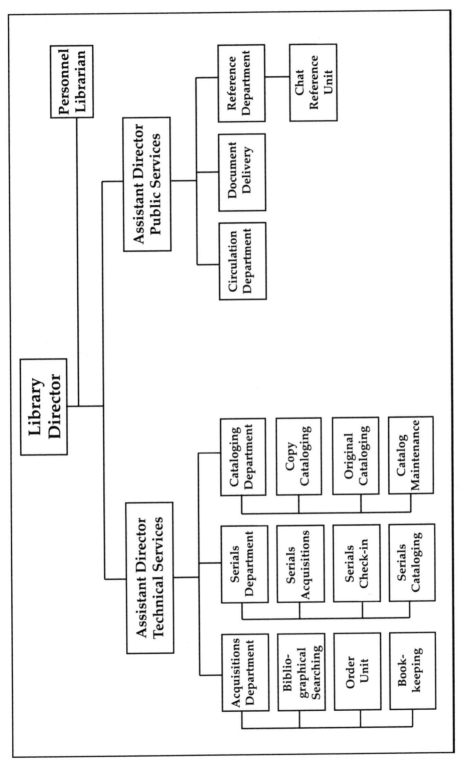

Figure 6-2 Block Diagram: Typical library organization chart.

notices, recalls, reserves, charging, and discharging. This block diagram does not show that some of the functions are performed in person, some via telephone, or over the Web, e.g., reserves and renewals. If there were a reason to show such information, the diagram could be modified accordingly. Remember the real purpose is to gain an overview of the activity to be studied.

If a library did not register patrons but just required a general I.D. card, did not fine or send overdue notices, and did not renew or reserve books, the block diagram would be greatly simplified as shown in Figure 6-3.

Final Thoughts

The block diagram is a very simple, but useful tool that can be used in a variety of ways. I've found it very helpful when explaining to staff the components of a process. The tool is equally helpful in briefing a study team about an activity that the team has been charged to study.

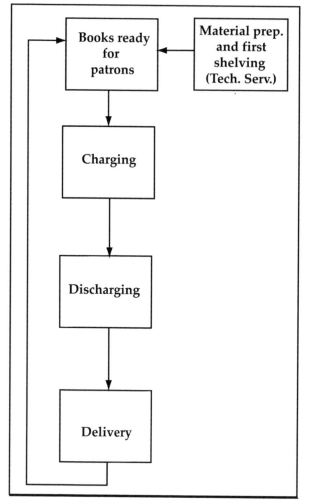

Figure 6-3 Block Diagram: Simplified circulation system.

Chapter Seven

Tools for Process Analysis

Scope note: This chapter is divided into four distinct parts. Each part describes a tool that can be used to analyze workflows and processes. Part one focuses on simple check sheets that are used to calculate the frequency with which an activity occurs. Part two introduces the work-flow diagram that is used to trace the movement of staff or products as they move from workstation to workstation. Part three explains how the flow process chart is used to chart any procedure that does not involve extensive decision making. Part four introduces the flow chart that can be used to analyze a wide variety of processes and workflows. Instructions and illustrations are included for each tool.

Part One: Check Sheets

A check sheet is a form on which data may be collected systematically and recorded in a uniform manner by means of tick marks or some equally simple symbol. It can be used to answer the question "How often does such-and-such occur?" A check sheet list enables one to gather a variety of data in a way that the data can be easily used and interpreted.

If the categories are complete and the check sheet is well organized, this simple tool can provide a clear and objective picture of the underlying facts. The following story illustrates how a simple check sheet can provide valuable information.

A few years ago an angry faculty member confronted me at the campus faculty club. He was unhappy about the quality of service he had been receiving from the library. Fortunately we had been collecting data about patron complaints using a simple check sheet because the reference department happened to be very interested in improving customer service. The data collected revealed that while there were occasional complaints, they were infrequent and isolated. Knowing that, I invited this faculty member to have a drink at the club where we could talk informally. While he was not likely to believe my "data," I felt sufficiently comfortable with them to ask what was really behind his complaint. He finally described an encounter with a staff member that caused him to go ballistic, and probably justifiably so. Once our unhappy faculty member had vented, he felt better about the situation. Based on the data collected, however, we decided he was generalizing from an isolated incident, which is an all too common reaction.

There are many well-known, traditional uses of check sheets. I suspect the best known application of the check sheet format has been to collect data about the reference desk. Traditionally such check sheets would have included categories such as research questions, ready-reference, and directional questions. Today other categories might include the number of queries received from patrons remote from the reference desk or questions involving use of the Web, etc. Figures 7-1 and 7-2 illustrate typical reference unit check sheets: one for a university library and the other for a college library. I find the differences between the two checklists illuminating. The university library check sheet includes only brief, extended, and referral reference. There is no mention of instruction in any manner. The college library check sheet lists directional, informational, and instructional. Clearly the nature of activity that occurs at these two libraries differs significantly. What is surprising is that there is no mention in either check sheet regarding assistance to patrons using the Web or Web resources. I was also surprised that the college library collected no data after its desk closes at 5:00 PM when a great deal of activity normally occurs during the evening hours.

My interpretations of the data aren't particularly important because there is only one day involved, and by the time this book reaches its readers, the specifics of these check sheets will be largely irrelevant. My purpose in making the interpretations is simply to point out that even the simplest data collection instruments can generate useful information.

Simple check sheets can also be used to collect data that can be used to help plan detailed diary or work sampling studies designed to determine times and costs. For more information about these two methodologies, consult Chapters 11 and 12.

Of course with the growth in automated systems and Web-based systems that generate detailed statistics, one can expect the use of traditional check sheets such as those depicted in Figures 7-1 and 7-2 to decline in popularity. Integrated library systems such as those offered by Innovative Interfaces or Ex Libris collect an enormous variety of data. In reference support systems such as RefTracker a wide variety of management data can be provided in the form of automated check sheets. Figure 7-3 displays a RefTracker statistical compilation that is comparable to what might be expected from a manually compiled check sheet.[1] The software's statistical package can be tailored to meet the specific desires of a client. Data on a variety of additional categories can be collected if desired. For example:

- which staff member answered the question;
- how the question arrived—desk, phone, email, online/chat;
- up to three attributes of the client asking the question—for example age, department, reason for making the request, level of response required, etc.;

Reference Center Statistics

Day __Tuesday__   Date_____

Time	Brief Reference	Extended Reference	Referral
8-9			
9-10	/ /	//// /	
10-11	⊬⊬/ /	⊬⊬ /	
11-12	⊬⊬ ⊬⊬ / /// /	////	/ /
12-1	⊬⊬ ⊬⊬ ⊬⊬ /	// //	
1-2	⊬⊬ ⊬⊬ ⊬⊬ /	/ /	
2-3	⊬⊬ ⊬⊬ // //	/ ///	
3-4	⊬⊬ ⊬⊬ /// /		
4-5	////		
5-6	⊬⊬ ⊬⊬ ⊬⊬ ⊬⊬ ⊬⊬ /// /		
6-7	⊬⊬ ///	//	
7-8	⊬⊬ /		
8-9	⊬⊬ ⊬⊬ / ///	\ \ \\	
9-10	⊬⊬ \	\ \	
10-11	\ \ \ \		
11-12	/		
12-1			
1-2			

Figure 7-1 Daily statistics checklist for a university library reference department.

Reference Desk Statistics			
Time	Directional	Informational	Instructional
9-10			‖ ∕∕
10-11		‖‖ ‖‖ ‖	‖‖ ‖‖ ‖
11-12			‖‖ ‖‖ ‖ ‖
12-1	‖ ‖	∕∕ ∕ ∕	
1-2	∕∕∕∕	∕ ∕∕∕	‖‖ ‖‖ ‖
2-3		‖‖ ‖‖ ‖‖ ‖‖ ‖‖	‖‖
3-4		‖‖ ‖‖‖	
4-5		‖‖ ∕∕∕	‖‖ ‖‖ ‖
Date_____			

Figure 7-2 Daily statistics checklist for a college library reference department.

• the length of time taken to answer the question;

• whether the question was successfully answered or referred on.

Note that the data collection form shown in Figure 7-3 includes not only the frequency of activity but also the time when the last transaction occurred. The data-collection capability can also be tailored to collect reference-related statistics as well as other desk-related activities such as document delivery.

No matter how sophisticated the system, however, the principles on which the automated systems record data are the same as those of the traditional pencil and paper method; that is, each occurrence is counted, sums are added, and the percentages are calculated.

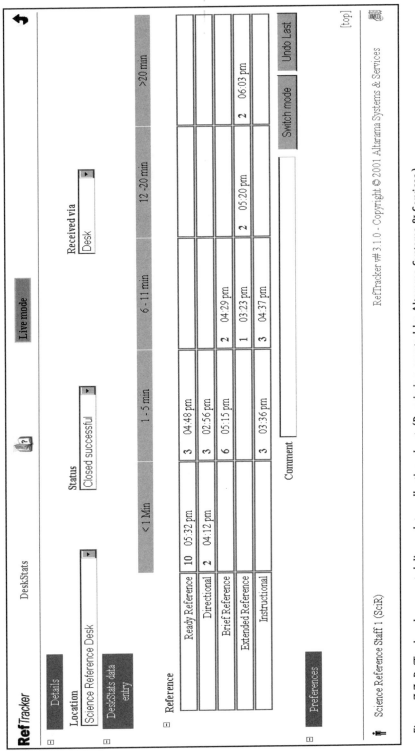

Figure 7-3 RefTracker document delivery data collection sheet. (Permission granted by Altarama Systems & Services.)

Purpose of a Check Sheet

It is important to think very carefully about the purposes a check sheet is intended to serve before putting it into use.

- Who needs the data?

- What are the categories of data that are needed? You want to be sure that all of the important categories are included.

- When should the data be collected? Collecting data over an extended period of time is likely to lead to increased errors. Would a sampling of data suffice?

- Where should the data be collected? What locations need to be included in the data collection?

- How should the data be collected and by whom? Should it be collected manually or by machine?

Concerns about Accuracy

It is often difficult to collect reliable data using check sheets when the data are recorded manually. A reference desk-related example illustrates the two most common problems. First, it is not unusual for a staff member who is busy at the desk to forget to record each transaction at its completion. Instead there is a tendency to wait until the end of a shift, and then try to reconstruct from memory what occurred. Second, staff members often have differing interpretations of a data category. For instance, one person records a reference transaction as ready reference, whereas another staff member records a similar transaction as a research question.

In either case the accuracy of the data collected will be adversely affected. Therefore, it is important to make sure that categories of data are clearly defined and understood by all staff, and that staff are instructed to record data as transactions are completed and not wait until the end of their desk assignment.

Part Two: Work-Flow Diagram

A work-flow diagram provides a two-dimensional layout of a work area upon which is superimposed the movement of people, paperwork, or materials. The product is a graphic representation of a workflow. People or products can be charted either separately or in combination. The instructions for developing a work-flow diagram are straightforward.[2]

Instructions

- Draw workstation to scale with depictions of the workstations, equipment, etc. so that lines to show movement can be drawn in.
- Draw and number circles to represent the specific tasks performed, placing the circle at the workstation at which that task is performed.
- Prepare a key that defines the location represented by each numbered circle and the distance traveled from the previous circle.
- Show movements by inserting lines connecting the circles. In some instances, movements can be plotted on an actual floor plan of the work area.
- Record the frequency of movement by differentiating the lines used to represent light and heavy traffic flows. For example, a single line might represent each trip; but a heavier line or one of a different color could be used to represent frequently traveled "roads."

The following items will help one draw a work area to scale: an office layout template, an architect's ruler, scaled grid paper, building floor plans, and a tape measure. Today various software packages such as SmartDraw and QuickDraw are available to assist in this work.[3]

Illustration

To illustrate the uses of a work-flow diagram, let's examine the layout of an interlibrary borrowing unit. Interlibrary borrowing and lending processes can involve considerable movement of staff, materials, and forms. In the following illustration the path depicted represents the flow of work as an ILB staff member processes patron requests for materials.

Figure 7-4 depicts the paths traveled by staff to process requests for monographs. Requests for articles are handled differently because online full-text copies are available for many requested articles. It is easy to see that this procedure involves a great deal of movement. Figure 7-5 represents the key to the movement that is shown in the work-flow diagram. The key provides enough explanation so that the reader can follow what is happening throughout the procedure.

Several points merit attention. First, the forms are brought from the reference department that is located in another part of the building. This operation occurs only once a day so this step could have been skipped because it skews the distance traveled. Second, if we had decided to diagram the movement of the ILB requests instead of the staff members who were processing the requests, the diagram would have looked different as several operations would have been replaced by delay symbols (D) because request forms were temporarily filed to await processing later. Steps 3-4, 9-10, and 10-11 in Figure 7-5 illustrate this point. Third, most requests are received via email or the Web. If we had been charting these forms, the work-flow diagram would have begun with the printing of the requests at workstation number 1. And finally, since we are focused on movement, we can ignore the decision points that occur throughout the procedure, e.g., if a request is RUSH it isn't filed temporarily but processed immediately. (See step 9-10 in the key.)

It should be fairly obvious that this procedure was badly in need of reorganization. As a matter of fact, once the floor plan and work-flow diagram were laid out, and staff members were given an opportunity to think about traffic flows, they immediately began to offer suggestions. For example, why not cluster the files and workstations in a single area? But what I found most fascinating was once staff began looking at traffic flows, they also began raising equally insightful questions about files and work methods. For example, why were so many paper files being maintained? Why couldn't some or all of them be eliminated? Why was there a special workstation for collecting tracking and workload data? This step in the procedure often caused backlogs because the software was so slow. One person asked why they were using a local software package when commercial packages were available. This person went on to add: "Why don't we use a software package that would allow us to use bar codes to keep track of progress?" Gradually the layout that evolved was much more efficient. Furthermore over the next few months this discussion led to an overhaul of the entire system, and the adoption of an entirely new interlibrary borrowing and lending system that permitted the elimination of a great deal of paperwork.

A work-flow diagram can also be used in conjunction with a flow process chart. Figure 7-6 depicts a flow process chart that describes the handling of requests from the point they are received until they are transmitted via OCLC or are mailed. This was a logical breaking point because no action occurs until the requested item is received. Figure 7-7 is a work-flow diagram that is keyed directly to the flow process chart.[4]

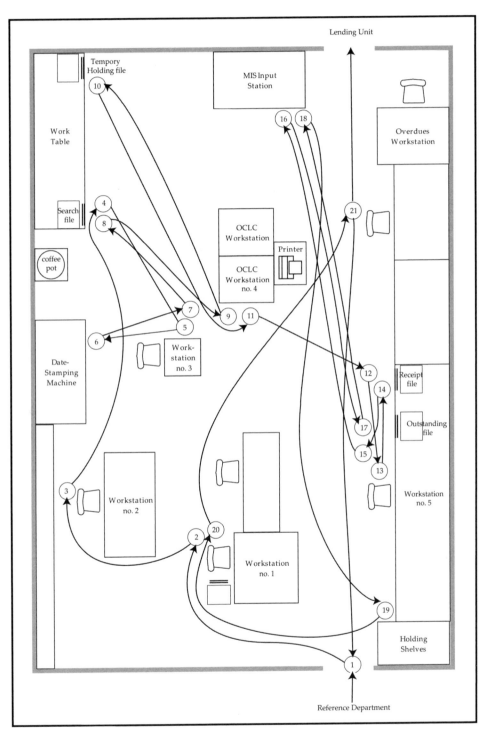

Figure 7-4 Work-flow Diagram: ILB request procedure.

Step#	Description of Movement, Task, and Distance Traveled
1-2	Reference department to workstation #1 where requests are ready for pre-search processing (1,400 feet, once per day).
2-3	Workstation #1 to workstation #2 where pre-search process is performed (12 ft).
3-4	Workstation #2 to search file where requests ready for searching are held until they are searched. Except for those designated as "rush," requests are processed on a First-In/First-Out basis (20 ft).
4-5	Search file to workstation #3 where requests are prepared for date-stamping (13 ft).
5-6	Workstation #3 to date-stamping machine where requests are date-stamped (9 ft).
6-7	Date-stamping machine back to workstation #3 where pre-processing is completed (9 ft).
7-8	Workstation #3 to search file (13 ft).
8-9	Search file to workstation #4 where OCLC searching is performed (11 ft).
9-10	Workstation #4 to temporary holding file where the searched forms are held until actual transmission occurs (17 ft).
10-11	Temporary holding file to workstation #4 where requests are transmitted via OCLC (17 ft).
11-12	Workstation #4 to receipt file where forms are held until requested book is received (10 ft).
12-13	Receipt file to workstation #5 where the receipt process is performed (10 ft).
13-14	Workstation #5 to receipt file (10 ft).
14-15	Receipt file to workstation #5. Because the workstation and file are not in the same location, the student assistant made numerous trips between the two while checking various records (10 ft).
15-16	Workstation #5 to MIS database input station (25 ft).
16-17	MIS workstation to outstanding file where forms are held until user returns item (25 ft). (Forms for non-returnables are sent to the lending unit where they will be archived.)
17-18	Outstanding file to MIS workstation where the local MIS system is updated (25 ft). (This step occurs after a returnable is processed for return.)
18-19	MIS workstation to holding shelves where books to be returned are shelved, until they are picked up and delivered to mailroom for processing (45 ft).
19-20	Holding shelves to workstation #1 where transactions and OCLC transaction are completed (8 ft).
20-21	Workstation #1 to lending unit where forms will be archived (70 ft).

Figure 7-5 Key to Work-flow Diagram: ILB request procedure.

Flow Process Chart					Summary			

						Pres. Meth.	Prop. Meth.	Diff.
Subject or Procedure Charted: **Processing ILB Requests**								
Present ☑ or Proposed ☐ Method			Type of Chart ☑ Man ☐ Product		Operations	13		
Chart Begins	Picks up requests at reference desk				Transportation	11		
Chart Ends:	Returns to workstation				Inspections			
Charted By: **KED**		Date: **April 4, 2007**			Delays			
		Sheet 1 of 1			Distance in feet	1542		

Dist. In feet	Time in Min	Symbol	Step no.	Description of Event
		●□□▽▷	1	Picks up requests at reference desk
1400		○■□▽▷	2	To pre-search workstation no.1
		●□□▽▷	3	Prepares requests for search
12		○■□▽▷	4	To workstation no.2
		●□□▽▷	5	Completes pre-search processing
20		○■□▽▷	6	To search file
		●□□▽▷	7	Files requests
		●□□▽▷	8	Picks up requests ready for date-stamping
13		○■□▽▷	9	To date-stamping machine
		●□□▽▷	10	Date stamps requests
9		○■□▽▷	11	To workstation no.3
		●□□▽▷	12	Completes pre-processing
13		○■□▽▷	13	To the seach file
		●□□▽▷	14	Picks up requests ready for processing
11		○■□▽▷	15	To workstation no.4
		●□□▽▷	16	Searches OCLC
17		○■□▽▷	17	To the temporary file (to await actual transmission)
		●□□▽▷	18	Files requests
		●□□▽▷	19	Picks up requests ready for transmittal
20		○■□▽▷	20	To workstation no.4
		●□□▽▷	21	Transmits requests
22		○■□▽▷	22	To receipt file (held until book arrives)
		●□□▽▷	23	Files requests
25		○■□▽▷	24	Returns to workstation no.2

Figure 7-6 Flow Process Chart: ILB request procedure.

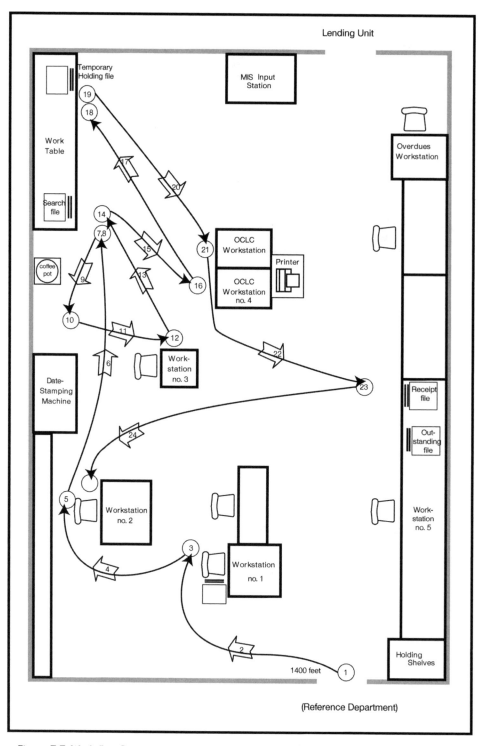

Figure 7-7 Work-flow Diagram: Processing ILB request—keyed to a flow process chart.

Part Three: Flow Process Chart

The flow process chart is one of the first tools used by analysts going as far back as the Gilbreth era.[5] This charting tool was particularly useful in documenting routine procedures that were highly repetitious and frequently performed. When the first edition of *Scientific Management of Library Operations* appeared, there were many library procedures that met the criteria of being frequently performed and highly repetitious, but in the intervening years, many of these procedures have been automated out of existence. For example, circulation procedures that required users to sign one or two book cards in order to check out a book, which was slow and cumbersome, have been largely replaced by streamlined procedures using bar code readers or sensitized plates used with RFID tags.

There are still many occasions when the flow process chart can prove to be a useful tool. For example, the interlibrary lending book-packing procedure depicted in Figure 7-16 (see page 79) describes a straightforward repetitious procedure that is frequently performed by ILL student assistants. Other commonly performed procedures that come to mind are: photocopying and mailing, preparing fax copies, book return procedures, mailroom packing and unpacking procedures, registration of new borrowers, and book preparation procedures. Even a cursory look in the typical library will uncover many more examples.

When a process involves a great deal of movement of staff and/or materials, the flow process chart can be an effective tool even if many decision points are involved. For example, when a new book arrives in the order department, what is the path it will travel until it finally reaches the shelf? Are the involved processes and procedures organized to minimize unnecessary movement? It was pretty clear that the ILB request handling procedure depicted in Figure 7-4 was poorly organized.

When movement seems excessive, charting all of the main decisions and simply ignoring all of the exception decisions will produce a clear picture of the situation. The resultant chart will clearly reveal the distances traveled. But if one desires to chart all of the decision points in order to develop a logical representation of the processes and procedures that comprise a workflow, then a flow chart would be the appropriate choice of tool. (See Chapter 7, part 4.)

The flow process chart is used to describe a procedure at a level of detail that makes it possible to identify each task as it is performed, e.g., stamp a book, shelve

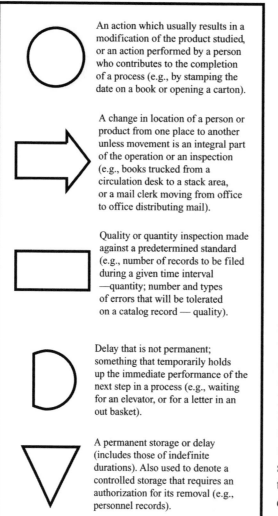

An action which usually results in a modification of the product studied, or an action performed by a person who contributes to the completion of a process (e.g., by stamping the date on a book or opening a carton).

A change in location of a person or product from one place to another unless movement is an integral part of the operation or an inspection (e.g., books trucked from a circulation desk to a stack area, or a mail clerk moving from office to office distributing mail).

Quality or quantity inspection made against a predetermined standard (e.g., number of records to be filed during a given time interval —quantity; number and types of errors that will be tolerated on a catalog record — quality).

Delay that is not permanent; something that temporarily holds up the immediate performance of the next step in a process (e.g., waiting for an elevator, or for a letter in an out basket).

A permanent storage or delay (includes those of indefinite durations). Also used to denote a controlled storage that requires an authorization for its removal (e.g., personnel records).

Figure 7-8 Flow Process Chart: Symbols.

a book, record the date, etc. By means of graphic representation and narrative descriptions, the flow process chart documents a procedure in which people, materials, or forms move from one workstation to another. As already mentioned, the flow process chart is especially valuable in identifying distances traveled, unrecognized delays, and unnecessary inspections.

The American Society of Mechanical Engineers (ASME) has issued a set of standardized symbols that are used with the flow process chart.[6] (See Figures 7-8 and 7-9.) The ASME has also made available special symbols that allow one to record two actions at the same time; for example, one might check the completeness of a form while walking from one workstation to another. (See Figure 7-9.) The flow process chart can also be used to show the creation of a form or the addition of information on an existing form. The basic ASME symbols are often included as part of preprinted forms. Figures 7-10 and 7-11 illustrate two typical pre-printed versions.

The only difference between the two formats is that the second version enables an analyst to jot down ideas for improvements while actual observations are being made. There is also no reason why a library can't design its own version for local consumption as shown in Figures 7-14, 7-15, and 7-16 (see pages 76, 77, and 79).

Description of the Flow Process Chart

The chart is usually organized into three sections. Normally one completes the basic information first, and then fills in the summary section after the observations are made. The major section describes the process being documented and the se-

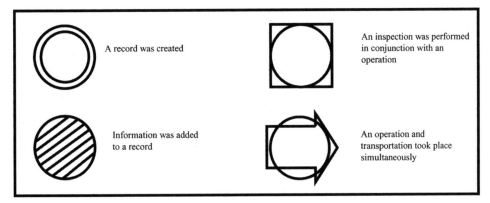

Figure 7-9 Flow Process Chart: Special symbols.

quence in which the tasks are performed. The distance moved, time taken, symbol, step number, and description of events are also recorded. As shown in Figure 7-11, the chart can be formatted to include prompts about possible improvements at the same time one is observing the staff worker.

When designing a flow process chart, one should include the following information in the header section:

1. who or what is being charted,

2. whether the chart represents a present or proposed process,

3. starting and finishing points of the process being charted,

4. name of the analyst,

5. date the charting was done,

Flow Process Chart					Summary			
Subject or Procedure Charted:						Pres. Meth.	Prop. Meth.	Diff.
Present ❑ or Proposed ❑ Method		Type of Chart ❑ Man ❑ Product			Operations			
Chart Begins:					Transpor- tation			
Chart Ends:					Inspections			
Charted By		Date			Delays			
		Sheet of			Distance in feet			
Dist. In feet	Time in Min	Symbol	Step no.	Description of Event				
		◯▢▢▽▷						
		◯▢▢▽▷						
		◯▢▢▽▷						
		◯▢▢▽▷						

Figure 7-10 Flow Process Chart: Pre-printed forms.

Flow Process Chart				Summary		
Subject or Procedure Charted:					Pres. Meth.	Prop. Meth.	Diff.
Present ☐ or Proposed ☐ Method	Type of Chart ☐ Man ☐ Product			Operations			
Chart Begins:				Transpor-tation			
Chart Ends:				Inspections			
Charted By Date				Delays			
Sheet of				Distance in feet			
Dist. In feet	Time in Min	Symbol	Step no.	Description of Event	Possible Improvements		
		○☐☐▽▷ ○☐☐▽▷ ○☐☐▽▷ ○☐☐▽▷					

Figure 7-11 Flow Process Chart: Pre-printed form with space provided to record possible improvements.

6. tabular summary block for comparing the present and proposed methods, and

7. description of events, flow process chart symbols, and step numbers.

The time and distance-traveled sections are optional but very useful. Times were not included in the figures because we were focusing on what work is done, and not how much time the work takes. Once the steps of a procedure are known, a time study can be conducted and the times added if desired. The symbol section can be designed in either of two ways: a single column where the analyst draws each symbol as needed or a column with all symbols arranged so that a line can be drawn through the column as one proceeds. The chart with all of the symbols displayed is faster to use, but it does reduce the amount of space available for describing each task. The multi-column form works well for charting a process, the single-column form for presentations in final reports.

Instructions for Preparing a Flow Process Chart

- Before observations actually begin, brief the person(s) to be observed. Those involved should understand what is going on, and how the results of the study will be used. Without such information some staff are going to feel threatened and a few even intimidated.[7]

- Decide what or who is to be charted. Will the analyst observe what a person does, or what is done to a product or form? Once decided, the subject of the chart should not be changed. One simple way to prevent inadvertent switching of subjects is to fill out the form in the active voice when one is observing a person and the passive voice when a product or form is being charted. In

Figure 7-6 the process would have been described differently had we been charting the request form and not the staff member. The forms not only moved around, they were frequently filed and stored to wait processing later.

- Choose a definite beginning and ending point. Be sure not to omit any part of the process or procedure. A block diagram providing an overview of the activities to be studied can help one avoid such oversights. Remember to distinguish between performing the work, and the preparation and put-away steps. (See Figure 7-16, page 79 for an illustration.)

- Make a few trial runs. This provides an opportunity to become familiar with the procedure and to observe which operations are performed during each job cycle. The trial period also helps the person being observed to become accustomed to the presence of the observer.

- Chart each step in the procedure even though an action may appear to be unimportant or superfluous. It is preferable to include too much detail than not enough. It might sound trite, but a task that is not recorded cannot be eliminated. A job should be charted as it is actually performed, and not as one thinks it should be performed. This error is easy to make when one is simultaneously observing and thinking of possible improvements. It is particularly easy to lose focus when one suddenly becomes conscious that a particular step, or series of steps, is not necessary. Keep in mind that the first objective is to chart the job, as it is performed, and then, and only then, to concentrate on how to improve it.

- When the charting has been completed, calculate the number of operations, transportations, the distances traveled, and the number of delays and inspections, and record these figures in the summary block.

Charting Procedures with Decision Points

One major limitation of the flow process chart is that procedures involving numerous decision points (yes-no decisions) can't be easily charted. When numerous decision points are involved, the flow chart, which is introduced in Chapter 7, part 4, is a better-suited tool. However, a flow process chart can accommodate procedures that consist primarily of a series of operations and involve only a few decision points.

A public library's book hold procedure outlined in Figure 7-12 illustrates such a case. Its purpose is to simply show how a flow process chart can accommodate a limited number of decision points which are highlighted with italics and underlines. Notice that the basic procedures have been divided into a series of sub-procedures, each initiated with a conditional statement, e.g., "If the title is already on hold." If the library also lent periodicals, we would have inserted a sub-procedure headed: "If requested title is a periodical." Also in an actual situation the work would have been organized so that tasks were batched; that is, all of the requests would have

Flow Process Chart					Summary			

Subject or Procedure Charted: Processing Holds

		Pres. Meth.	Prop. Meth.	Diff.
Present ☑ or Proposed ☐ Method	Type of Chart ☑ Person ☐ Product	Operations	22		
Chart Begins: Walks to the circulation desk		Transportation	12		
Chart Ends: Returns to work area		Inspections			
Charted By: APD	Date	Delays			
	Sheet 1 of 1	Distance in feet	2000		

Dist. In feet	Time in Min	Symbol	Step no.	Description of Event	Proposed Improvements
65		O D □ ▽ ■	1	Walks to the circulation desk	
		● D □ ▽ D	2	Picks up accumulation of requests	
65		O D □ ▽ ■	3	Walks to the work area	
		● D □ ▽ D	4	Arranges requests by author and title	
		● D □ ▽ D	5	Checks OPAC to see if library already owns title or if the title has been purchased but is not yet cataloged	
		● D □ ▽ D	6	Checks OPAC to determine whether title is available	
				If the library already owns the titile and it is already in circulation	
		● D □ ▽ D	7	Adds patron's name to hold list	
		● D □ ▽ D	8	Notifies patron via email that book is available and how long the book will be held	
				If the library already owns the titile and it is available	
		● D □ ▽ D	9	Records call numbers and locations	
705		O D □ ▽ ■	10	Walks to shelf	
		● D □ ▽ D	11	Retrieves book	
160		O D □ ▽ ■	12	Returns to the work area with requested titles	
				If the library has purchased the title but it has not yet been cataloged	
350		O D □ ▽ ■	13	Walks to the cataloging unit	
		● D □ ▽ D	14	Checks the new book holding shelves	
55		O D □ ▽ ■	15	Walks to the desk of the unit supervisor	
		● D □ ▽ D	16	Places RUSH flier in book and requests that book be cataloged	
295		O D □ ▽ ■	17	Returns to work area	
				If a title is neither owned nor on order	
		● D □ ▽ D	18	Places request in the "consideration" file	
				Preparing requested books for circulation	
				If patron requests notification via email	
		● D □ ▽ D	19	Notifies patron via email that book is available and how long the book will be held	
		● D □ ▽ D	20	Places request form in book	
75		O D □ ▽ ■	21	Walks to the holding area in the circulation	
		● D □ ▽ D	22	Shelves book according to patron's name	
				If patron doesn't have an email address	
		● D □ ▽ D	23	Fills out notice to be sent to patron	
		● D □ ▽ D	24	Places postage stamp on card	
40		O D □ ▽ ■	25	Walks to mail box	
		● D □ ▽ D	26	Drops reserve post cards into box	
		● D □ ▽ D	27	Places request form in book	
40		O D □ ▽ ■	28	Walks to the holding area in the circulation	
		● D □ ▽ D	29	Shelves book according to patron's name	
				Processing "not called for" titles	
75		O D □ ▽ ■	30	Walks to holding area	
		● D □ ▽ D	31	Checks dates	
		● D □ ▽ D	32	Removes books from the shelf	
		● D □ ▽ D	33	Places titles on the "to be shelved" book truck	
75		O D □ ▽ ■	34	Returns to the work area	

Figure 7-12 Processing book holding requests which involve a series of decisions.

been checked in the relevant catalog(s), all of the books would have been retrieved during the same trip, etc. The arrows in Figure 7-12 indicate steps that would have been repeated until all holds were processed.

First Illustration

Let us briefly examine the process of loading a dishwasher. This illustration might seem a bit contrived, but the procedure as described was my method until my wife suggested there might be a more efficient way. It was my practice, without much thought, to fill the dishwasher by removing each setting of dirty dishes from the table and transporting them to the kitchen work area, where I scraped and rinsed them. The dishes were then carried to the dishwasher, where they were loaded into the unit. The work-flow diagram depicting my movements appears as Figure 7-13. (What I found most intriguing about this set-up was the location of the dishwasher. Obviously the owner of the apartment didn't utilize a work-flow diagram when laying out the kitchen.) The obvious way to reduce movement was to batch the work, and carry out all of the plates, silverware, etc. at the same time. A flow process chart description of the procedure I initially followed is shown in Figure 7-14 and the improved procedure is shown in Figure 7-15. There is certainly a difference in the tasks performed and the distance traveled.

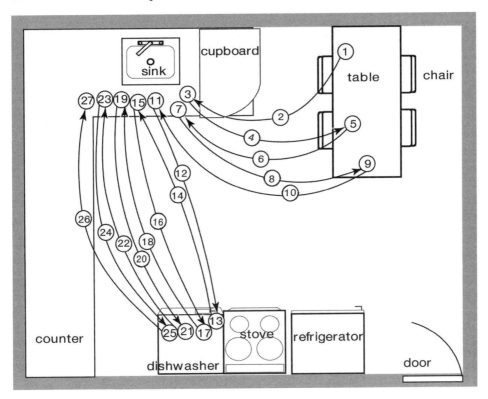

Figure 7-13 Work-Flow Diagram: Loading a dishwasher.

Flow Process Chart					Summary			
Subject or Procedure Charted: **Loading a dishwasher**						Pres. Meth.	Prop. Meth.	Diff.
Present ☑ or Proposed ☐ Method		Type of Chart ☑ Man ☐ Product			Operations	15		
Chart Begins: **Stacks one place setting of dishes**					Transportation	14		
Chart Ends: **returns to table**					Inspections	0		
Charted By:		Date			Delays	0		
KED		Sheet 1 of 1			Distance in feet	136		

Dist. In feet	Time in Min	Symbol	Step no.	Description of Event
		○	1	stacks one place setting of dishes
12		▷	2	takes dishes to sink
		○	3	places dishes in sink
12		▷	4	returns to table
		○	5	stacks 2nd place setting of dishes
12		▷	6	takes dishes to sink
		○	7	places dishes in sink
12		▷	8	returns to table
		○	9	stacks 3rd place setting of dishes
12		▷	10	takes dishes to sink
		○	11	rinses dishes
8		▷	12	places 1st setting in dishwasher
		○	13	
8		▷	14	returns to sink
		○	15	
8		▷	16	places 2nd setting in dishwasher
		○	17	loads dishes
8		▷	18	returns to sink
		○	19	
8		▷	20	places 3rd setting in dishwasher
		○	21	
8		▷	22	returns to sink
		○	23	removes soap from under sink
8		▷	24	returns to dishwasher
		○	25	adds soap
		○	26	starts dishwasher
8		▷	27	returns to sink
		○	28	returns soap to sink
12		▷	29	returns to table

Figure 7-14 Flow-Process Chart: Loading a dishwasher.

Flow Process Chart					Summary			
Subject or Procedure Charted: Loading a dishwasher						Pres. Meth.	Prop. Meth.	Diff.
Present ☐ or Proposed ☑ Method		Type of Chart ☑ Man ☐ Product			Operations	15	13	2
Chart Begins: **walks to storage cuboard from table**					Transpor-tation	14	6	8
Chart Ends: **sits down**					Inspections	0	0	0
Charted By: Date					Delays	0	0	0
KED			Sheet 1 of 1		Distance in feet	136	46	90

Dist. In feet	Time in Min	Sym-bol	Step no.	Description of Event
2		▢	1	walks to storage cuboard from table
		◯	2	removes tray from cupboard
2		▢	3	walks to table
		◯	4	places all dishes on the tray
12		▢	5	walks to sink with tray of dishes
		◯	6	places tray on counter
		◯	7	rinses dishes
		◯	8	sets dishes on tray
		◯	9	removes soap from under sink — puts it on the tray
8		▢	10	walks to dishwasher with tray and soap
		◯	11	laods dishwasher
		◯	12	adds soap
		◯	13	starts machine
8		▢	14	returns to sink
		◯	15	returns soap to sink
12		▢	16	walks to storage cupboard
		◯	17	returns tray to storage cupboard
2		▢	18	returns to table
		◯	19	sits down

Figure 7-15 Flow Process Chart: Loading dirty dishes into a dishwasher—proposed method.

Second Illustration

Let us now examine how a library's interlibrary library loan unit prepared books for shipment to requesting libraries. Figure 7-16 depicts the current work method. Note that the chart is organized to highlight the steps that are repeated for each address to which books will be mailed. The initial (preparation) and ending (put-away) steps are performed only once.

In this particular illustration, the analysis reveals that the work being performed in the loading dock area could be completed more efficiently and easily if the work were performed in the interlibrary lending unit work area itself. At present the student assistant must create a special workspace on each trip because there is no space in the loading dock area dedicated to the packing procedure.

I'm sure that experienced interlibrary lending staff can offer additional suggestions on how the procedure could be further streamlined. Chapter 16 presents suggestions and tips on how to develop improved methods for procedures such as this one. But it is never too soon to begin posing a series of Why, What, When, Where, Who, and How questions to explore how procedures might be streamlined.

Flow Process Chart

					Summary		
						Pres. Meth.	Prop. Meth.	Diff.

Subject or Procedure Charted: Preparing Book for Shipment

	Pres. Meth.	Prop. Meth.	Diff.
Present ☑ or Proposed ☐ Method — Type of Chart ☑ Man ☐ Product	Operations	**20**		
Chart Begins: **Wheels book truck to mail shelves**	Transportation	**7**		
Chart Ends: **Returns to ILB unit**	Inspections			
Charted By: **RMD** — Date	Delays			
Sheet 1 of 1	Distance in feet	**1,993**		

Dist. In feet	Time in Min	Symbol	Step no.	Description of Event
				Preparation
20		○ D □ ▽ ▬	1	Wheels book truck to "outgoing" mail shelves
		● D □ ▽ D	2	Removes batch of books from the "outgoing mail" shelf
		● D □ ▽ D	3	Places books on book truck
950		○ D □ ▽ ▬	4	Transports truck from the ILB unit to the mailing area
		● D □ ▽ D	5	Opens the storage cabinet
		● D □ ▽ D	6	Retrieves supplies from the storage cabinet
		● D □ ▽ D	7	Places supplies, i.e., tape, scissors, envelopes, etc., on truck
16		○ D □ ▽ ▬	8	Wheels truck to the designated work area
		● D □ ▽ D	9	Clears work space
				Process
		● D □ ▽ D	10	Tapes label onto padded mailer (When all of the books have been packed, the packages will be placed in a mailing sack)
		● D □ ▽ D	11	Opens first padded mailer
		● D □ ▽ D	12	Takes first book from book truck
		● D □ ▽ D	13	Removes pre-printed mailing label from book
		● D □ ▽ D	14	Places book in the mailing envelope
		● D □ ▽ D	15	Closes mailer by folding one end over
		● D □ ▽ D	16	Staples folded end three times
		● D □ ▽ D	17	Places tape over staples and wraps around the entire envelope
19		● D □ ▽ D	18	Moves truck to mailbag area
		● D □ ▽ D	19	Places package in USPS mailing bag
		● D □ ▽ D	20	Fills out green mailing card
		● D □ ▽ D	21	Places green card inside the mailing bag
		● D □ ▽ D	22	Places mailing bag in outgoing mailing cart (More than one mailing bag may be necessary)
19		○ D □ ▽ ▬	23	Returns to work area
				Put-Away
		● D □ ▽ D	23	Picks up supplies
19		○ D □ ▽ ▬	24	Returns to supplies cabinet
		● D □ ▽ D	25	Places unused supplies in cabinet
950		○ D □ ▽ ▬	26	Returns to the ILB unit

Figure 7-16 Flow Process Chart: Preparing books for shipment.

Part Four: Flow Chart

The flow chart is designed to document the key steps of a process, the yes-no decisions, to identify responsibility for individual tasks, and show where in the process tasks occur. Flow charts can also be formatted so that it is relatively easy to keep track of time and distance traveled. This tool is particularly helpful in analyzing complex workflows and processes that involve decisions, e.g., reference and cataloging-related activities.

Of course, the flow chart was originally designed as a tool for developing computer software. It didn't take long, however, before analysts realized that this tool could also be used to analyze and document processes and procedures that were independent of any computer activity.

Flow charts are very versatile. They can be used to analyze complicated activities, e.g., training, advertising, or market research programs. But the primary application in libraries is their use in analyzing processes and procedures that involve many decision points, e.g., copy cataloging, preparation of books for digitizing, interlibrary lending and borrowing, etc. This tool can also be used to develop Web sites and computer interfaces.

A standardized set of symbols is used to communicate the flow of the actions and the decision points. These symbols are described in Figure 7-17. A typical flow-charting template is shown in Figure 7-18.

Instructions

The simple procedure of starting a car shown in Figure 7-19 illustrates most of the principles of flow charting. The easiest way to master the principles is by flow charting something simple and familiar. The basic instructions for flow charting are straightforward:

- State the objectives of the process or procedure. It is important to be clear about what is to be analyzed. An overview chart such as the one shown in Figure 7-20 can be helpful.
- Decide on the level of detail to chart. It is usually best to err on the side of too much detail. As noted earlier, a step that isn't charted can't be reviewed later.
- Identify the major steps in the process. Again an overview chart can prove helpful.

- Phrase questions so that they can be answered by a yes-no. **All** questions must be answerable with either "yes" or "no" responses. If you are unable to do this, the original question must be rephrased or divided into two or more questions so that a "yes" or "no" is possible. There should be only one output arrow per process box; when this is not possible, a decision point may be involved so that additional questions will need to be posed.

- Chart the tasks in the sequence as they are presently performed.

- Determine the beginning and end of the activity to be charted. Each chart should have a logical starting and stopping point. The flows should eventually reach a point where no additional action is necessary, or a point where the action is passed on to another process.

Symbols	Name	Explanation
◇	Decision	The question must always be answerable with a "yes" or "no." If there are more than two choices, additional questions must be posed.
▭	Process	Any processing function: defined operation(s) causing change in value, form, or location of information.
○	Start/Stop	Beginning or end point in a flow chart; also used to depict an interrupt or delay.
⬠	Off Page Connector	From another chart or from another part of the same chart. Symbolizes entry to or exit from a page.
○	On Page Connector	Exit to, or entry from another part of the chart.
⌐ ⌐	Comment/ Annotation	Additional descriptive clarification, comment. (Dashed line extends to symbols as appropriate.)
←Y—	Yes Line	Leads from a question box to the box which answers "yes."
←N—	No Line	Leads from a question box to the box which answers "no."

Figure 7-17 Flow chart symbols.

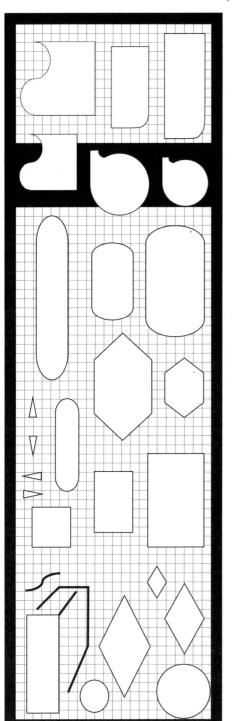

Figure 7-18 Flow chart template.

- Organize the chart so that the main flow of the trunk proceeds from the top of the page downward, or moving from the left-hand margin to the right recording the decisions and processes as they occur in the process. The branch-flows represent alternative decisions and actions—exceptions to the norm. For example, in Figure 7-19, when the ignition key is turned on, the normal reaction is for the engine to start. Therefore, the "yes" response to "engine start?" is located along the main trunk. But since the engine does not always start, a series of alternatives is represented to the side of the main trunk by additional questions and actions.

- Write descriptions that are brief yet lucid; otherwise readers may find it difficult to follow the flow. When an explanation to the process is deemed necessary, a box off to the side can be used. In Figures 7-21 and 7-22 a comment/annotation box (dashed lines) was used to provide additional information.

Common Pitfalls to Avoid

- Switching of subjects. One should decide on a subject (person, form, book, etc.) and stick with it. Switching subjects can produce a confusing chart. As mentioned previously, a chart that describes what a person is doing with an interlibrary borrowing request would be different than a chart that analyzes what actions occur to a form.

- Creating an endless loop. One must be able to get out of the chart on all of the paths.

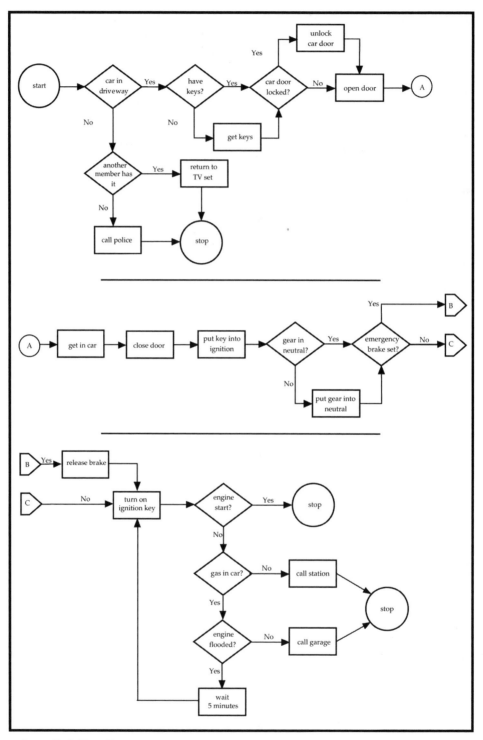

Figure 7-19 Flow Chart: Starting an automobile engine.

- Using conditional statements in the comment or annotation box. One should transform conditional statements into decision statements.

- Creating different levels of detail in the present and proposed methods—this can be described as the "kidding oneself technique." Before and after charts should always be constructed with the same level of detail.

Working with the Data

Constructing a flow chart is often not as intellectually demanding as it is physically cumbersome. I recall on one occasion posting many pages of computer printout paper on the walls of a meeting room. The chart covered almost 30 feet of wall space. We were charting all aspects of operations in a technical services division. Today I'm more likely to tape newsprint on a wall, and use stickies to represent the workflows. I've found that using wall space to display a flow chart helps to identify relationships among a group of related processes and procedures.

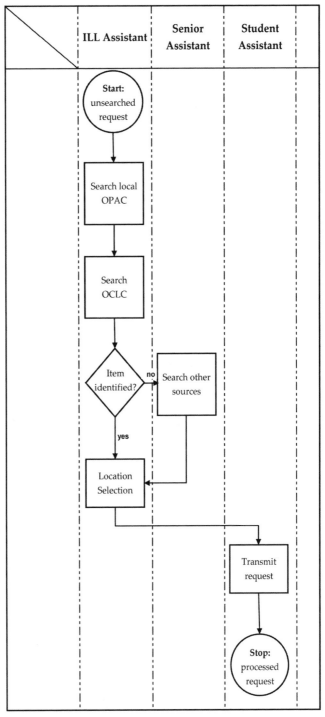

Figure 7-20 Flow Chart: Overview of searching an ILB request chart is organized to show who performs the various tasks.

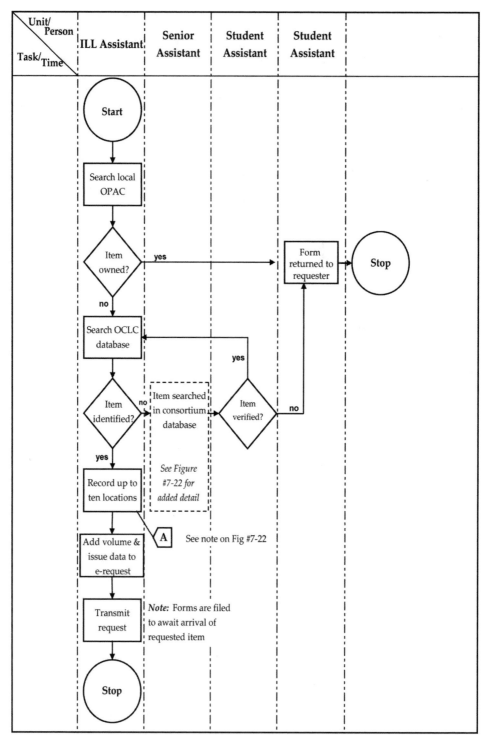

Figure 7-21 Flow Chart: Charting an ILB request.

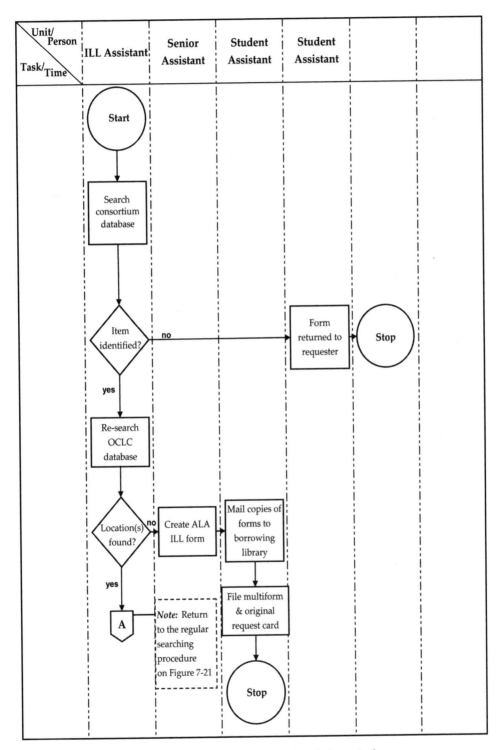

Figure 7-22 Flow Chart: Searching a local consortium data (sub-routine).

I've found that posting drafts, and inviting staff who are familiar with the workflows to comment on them, often improves accuracy. In the project that produced the 30-foot-long charts, staff members were particularly helpful in identifying logical errors. Moreover, in this project, once staff began to examine the charts, several of them offered constructive suggestions on how the workflows might be streamlined.

It is really surprising how complex some library processes can be at times. I recall charting the path of a periodical subscription request as it progressed through the various stages of review. The resulting flow chart measured 13 feet in length. It wasn't difficult to understand why it often took up to one year before a requested title was actually acquired.

Finally, once the process has been charted and critiqued, a commercial software package can be used to construct a polished version of the work. There are a variety of software packages available on the Web, including SmartDraw, which I found very useful.[8] Tools such as QuickDraw can be used to transform a 30-foot draft into a polished final version.

Useful Enhancements

The interlibrary borrowing searching procedure illustrated in the preceding series of figures serves to illustrate the versatility of a flow chart. Figure 7-20 provides a simple overview of the procedure and identifies the classification of those responsible for performing the work. Figure 7-21 represents a more detailed description of the searching procedure. Figure 7-22 depicts a sub-routine of searching a consortium's database when the requested item couldn't be located in OCLC's database. Figures 7-21 and 7-22 are also formatted so that the time required to perform specific tasks could have been recorded along with the classification of the person who performed the work. And, as shown in Figures 7-23 and 7-24, the charts could have been organized to record the work of specific individuals or to focus attention on the units where the work was performed.

Final Thoughts

One of the questions staff members who are just learning to analyze workflows will ask is "What tool should I be using?" While there is no pat response, I would say that if the procedure or process involves lots of movement of staff or forms, begin by constructing a work-flow diagram. It is amazing how easy it is to take movement for granted. For example, the layout of an information commons could have an enormous long-term impact on how much time is spent walking from one workstation to another. Keep in mind that while walking is a healthy activity, it doesn't qualify as a productive activity in a work setting.

If an analysis reveals a long series of operations along with transportations, a flow process chart along with a work-flow diagram might be the best way to start. There is also no reason why one can't use flow process charts and flow charts

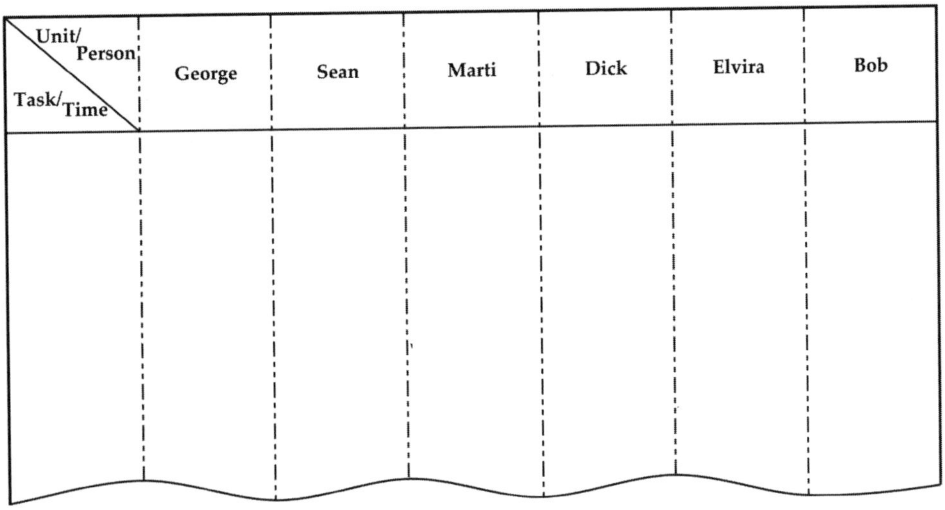

Unit/Person — Task/Time	George	Sean	Marti	Dick	Elvira	Bob

Figure 7-23 Flow Chart: Charting staff activity.

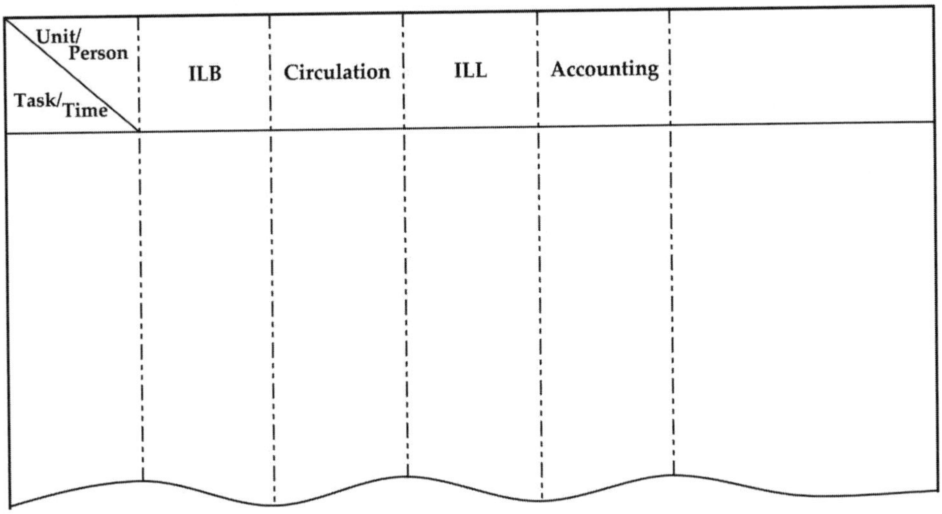

Unit/Person — Task/Time	ILB	Circulation	ILL	Accounting	

Figure 7-24 Flow Chart: Charting involvement of units.

in combination when the process under review involves both decisions and long sequences of operations, transportations, and delays. Finally, while many library employees are not comfortable in reading and thinking in terms of symbols strung together by a network of arrows, the charting information that will be produced using the tools described in this chapter can be used to create practical procedure manuals and other training aids.

Notes

1. This compilation of reference activity is based on the RefTracker system created by Altarama Information Systems. Permission to use this table has been granted.

2. There is a great deal of relevant information available on the Web. I found useful suggestions on how to organize an efficient office layout at Integrated Publishing's site, http://www.tpub.com/ask/19.htm (17 May 2007).

3. Any of the popular search engines will produce plenty of available software packages. Two packages that I found particularly relevant are SmartDraw and QuickDraw. These commercial packages offer free trial periods. SmartDraw software packages can be found at http://www.smartdraw.com/exp/dia (18 October 2006).

4. Lawrence S. Aft, *Measurement and Methods Improvement* (New York: Wiley-Interscience, 2000), 54-63. Aft provides several illustrations of how a flow process chart and a work-flow diagram can be used together.

5. Ben B. Graham of the Ben Graham Corporation publishes extensively on the subject of process analysis and work simplifications. While it is a commercial firm, Graham's Web site includes a great deal of free material on the subject, http://www.worksimp.com (17 May 2007).

6. In the 1940s the American Society of Mechanical Engineers (ASME) established a set of symbols that have remained fairly standard over the years. Today it is easy to consult the Web for lists of specialized symbols along with definitions. For example, http://www.breezetree.com/article-excel-flowchart-shapes.htm (25 May 2007).

7. The importance of briefing staff in advance of a study is mentioned at several points in the book because of its importance when undertaking any form of study. In most cases once staff members understand the purpose, they will relax and sometimes even be willing to volunteer helpful suggestions on how to improve the procedure. Library staff members are pretty good at exercising common sense about what really needs to be done and what doesn't. This admonition is discussed in greater detail in connection with conducting diary studies in Chapter 11 and work sampling studies in Chapter 12.

8. These are the same packages referenced in footnote 3. The packages can be useful for designing work-flow diagrams, flow charts, or other tools for process analysis.

Chapter Eight

Tools for Special Situations

Scope note: *This chapter describes a series of tools and techniques that can be used to collect data and analyze special situations. These specialized tools include: the control chart, the operations chart, and the worker-machine chart. The control chart can be used to identify seasonal fluctuations in activities. The operation chart is used to analyze frequently performed activities. The worker-machine chart can be used to study the interactions between a worker and a computer workstation. This chapter also introduces usability testing, techniques for collecting data unobtrusively, and basic principles of motion economy.*

In previous chapters, I presented tools designed to analyze workflows that involve staff or materials that move from one workstation to another. As noted several times, these workflows may or may not involve decisions, but in reality most library processes and procedures do include decision points. The tools already presented will suffice 98 percent of the time. Occasionally, however, situations arise that will require the use of a specialized tool. Let's begin with the control chart.

Control Chart

Many library-related processes reflect sizeable seasonal fluctuations in activity. For example, orders for new books and journals begin to rise in the fall as school begins, and drop off during the December and January holidays. Likewise, interlibrary loan requests peak in the fall and mid-spring, and significantly decline during the summer vacation months. When such peaks and valleys of activity occur, temporary staffing problems may occur, which may justify an adjustment to regular staffing patterns. The control chart can be a useful tool in documenting fluctuations in activity.

The control chart is a special form of line graph that can be used to discover how much of the variability in a process is due to random variation, and how much is due to unique events and/or individual actions. It gained popularity as one of Deming's TQM tools. In industry, control charts are normally derived from collected statistical data. They are used to examine trends and variability within a process.[1]

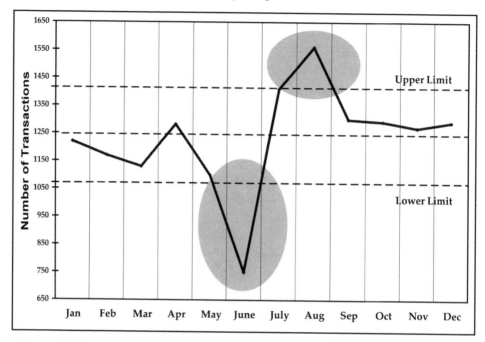

Figure 8-1 Control Chart: Staff capacity to process requests without delays.

The concept of a control chart can be applied to library situations without getting bogged down in statistical analyses. Figure 8-1 depicts how a control chart is used to identify time periods when work backlogs are either likely to accumulate and/or time periods when staff might be underutilized. In this illustration the monthly number of new book orders is plotted. This type of data, which is an easily captured statistic, is shown in Figure 8-2. The order unit knows that it has the capacity to process approximately 1,400 new order requests each month. The chart clearly shows that during the later stages of the summer and early fall, staff may not be able to keep up with the influx of new order requests using current processes and procedures. Backlogs of unprocessed requests are most likely to accumulate at this time. When the volume of work declines significantly as typically occurs during the early months of summer, staff will probably not be fully engaged by regular duties. I'm aware of situations where selected acquisitions staff workers have been cross trained so that they can perform tasks in cataloging during such lulls.

Month	No. of new orders
Jan	1220
Feb	1170
Mar	1130
Apr	1282
May	1100
June	750
July	1410
Aug	1560
Sep	1300
Oct	1292
Nov	1270
Dec	1290

Figure 8-2 Monthly receipt of new order requests.

An analysis using a control chart can prove useful in tracking the level of activity in any process that typically experiences significant fluctuations in work activity over time. Shelving of books and the receipt of interlibrary lending and borrowing requests are other common examples.

Data collected using a control chart can be helpful in a variety of ways: to justify temporary staffing; to explain to management why backlogs exist or persist; or during periods of slack activity, to justify a request to cross train staff so that they can be assigned temporarily to other duties.

Operation Chart

As already noted, flow process charts and flow charts will suffice for most studies. Both of these tools are particularly helpful in charting work as it progresses from one workstation to another. But if one wants to analyze the work at a single workstation or service desk, the appropriate technique is known as operation analysis or left-right hand analysis.

The operation chart was designed to analyze tasks that are frequently performed and are repetitive in nature. Several circulation routines fit this description very well. Separating multiple part forms in acquisitions, scanning materials or inserting RFID tags in book preparation are two other typical library illustrations.

Initially I was not going to cover operations analysis and the operation chart since there are so few library processes that justify a left-right hand analysis. Then I visited several public libraries, and observed their automated circulation checkout and discharge routines, which made me change my mind. What I often observed during my visits were lines of patrons waiting to checkout piles of books, videos, CDs, etc. If ways could be found to reduce patron waiting times, patron satisfaction undoubtedly would be enhanced.

Preparing an Operation Chart

The operation chart is also known as a left-right hand chart because it is designed to focus attention on the motions of a worker's hands or feet. The first step in analyzing an operation is to prepare a simple diagram of the work area. (See Figure 8-3.) Sometimes, just the diagram by itself will lead to an improved arrangement. The diagram should display the arrangement of all relevant equipment and materials. In Figure 8-3 the layout of the workstation was designed so that the desk attendant had sufficient space to open each book and quickly scan it.

The symbols used with operations charts are almost identical to those used with the flow process chart, although with the operation chart they apply to parts of the body, i.e., hands or feet instead of the entire body. (See Figure 8-4.)

Once again, the staff members who will be observed need to be briefed about what is going to happen, and how the results of the analysis may affect them. Some staff will experience stress at the prospect of being observed, but once they understand what will occur, their level of stress should decline.

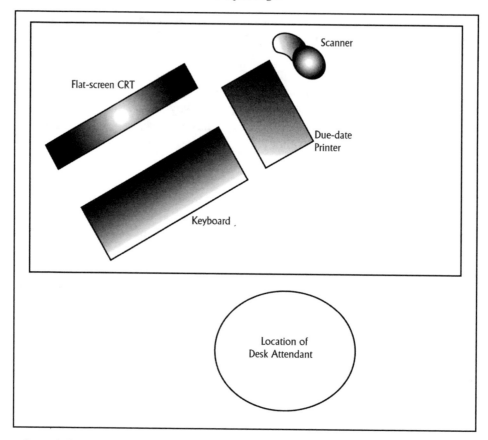

Figure 8-3 Layout of a well-designed public library circulation checkout station.

Technology has made conducting an operation analysis much easier than it was a few years ago. Today, digital camcorders can be used to record the observations.[2]

Instructions

The guidelines for preparing an operation chart are similar to those used to prepare a flow process chart.

- Choose a definite beginning and ending point. Be sure not to omit any part of the procedure being observed.

- Record a few trial runs. This provides an opportunity to become familiar with the activity and to observe which tasks are performed during each cycle. For example, if an overdue fine has to be collected, this sub-procedure would not be part of the regular checkout routine. The fine collection/ procedure would be handled on a separate chart. The trial period also helps the staff worker being observed to become more comfortable with the presence of an observer.

- Record the movements of each hand from the beginning to the end of the cycle. Several cycles should be observed until you are confident that the essence of the procedure has been recorded. You also want to record enough cycles so that you can chart the individual tasks that are performed simultaneously with both hands. Occasionally one hand will perform several steps while the other hand stays at rest. In such cases the description for one hand will have to be repeated for two or more steps in succession.

- Record each step in the cycle even though an action may appear to be unimportant or superfluous. This is easy to do with a camcorder. Keep in mind that it is always preferable to include too much detail than not enough.

- Once the chart is created, calculate the number of operations, transportations, and the number of delays and inspections, and record these figures in the summary block.

- As is true with the flow chart and the flow process chart, be sure to record the work actually performed, and not how you think the procedure *should* be performed. Keep in mind that the first objective is to record the series of steps, as they are performed, and then, and only then, to concentrate on improving the procedure.

Figure 8-5 is an operation chart of a typical library charging procedure. It is a very good example of how to analyze a frequently performed activity. Note in Figure 8-6 that the attendant is scanning a barcode that is adhered to the front cover, and in Figure 8-7 she is scanning a bar code that is located inside the front cover. The fact that the barcodes were not located in the same place did affect the staff worker's rhythm as she checked out a series of books. I asked her why she used one hand on some occasions, and two hands on others. She replied that she used one hand when the volume was light or thin, and two hands when the volumes were heavier or when she saw that the barcode was located inside the front cover.

Symbol	Name	Explanation
◯	Operation	The body member (hand) does something, except when the hand is moving toward or from an object, or holding an object. (Examples: picking up, putting together, taking apart, or writing.)
⇨	Transportation	The body member (hand) moves toward or from an object.
▽	Hold	The body member (hand) maintains an object in a fixed position so that work can be performed with it or upon it.
D	Delay	The body member (hand) is idle or is moving, but without purpose.

Figure 8-4 Symbols for operations charts.

Summary						Library: Any Place
	Present		Proposed		Difference	Department: Circulation
	LH	RH	LH	RH	LH	RH	Operation: Checking out books
Operation	12	11					
Transportation	4	6					Operator: KED
Holds	2	0					Data:
Delays	7	8					Present ☑ Proposed ☐
Total	25	25					Sheet 1 of 1

Left Hand	Symbol	No.	Symbol	Right Hand
Idle	D	1	⇨	Reaches for customer's ID card
Idle	D	2	◯	Picks up customer's ID card
Idle	D	3	⇨	Moves card to scanner
Idle	D	4	◯	Scans barcode
Idle	D	5	⇨	Returns ID card to customer
Idle	D	6	◯	Gives card to customer
Moves toward first book	⇨	7	⇨	Moves toward first book
Picks up first book	◯	8	D	Idle
Moves toward scanner	⇨	9	D	Idle
Scans barcode	◯	10	D	Idle
Sets scanned book aside	◯	11	D	Idle
Moves to second book	⇨	12	D	Idle
Picks up second book	◯	13	D	Idle
Passes book past scanner	◯	14	D	Idle
Sets scanned book aside	◯	15	◯	Picks up second book
Moves book toward scanner	⇨	16	⇨	Moves book toward scanner
Scans barcode	◯	17	◯	Scans barcode
Sets scanned book aside	◯	18	D	Idle
Idle	D	19	◯	Picks up third book
Holds book	▽	20	◯	Opens cover
Scans barcode (inside front cover)	◯	21	◯	Scans barcode (inside front cover)
Holds book	▽	22	⇨	Reaches for date due printout
Opens book	◯	23	◯	Places date due inside book
Picks up checked-out books	◯	24	◯	Picks up checked-out books
Hands books to customer	◯	25	◯	Hands books to customer

Figure 8-5 Analysis of a book charging procedure.

Figure 8-6 Scanning a front cover barcode.

Case Study: Checking Out Books

The following evolution of a circulation checkout routine illustrates how useful an operation analysis can prove to be at streamlining a frequently performed library routine.

Phase One

When the library initially began to use barcodes and hand scanners, barcodes were affixed to the inside of the book's front cover. Barcodes weren't affixed to the outside cover because staff felt that the barcode detracted from the book's appearance.

Observation: Each time a book was checked out, the circulation attendant opened the book to locate the bar code. With the book cover open, the bar code was wanded using a hand scanner. The scanner was held in the left hand, and the book was closed with the right hand and set aside, and the next book to be checked out was moved into position. One circulation attendant pointed out to me that opening the cover of the book to locate the bar code took time, and suggested that the barcode be affixed to the front cover in a standard location.

Phase Two

Based on staff suggestions, the library began to affix barcodes to the front covers in a standard location. With barcodes located outside on the front cover, the attendant could now simply scan the barcode without opening the book's cover.

Observation: This change did speed up the checkout process, but still each book had to be scanned by sweeping the scanner over the barcode.

Figure 8-7 Scanning an inside front cover barcode.

Figure 8-8 Streamlined scanning of a barcode.

Phase Three

Further analysis led to the introduction of a fixture that made it possible to simply sweep each book under the scanner (See Figure 8-8.)

Observations: The introduction of a fixture made it possible for the desk attendant to make use of two hands to scan each barcode. Two-handed work is always quicker and less fatiguing than one-handed work. One downside of placing barcodes on the outside of covers was that some barcodes began to show wear and tear. As a result, discussions occurred as to whether it was more important to protect barcodes or to speed-up the checkout process.

This debate was never settled because it became moot as the library introduced a checkout system based on RFID tags. This new technology permits the library to affix the tag inside the book cover because the volume can be checked out by simply passing it over a station reader. There is no need to read a barcode. It is a much quicker procedure. In fact the RFID technology allows an attendant to check out books one at a time or a batch of books with a single pass over a reader. The RFID technology also speeds up the discharging of books, and with some systems I've observed, it also greatly speeds up shelf reading and inventory control since missing or out of place books can be easily identified.[3]

Improving an Operation

Chapter 16 focuses on how to streamline workflows and processes. The same principles that apply to workflow improvement also apply to work that is analyzed using an operation chart. This usually means paying particular attention to "idles" and "holds." In our initial illustration, after observing the checkout procedure (see Figure 8-5), my recommendation was to encourage desk attendants to use two hands when scanning a book. I also raised the issue with management about the location of the barcodes because the use of multiple locations interfered with the attendant's working rhythm.

Other Benefits

A library that is concerned about the speed and efficiency of frequently performed tasks, particularly those that impact patron service, is also advised to keep abreast of new technological tools. For example, some libraries have been taking a leaf from banks, department stores, and supermarkets by introducing easy-to-use self-checkout stations. The use of self-checkout devices can not only help to take pressure off checkout lines during peak periods of activity, but also provide an outlet for patrons who enjoy doing things themselves.

Analyzing Relationships between Staff and Computers

The interaction between workers and machines has been the subject of analysis since the early days of Industrial Engineering. The goal of such analyses was to minimize operator and machine idle time. In industry the motivation for such analyses stemmed from the fact that a great deal of time and money were at stake. Oftentimes tens of thousands of parts were produced, and thus if machine idle time could be reduced, significant savings would be realized. Today, industrial robots perform much of the work that was formerly the focus of such studies. But in-depth study techniques are still very useful in situations where workers assemble complicated electronic products, such as laptop computers, cell phones, etc.

Worker-Machine Chart

The worker-machine chart was designed to study the interaction between a worker and one or more machines. The checkout routine shown in Figure 8-9 illustrates how a worker-machine chart could be applied in a library situation. This illustration depicts a very efficient routine because the staff worker isn't idle at any time. And in this analysis it makes no difference whether the scanner is active or idle. The illustration also highlights the benefits of a streamlined procedure because the patron is idle through the entire process: the slower the checkout process the longer the patron has to wait.

While the use of worker-machine charts hasn't had much utility in libraries, the benefits of analyzing work performed at computer workstations has mushroomed. Information on computer screens needs to be laid out clearly, otherwise information seekers as well as library staff workers are likely to become frustrated; productivity will also be adversely affected. It is still very common to encounter Web sites that are so poorly designed that one quickly exits the site feeling frustrated, and worse, never returns.

The growth of searching online catalogs or discipline-oriented databases such as BIOSIS, INSPEC, Lexis/Nexis, ProQuest, or ABInform, coupled with the growing popularity of chat reference services, have greatly increased the need for specialized training. In most libraries there now exists a work environment that justifies the analysis of work performed at computer workstations.

Direct observation of work performed at computer workstations can quickly reveal the level of skill a worker possesses, particularly if a transcript is produced as a by-product of the work performed. Transcripts are commonly used as training aids. Some libraries have also begun to employ transcript reviews as a means to evaluate the skills and subject expertise of staff who provide virtual reference

Worker/Machine Chart

Activity Charted: Check out books

Chart Begins: Greets patron   **Charted By:**

Chart Ends: Says goodbye to patron   **Date:**

Method: ☑ current   ❑ proposed   **Sheet: 1 of 1**

Man				Machine	
Patron	**Time/ Sec**	**Circulation Assistant**	**Time/ Sec.**	**Light Pen**	**Time/ Sec.**
idle	5	greets patron	5	idle	5
hands books and library card to circulation assistant	10 / 15	takes books and library card from patron	10 / 15	/ idle	10 / 15
idle	17	places ID card under scanner	17	read barcoded label	17
idle	20	passes light pen over barcoded area of first book	20	read barcoded label	20
idle	23	scans second book	23	read barcoded label	23
accepts books and library card	25	returns books and card to patron	25	idle	25
idle	30	says goodbye to patron	30	idle	30

Worker/Machine Chart Summary

Activity:

Method: ❑ current   ❑ proposed

Times	Patron	Circ. Clerk	Light Pen
idle time	95	-0-	85
working time	50	145	60
total time	145 sec	145 sec	145 sec
percent of utilization	35%	100%	41%

Figure 8-9 Worker-machine chart.

services. Hopefully improved training will lead to improvements in productivity and enhanced patron satisfaction.

Principles of Motion Economy

It seems appropriate to introduce the topic of Motion Economy in conjunction with our discussion of the layout of workstations. These principles are not new. They were introduced by the Gilbreths in conjunction with their detailed analyses of work and are as relevant today as they were when they were first introduced. Their application to highly repetitive operations can reap sizable benefits. The principles most relevant to library situations are presented in the following paragraphs.

Two-Handed Work

Two-handed work is faster than one-handed; more units can be produced with less effort. If the hands need to be idle, they should be idle at the same time during a cycle of work. Motions of the arms should be made in opposite and symmetrical directions. Holds and delays should be minimized because they are not productive. For example, in the previous case study when a fixture to hold the scanner was introduced, productivity immediately increased because this enabled the desk attendant to pass the book under the scanner using two hands. (See Figure 8-8.)

Some people express skepticism when I assert that two-handed work is faster and less fatiguing than one-handed work. I know I was dubious when this principle was first introduced to me. A quick way to dispel doubts is to place a pegboard in front of a skeptic, and ask that person to place a peg into each hole, working as quickly as possible using one hand. Record the time it takes to complete the task. Then ask this same person to divide the pegs into two piles, one for each hand, and repeat the cycle, this time using two hands to fill up the pegboard. The results of this experiment are interesting. Try it. Studies have shown that people who are skilled at performing jobs with one hand will also be good at two-handed work, and those who are slow with one-handed work will probably also be slow at two-handed work.

Normal and Extended Work Areas

It is not uncommon to see a workplace, such as a desk or table, laid out inefficiently. Layouts run the gamut from complete disorganization to arrangements in straight lines, the latter being the usual approach. A straight-line layout ignores the fact that a person works naturally in areas bounded by symmetrical arcs. The normal work area includes the surface that can be covered by the forearms as they pivot from the elbow with the upper arms hanging straight from the shoulders. (See Figure 8-10.) The area bounded by the inner intersecting arcs (solid lines) is the prime-working zone. The extended work area is formed by arcs (dashed lines) that circumscribe with the area covered by the arms extended from the shoulders. These two maximum arcs depict the zone that should be avoided. If a task requires

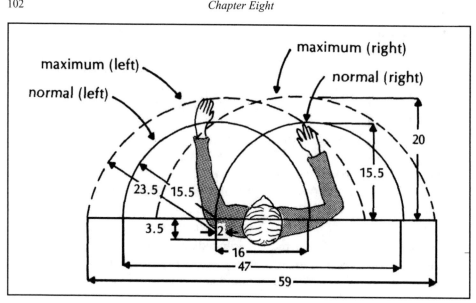

Figure 8-10 Dimensions of normal and extended work areas for a typical worker.

frequent motions into this zone, the worker will become fatigued. Because the natural motion of the arms is circular, tools and equipment should be built as close as possible around the workstation.

A typical dinner-table arrangement illustrates the difference between the normal and extended work areas. The plate and silverware occupy the prime zone, where most activity occurs. Around the immediate periphery, but in the extended zone are located the cup and saucer, wine glass, water glass, and salad plate. Beyond the extended zone it is customary to ask that food be passed into the working zones. One can appreciate the effect of a poor arrangement by imagining a reversed arrangement, that is, place the salad bowl in the prime zone and the plate in the extended area. Eating a meal under such conditions would undoubtedly prove more fatiguing and certainly less satisfying.

Placement of Tools and Materials

Tools should be positioned in fixed locations. Ordinarily, when the hand is moved, the eye precedes the hand. If tools and materials are pre-positioned, however, the hand will automatically become accustomed to the proper location, and movements will become reflexive so that the eye is able to remain at the point of activity. The fixed location of the scanner in Figure 8-8 at the circulation desk illustrates this principle very nicely. The discussion in Chapter 17 regarding the design of special workstations also offers additional illustrations of this principle. (Chapter 17, page 230.)

Usability Testing

As the number of people who work at computers expanded in the 1990s, a new engineering specialty gradually emerged. New techniques to analyze the interface and interactions between workers and computer software were developed. This specialty is known as Human-Computer Interaction (HCI).[4] HCI also led to another specialty termed "usability testing." The objective of usability testing is to improve the usability of products. Usability testing can also help break down walls between those who create products and those who use them. As we shall see shortly, this aspect of usability testing has special relevance to library situations.

Usability testing has been used in industry to test a broad range of products including regular and HD TVs, VCRs, cordless telephones, telephone/answering machines, telephone trees, electronic mail software packages, spread sheets, and time management software.[5] This represents only a small sampling of products that are routinely tested.

In library work environments, the usability of software should be of particular interest to analysts. In fact, usability testing of Web sites in libraries has become rather popular. A number of instructive case studies have been reported in the literature.[6]

Since usability testing is intended to help people accomplish their purposes, as quickly and easily as possible, the goal is to focus on busy users who want to be productive, and avoid frustration when using a product. More importantly, it is the user not the producer who decides when a product or software package is easy to use. Once again, the customer is always right. In this regard, I have personally used software packages that I found very difficult to use even though the vendor representative was convinced that my frustrations were really due to my inadequacies. While the vendor was probably right, the bottom line was that I quit using his product in favor of a competitor's version. So who lost in the end?

I believe that the techniques and tools that usability specialists employ can help librarians who must deal with vendors when trying to convince them to modify their product or software. Vendors need to be reminded, as I just said, that it is the customer, not the producer, who decides whether or not a product or software package is easy to use. Librarians can use the same techniques employed by usability specialists to identify shortcomings of software packages and to provide meaningful feedback to vendors.

Several years ago I interviewed several library staff members who were in the process of testing a new serials check-in module of a system that was offered by a well-known library vendor. The staff weren't happy, and I too was taken aback by the clunkiness of the module. It was clear that the library's previous serials module was more efficient, and much less frustrating—at least from the staff's point of view. In spite of staff objections the new module was introduced, and yes, staff in this unit became less productive. In time the vendor provided the library with an upgraded version of the module, that eliminated the clunky routines.

In part, it was staff feedback concerning the problems with the module that prompted the vendor to issue an easier-to-use version. The lesson is that one should never assume that a new software package will be more productive or easier to use than its predecessor. One needs to be ready to evaluate new and/or upgraded software packages, and be willing to speak out and provide vendors with feedback, and if necessary, badger them to improve their software.

The process of conducting a usability test is really straightforward. To begin one needs to decide on the goals and objectives of the test. Without a clear understanding of what information is being sought, there is a danger that key questions will not be asked. For example, I recall working with a library's staff that was evaluating its Web site. The analyst asked students about the terminology used on the page. "Did the students understand the terms, e.g., holds, recalls, journals, etc.?" He found that students often didn't understand the terminology that was being used. But it never occurred to the analyst that he should have interviewed staff members who also used the homepage. As a result the analyst never discovered that many new staff didn't understand the terminology any better than did the typical student.

Tests should represent real users. The test participants should engage in real tests. The investigators need to observe and record what participants do and say. It is the responsibility of the person who is conducting the study to analyze the data, diagnose the problems, and provide recommendations on how the problems can be remedied.[7]

Focus groups of actual users can also serve as an effective way to assess a product, software package, or Web site. Focus group participants may not only identify problems, but also offer suggestions on ways to improve the product. More information about the use of focus groups is presented in Chapter 4, page 26.

Unobtrusive Data Collection

I don't believe that many libraries collect data unobtrusively, but there are some service organizations that do use such techniques. When most libraries decide they need information for a project, they immediately think in terms of surveys, interviews, and questionnaires. Few consider that the wealth of information already collected may also be helpful. These are a form of "unobtrusive measures" because people are not asked to stop what they are doing and fill out forms or speak to consultants.

Organizations record a variety of information. Some common examples of data that are collected routinely:

- Absenteeism, lateness, and other "behavior" records;
- Turnover, accident, and grievance statistics;
- Who orders new books;
- Categories of patrons using the virtual reference service;

- Student assistant demographic data;
- Existing memos and letters and email.

Unobtrusive measures involve any method for studying behavior where individuals do not know they are being observed. In the world of librarianship, the most well-known studies involving the use of data collected unobtrusively have been numerous studies of reference performance. Among the best known were those conducted by Crowley, Childers, McClure and Hernon.[8] Undoubtedly the most extensive study using unobtrusive techniques is a Canadian study of government documents reference service.[9] In all of these studies, the objective was to pose questions to reference librarians who didn't know they were being tested in order to measure the accuracy of answers provided. These studies spawned a series of rebuttals and criticism about the methodology.[10]

Another form of gathering data unobtrusively that has gained some traction in the commercial world is the use of mystery shoppers. Of course in organizations where the quality of customer service is paramount, it is understandable why an organization might employ mystery shoppers in order to evaluate the quality of customer service. I am familiar with only one library that has used mystery shopper techniques, and even this library didn't use the technique as an evaluative tool, but as a training tool for its employees.[11]

Advantages

Although I have personal reservations about using data collected unobtrusively, there are some worthwhile advantages:

- When formal surveys are conducted, the individuals surveyed expect actions to be taken, but when data are collected unobtrusively raising expectations is avoided.
- With formal surveys staff or patrons may also alter their answers, often without realizing it, to conform to organizational norms, to match the surveyor's expectations, or for political reasons. Unobtrusive techniques avoid these problems.
- Unobtrusive measures can be analyzed, just as surveys can be. Letters, memos, and other "qualitative" information can be content-analyzed as can interviews and direct observations.
- Unobtrusive measures can save a great deal of time and money because existing data can be used instead of collecting new data. The information may also be more credible than survey findings.

Disadvantages

There are some significant disadvantages in using unobtrusively collected data:

- Ethical concerns may arise. Some staff members consider such a technique an invasion of privacy and a demonstration of management's lack of trust. At some institutions, a research review board would likely object to a study that didn't fully inform subjects that they were being studied.

- Legal or contractual restrictions often prevent the use of certain categories of personal information.

- Issues of validity must be considered. Numerous observations of a representative sample need to take place in order to generalize the findings. Replication is difficult when using unobtrusive observations. This is the basis for one of Hubbertz's chief criticisms of most reference service oriented research studies.[12]

- The quality of an organization's record keeping must be considered. The data available may not be accurate, reliable, valid, or easily used, even if people within the organization find it to be adequate.

Balancing the Pros and Cons

Today many staff members don't feel comfortable with any form of evaluation, but more and more libraries are placing greater emphasis on assessment and accountability. If staff members are to be formally evaluated, the methods used ought to be clearly understood by those affected by the evaluation. I believe that evaluations should be based on direct observations made by those who will do the evaluating, i.e., supervisors and/or peers.

While it is important for librarians to understand the basics of collecting data unobtrusively, I'm still not convinced that there is a place for using data collected unobtrusively as the basis for staff evaluations. One exception could be the use of mystery shoppers to evaluate staff behavior at a service desk, but even here I'd counsel caution.

Notes

1. Aluri suggested the use of control charts along with other TQM tools such as check sheets, Pareto charts, and cause and effect diagrams to evaluate reference services and also create an environment for continuous improvement. *See* Rao Aluri, "Improving Reference Service: The Case for Using a Continuous Quality Improvement Method," *Reference & User Services Quarterly* 33, iss. 2 (Winter 1993): 220-36.

2. Digital camcorders and software such as IMovie have not only simplified the analysis of frequently performed operations, they have provided a resource that can be used for other purposes, such as selected digital film clips as useful training aids.

3. When RFID technology was introduced in libraries, a number of librarians raised concerns about customer privacy. In this particular library, care was taken so that personal information was not recorded. A useful article on RFID technology has been written by Jay Singh, Navjit Brar, and Carmen Fong, "The State of RFID Applications in Libraries," *Information Technology and Libraries* (March 2006): 24-32.

4. The design of human/computer interfaces (HCI) is a very technical specialty, and its literature is extensive. A typical monograph is Dan R. Olsen, Jr., *Developing User Interfaces* (San Francisco, Calif.: Morgan Kaufmann Pub., 1998). Also a quick search of the Web under the heading "Human Computer Interface" will produce a wealth of sources including usability testing.

5. Joseph S. Dumas and Janice C. Redish, *A Practical Guide to Usability Testing,* rev. ed. (Portland, Ore.: Intellect, 1999). The authors provide a comprehensive work on the subject of usability testing. The treatment is in considerable depth as contrasted with the studies that have been published in library literature. I believe one reason for the greater complexity in methodologies that are common in the corporate sector is the considerable amount of money that is involved. One is motivated to take extra steps in order to avoid costly mistakes. Another comprehensive treatment of the topic is Jeffrey Rubin, *Handbook of Usability Testing* (New York: Wiley, 1994).

6. A study conducted by a group of librarians at Hunter College provides excellent guidance for those who desire to conduct studies of their Web site. This article also cites a number of similar library-oriented case studies. *See* Laura Cobus, Valenda Frances Dent, and Anita Ondrusek, "How Twenty-Eight Users Helped Redesign an Academic Library Web Site: A Usability Study," *Reference & User Services Quarterly* 44, no. 3 (Spring 2005): 232-46. Another useful study reports on the work of the UCLA Library Web site Redesign Team to develop a new library Web site that would be responsive to the needs of a broad spectrum of UCLA library users. The UCLA usability study employed a combination of methodologies which the authors describe in some detail. Their methodologies included surveys, card sort, and a usability test called "think aloud protocol." *See* Dominique Turnbow, Kris Kasianovitz, Lise Snyder, David Gilbert, and David Yamamoto, "Usability testing for Web Redesign: a UCLA Case Study," *OCLC Systems & Services* 21, iss. 3 (September 2005): 226-34. Another report describes how a public library conducted a study without having to bear the expense of hiring expensive consultants. *See* David King, "The Mom-and-Pop-Shop Approach to Usability Studies," *Computers in Libraries* 23, no. 1 (January 2003):12-14, 71-72.

7. It should come as no surprise that the person conducting a usability test needs to be a skilled interviewer. Usability specialists have also developed an interviewing technique that is termed "contextual interviewing." It is described as a technique for interviewing and observing users individually at their regular places of work as they do their own work. The following work is suggested for those interested in learning more about this approach to interviewing. *See* D. Wixon, K. Holtzblatt, and S. Knox, "Contextual Design: An Emergent View of System Design," *Proceedings of the ACM CH'90* (1990): 332.

8. Terence Crowley and Thomas Childers, *Information Service in Public Libraries: Two Studies* (Metuchen N.J.: Scarecrow, 1971) and Peter Hernon and Charles R. McClure, "Unobtrusive Reference Testing: The 55% Rule," *Library Journal* 111 (April 15, 1986): 37-41.

9. Juris Dilevko, *Unobtrusive Evaluation of Reference Service and Individual Responsibility: The Canadian Experience* (Westport, Conn.: Ablex Pub., 2000). All aspects of this nationwide study are thoroughly reported including a discussion of the controversy surrounding the methodology itself. This study also includes a thorough bibliography of relevant readings.

10. Andrew Hubbertz has done a nice job of explaining why most studies using unobtrusive measures to evaluate reference performance have fallen short of the mark. See Andrew Hubbertz, "The Design and Interpretation of Unobtrusive Evaluations," *Reference & User Services Quarterly* 44, iss. 4 (Summer 2005): 327-35.

11. Marlu Burkamp and Diane E. Virbick, "Through the Eyes of a Secret Shopper," *American Libraries* 33, iss. 10 (November 2002): 56.

12. Hubbertz, "The Design and Interpretation of Unobtrusive Evaluations," 327-35.

Chapter Nine

Forms and Templates

Scope note: The introduction of powerful and sophisticated integrated library systems has impacted all phases of library work, but no aspect has been more affected than the use of, and the need for, paper-based forms. Nonetheless, libraries continue to use a wide variety of forms. This chapter presents methods for tracking the flow of paperwork. Also covered are some basic principles that apply to the design of forms and Web-based templates.

In spite of the ubiquity of databases, paper documents still play important roles in our lives. Many actions in contemporary society must be preceded by a correctly completed form, and entry of that information into a database. For example, in order to use a public library a prospective patron may be required to fill out a "Patron Registration Form," which in turn authorizes the issuance of a plastic "Patron I.D. Card." To qualify for a driver's license one must fill out the "Request for a Driver's License" and often this involves completing a test that is still paper-based in some locations. Even to pick up one's clothing at the cleaners or prints from a camera shop requires a claim check (a form that includes processing numbers, dates, names, addresses, phone numbers, and so on). Of course, in most of these instances the data on the form is usually coordinated with a database.

In the pre-automation era, libraries were notable for the variety of forms they required in order to conduct business. To name just a few: order-request forms, multiple-part order forms, invoices, vouchers, reports on book funds, check-in cards, and Kardex forms; specification cards for bindery preparation, bindery slips; card-ordering forms, pre-cataloging forms, catalog-correction forms; borrowers' cards, date slips, transaction slips, overdue notices, reserve forms, ILL requests.

Integrated library systems made it possible for libraries to reduce greatly, if not eliminate entirely, traditional forms in acquisitions, serials, cataloging, circulation, and interlibrary lending and borrowing.[1] In fact, if a library using an integrated system discovers that it is still using paper to transact business, this discovery should be interpreted as a red flag; someone should immediately begin asking why the form(s) are necessary.

Of course, integrated systems haven't eliminated all forms; furthermore, many libraries still can't afford or justify the cost of an integrated system. Fortunately, many libraries have been able to share systems, which has helped smaller libraries to also enjoy the benefits of technology.

I recently posted a message on a listserv about the current use of paper-based forms. I was surprised by the number of responses and staggered by the variety of paper-based forms cited by the respondents as still in use. (See Figure 9-1.)

Patron registration	Purchase orders
Registration holds releases	Claims
Hold/Recall request	Payment vouchers
Storage (retrieval request)	Book order requests
Guest borrower's card	Travel expense forms
Copy card purchase form	Leave requests
Reserve guest form	Multi-part overdue and fine notices
Back issues form	Multi-part order forms
Periodical check-in	Checklists for book processing
and payment cards	Reference question recording form
Bindery specifications form	Immigration and employment forms
Bindery shipment box	Wage and hours forms
contents form	Gift/memorials
ILL requests	Non-print checkout form
Student satisfaction surveys	

Figure 9-1 Sampling of paper-based forms still in use.

This figure shows that many libraries are still dependent on paper versions of these forms. Another sign that paper-based forms are still necessary is the number of vendors that continue to offer forms for sale.[2] After examining the offerings of several vendors, however, I believe that paper-based forms are finally declining in popularity.

The bottom line is that there is obviously still a great deal of paper and paperwork associated with library work. It still isn't uncommon to hear library staff workers bemoaning the fact that they are still swimming in paperwork. "Swimming" is probably an exaggeration, but many administrative procedures still require forms in order to conduct business, e.g., various personnel and budget documents.

While the need for forms has been greatly reduced, the use of Web-based fill-in forms (templates) as a means for transmitting and organizing data has greatly increased, e.g., library user surveys, research and help requests, interlibrary requests, and comment and suggestion templates. The design of templates is not a trivial matter. In recent years I've encountered some real abominations. One form that sticks out in particular was an early version of an OCLC ILB request template. I can still recall observing an interlibrary staff worker who was poring over a computer screen struggling to locate information on the template. The needed data was virtually buried in the middle. I wasn't surprised to hear this worker begin to complain about eyestrain. I'm sure that a systems person with no library experience, or at least no first-hand knowledge of how the information would be used must have designed that early version of this template. Later versions were laid out much better.

Whenever paper-based forms are involved, a systematic review of the processes may lead to significant efficiencies by reducing red tape, thus, making it easier for patrons to obtain services and materials. Reduced red tape also permits a freer flow of information, helps to fix responsibility, produces better work methods, and reduces employee training time.

Getting Started

When the issue of the flow of paperwork and the use of forms is raised, a good place to begin is with an inventory of the organization's forms. What forms are currently in use? How are they used? Is the information recorded actually needed? Who needs it? Could the information on the form be obtained elsewhere? The point is to simply take a hard look at not only the forms and information they contain, but also how they are designed and used. Moreover, bringing together and comparing forms also provides an opportunity to discover instances where the information between forms overlaps. In such cases it might be possible to consolidate two or more forms into one.

Paperwork-related problems are often discovered as part of a diagnostic process using either a Pareto chart or a Fishbone diagram. For example, we once discovered that patrons had difficulty in correctly filling out a reference request form. Was it a patron-related problem, or was it possible that the language on the form was vague or confusing? We eventually learned that some of the terms were partially responsible for the problem because basic terms like "full-text database," or "recalls" were meaningless to many patrons.

One of the great advantages of databases that are linked to different functions is that data only have to be entered into the system once, e.g., the title of a book or the name of the requester. This capability definitely reduces the number of times a piece of data needs to be input.

Charting the Flow of Forms

Single Copy Forms

There are many instances when a flow chart format can be used to follow the track of a form. Figure 9-2 depicts a straightforward description of a borrower registration procedure. The rules for preparing such a chart are exactly the same as

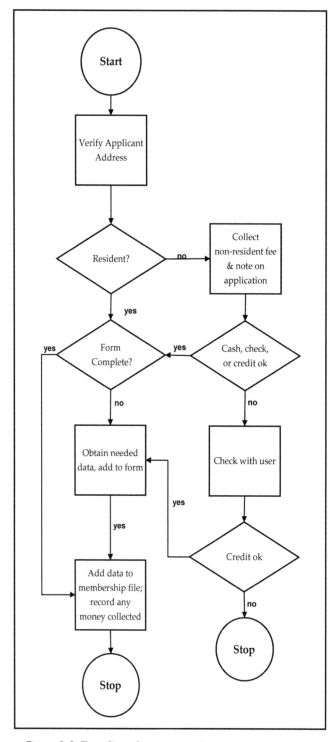

those presented for flow charts in Chapter 7 part 4, page 81.

Interestingly when a new director reviewed this straightforward procedure, she asked why the library was going to the trouble of checking credit information for non-resident applicants. She was told, "this is the way we have always done it." "But why?" she persisted. And the reply was; "The trustees enacted the policy years ago." The issue was taken back to the trustees. After an explanation of the pluses and minuses regarding costs and benefits and public relations, the policy was rescinded.

Charting the Flow of Multi-part Forms

In the pre-automated era, technical services routinely performed numerous processes and procedures that involved multi-part forms. These forms were intended to serve numerous purposes, e.g., proof of receipt, record cataloging data, verify financial data, document requester notification, etc. Technical services units also maintained numerous

Figure 9-2 Flow Chart: Borrower application procedure.

large, and often expensive-to-maintain, files, but as already noted, the need for such forms and files disappeared once integrated processing systems became available.

But for a variety of reasons some libraries still use multi-part forms with different copies designed to serve different purposes. Each copy travels a different route. For example a library not using OCLC's ILLiad interlibrary loan management software might produce a printout of an interlibrary loan template available through OCLC's First Search resource sharing system.[3] Or, a library that has not automated its ILL processes can obtain copies of the ALA form from either a library vendor or from an online PDF file.[4] Libraries that have not fully automated their ILL/ILB processes may still create multiple copies of an ILL form. For example, if a fee is involved, one copy of the form is sent to the bookkeeping office, and another copy accompanies the material to the requesting library. Figure 9-3 depicts the paperwork flow of an ILL multi-part form. The chart illustrates how multiple copies of the same form can be tracked.

Charting Forms from Unit to Unit

Charting multi-part forms that flow from unit to unit can be cumbersome. Although it is possible to chart each copy of the form separately, the resulting charts are difficult to analyze because they provide no easily interpretable overall picture. Since the principal objective in charting forms is to track the flow of each and every copy, a multiple-column charting technique is recommended. There are a number of ways this can be accomplished. For example, in Figure 9-4 the chart is organized to include the units through which a typical multi-part order form travels.

If the process is complicated and involves many steps, I recommend that sheets of newsprint be taped on a blank wall, and divided into several columns, one for each workstation or location. Then, using the flow chart symbols, including the information symbol, chart step-by-step what happens to each copy of the form. By employing the information symbol, it becomes possible to record what data are transmitted, when the data are recorded, and what happens to the data later in the process. An example would be the bibliographic information printed onto a form (a processing slip or a multi-part form) when a new book arrives, and which accompanies the book into the cataloging department. The bibliographic information collected during the ordering process might be revised later by cataloging staff because the quality of data recorded by the acquisition staff member was judged unacceptable. Whether such revisions are justified or not is not the issue here; the point to keep in mind is that by charting the flow of the form we have the ability to determine that such revisions occur.[5]

Simplifying the Flow of Paperwork

Chapter 16 focuses on streamlining workflows, processes, and procedures, but it seems appropriate here to mention that the use of forms and information in data-

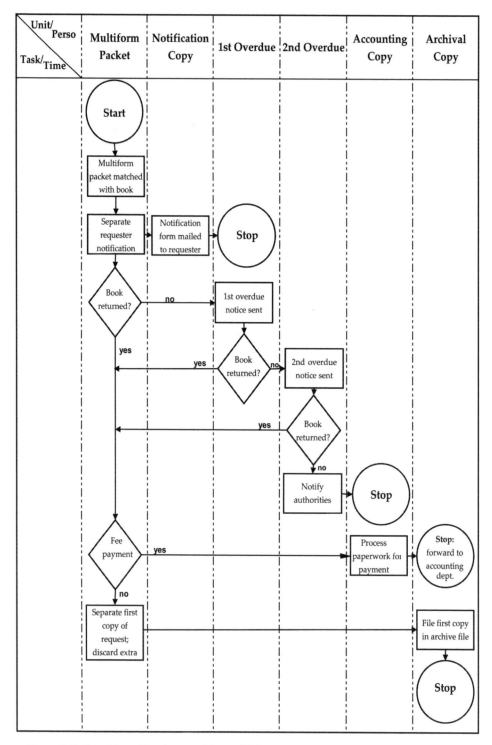

Figure 9-3 Flow Chart: Charting a multi-part ILL form.

	Requester	Searching Unit	Order Prep.	Vendor	Receiving Unit	Cataloging

Figure 9-4 Flow Chart: Tracking a multi-part purchase form through acquisitions and cataloging.

bases can often be streamlined. Actually in this age of integrated systems and the Web, one should begin a review of any form by asking whether the form is really necessary. Asking the same questions we've mentioned previously—What, Where, When, Who, How, and then Why—is an effective way to begin an examination of a form's utility and necessity. In the case of the interlibrary multi-part form, it was discovered that the file copy, which traditionally had been retained, really wasn't necessary because the same information was already in the library's database; moreover, questions began to be raised about patron privacy. Oftentimes a simple checklist such as the one depicted in Figure 9-5 can serve to stimulate thinking about how to streamline a process involving the use of forms.

Forms Design

The design goal with forms or templates is to create an easily understood form that produces reliable and accurate information. One of the underlying principles when designing forms and templates is to keep in mind that most people don't like filling out forms. They can be easily dissuaded from filling out a form or question-naire if it is perceived to be complex, hard to understand, or if the directions appear to be vague or confusing.[6]

A well-designed form can be a great aid in gathering, recording, processing, and communicating information. The following suggestions should be equally helpful to those who are responsible for designing traditional paper-based forms, or fill-in templates for computer or Web-based systems. The principles underlying the design of newsletters, books, questionnaires are very similar to the principles that apply to developing forms and computer screen templates, also, keep in mind patron privacy considerations. The transcending principles of good visual design are balance, regularity, economy, clarity, symmetry, and a logically developed sequence.[7]

- Instructions should precede the section to which they apply. Whenever possible include instructions directly on the form or template. With a paper form the reverse can also be used for complicated instructions. Using a second screen for a template is to be avoided.

- Information needed for a task should be included on one form or grouped into one section of a form. One request for information should follow another logically in the order the information is needed. For example, personal information such as name, address, telephone number followed by business information such as employer, address, telephone number, fax number, e-mail address, etc. This section might also request the preferred address.

- Forms and screens should be clearly organized. Only needed information should be requested. Avoid asking for information that you would like to have, but is not required for the task. Minimize the effort required wherever possible, e.g., allow boxes to be checked instead of writing answers.

Sample Forms Analysis Checklist

1) Can any form or copy be eliminated?

2) Can two or more forms be combined?

3) Can any steps in the process be eliminated?

4) Is more than one administrative unit maintaining a file when one file would suffice?

5) Can forms be presorted at some point during processing?

6) Can any files be eliminated? Will this form be used in the future? How often? What would be the consequences if this information were lost?

7) Can any steps be combined?

8) Can the form's originator furnish additional information?

9) Can work be eliminated by supplying copies to additional departments?

10) Can needless backtracking of forms be eliminated?

11) Can the amount of time that the form is delayed while awaiting action be reduced?

Figure 9-5 Forms Process Improvement Checklist.

- Arrange items so that writing proceeds from left to right and from top to bottom. On some forms it is also possible to order the items so that the most frequently required blocks are organized appropriately. If the data to be transcribed are listed on the source document, lay out the form or template entries in the same sequence.

- Group related data together. If seven people consult a form to obtain seven bits of data for seven different reasons, the form should be organized into seven zones. For example:

1	2
3	
4	
5	
6	7

Grouping data can be especially useful when an extensive array of data is presented in blocks that can be easily interpreted with a single inspection. Creating distinctive groupings is not always easily accomplished. Some information may have to be recorded more than once, and the cost of this repetition must be weighed against the cost of requiring workers to gather data from two zones on the form.

- Align boxes vertically to reduce the need for tab stops.

- Use the box design with descriptive captions in the upper left-hand corner of the box, whenever possible:

Name:

This format is usually superior to using captions followed by a line:

Name:_____

- Preprint as much information as possible. This will aid clarity and reduce the amount of writing or keying that is required to complete the form.

- Highlight certain areas and headings by using distinctive typefaces, heavy rules, shaded areas, or colors. However, attention-getting characters, print, or symbols should be limited. Background colors should contrast well with characters. Keep in mind that color-blind people and some senior citizens have difficulties with certain colors.

- Avoid jargon. Language should be positive and understandable; use symbols and abbreviations only when there can be no mistaking their meaning.

- Provide opportunities for open-ended feedback on forms designed for patrons. Borrower applications, friends' groups, and surveys should always conclude with a "thank you."

Template Designs Only

Libraries frequently use their Web sites to request information from patrons, therefore, the design of Web fill-in requests is now quite common. Although fill-in forms have become common, it is still worthwhile to keep in mind that most people don't enjoy filling out forms regardless of the environment. Patrons can be easily discouraged, and not bother to complete a screen form or questionnaire that is poorly designed. The following guidelines will help produce fill-in forms that are most likely to be acceptable to patrons.

- Screens should not be cluttered. No more than 30 percent of a screen should be covered by print or graphics. Blank space aids the reader to read accurately.[8]

- Information requests should be kept to a minimum. The number of data elements should not exceed seven on any given screen. Psychologists have found people have trouble keeping track of more than seven chunks of information.

- Lines in the request should be no longer than forty to sixty characters.

- Paragraphs and sections should always be separated by one or more blank lines.

- Text should be one and one-half or double-spaced. Single spacing makes the text look too dense for some readers.

- Text can be centered on the screen, but a justified left and a ragged right margin are recommended.

- Standard alphabet characters, upper and lower case, are used with standard punctuation.

- "Quit," "Next," "Continue to Next Screen," or "Return to the Beginning" prompts need to be provided if the template occupies more than one screen.

- Provide an easy method for backtracking if multiple screens are necessary.

Paper Forms Only

- Use the standard 3/5 spacing rule. This permits three lines per inch and five characters per inch. Three lines per inch corresponds to standard double-spacing. Other guides to keep in mind are five characters can be handwritten in an inch of space and most commonly used typefaces can accommodate ten characters per inch.

- Use standard-sized forms, such as 3 x 5, 4 x 6, 5 x 8, or 8.5 x 11 inches. Odd sizes usually cost more to produce and are more difficult to store.

- Use non-glossy paper with good opacity so that one cannot see through the form.

- Design forms so that mailing addresses are visible in standard window envelopes. Allow space for both the addressee and address if the form is designed for the addressee to return a copy complete with a reply to the originator.

- Assign a number to each form and a title that describes its function. Code designations will facilitate identification and retrievability. Be sure to add the date of preparation: a date alerts the person responsible for producing and maintaining forms that a revision might be in order.

Another Design Consideration

A trial might not always be possible because of time constraints, but since even the most experienced designer will occasionally let a blunder pass undetected, trying out a new form or a Web fill-in template before it is put into use is a wise course of action. Getting feedback as early as possible can avoid problems later. Once a problem is spotted the designer can make the necessary corrections before the final version is put into use.[9]

Final Thoughts

In the second edition of *Scientific Management of Library Operations*, considerable attention was paid to how records should be retained and how to maintain a regular inventory of forms in use. Since most libraries today do not create, maintain, or retain a wide variety of forms unless dictated by institutional or government regulations—that discussion has been dropped. If, for some reason, a library still employs a large number of paper-based forms, I suggest the second edition be consulted for a detailed description of record retention and inventory control programs.

As the number of Web-based fill-in templates proliferates, it is a good idea to create a database to manage templates that are currently in use. Coordination makes sense because excessive request forms can result in needless expenses. The information maintained in the database should include the reason why the template is being used. It also makes sense to review template fill-in request forms on a regular basis because needs and requirements frequently change. One way to avoid a clutter of unnecessary requests for information is to appoint an oversight group composed of department heads or their representatives. Such a group should maintain an overview of what each department is doing, and how the activities relate to each other; furthermore, the group should also be able to decide when a new form is needed.

Notes

1. I've encountered libraries that still maintain back-up files even though they are using an integrated system. Some of these files are really unofficial; that is, not sanctioned by the library's administration.

2. Well-known library vendors such as Gaylord, Brodart, and Demco still offer a variety of forms and notices for sale. Those libraries that still rely on forms sold by commercial vendors should keep in mind that the inclusion of a form in a supplier's catalog does not guarantee its efficacy or necessity. Forms listed in commercial catalogs, by and large, represent what libraries request, and what has been in use over the years. The forms offered by vendors are tested; nevertheless, each library should exercise judgment as to which forms are necessary in its particular circumstances.

3. A library that is committed to ILLiad wouldn't require a printout in order to process a request.

4. A replica of the ALA interlibrary lending form can be found at: http://www.ala.org/ala/rusa/rusaprotools/referenceguide/illformprint.pdf (17 May 2007).

5. An analysis of a complex workflow involving multi-part forms can be found in Richard M. Dougherty and Fred J. Heinritz, *Scientific Management of Library Operations 2nd ed.* (Metuchen, N.J.: Scarecrow Press, 1984), 208-9.

6. The Business Forms Management Association (BFMA), an organization intended to support the needs of forms designers and managers, should prove helpful. The function of forms design and analysis and usability testing now includes everything from traditional paper-based forms to electronic data capture and the databases and applications that support such activities. The Association also makes available for sale a range of relevant publications. http://www.bfma.org/membership/main.htm (17 May 2007).

7. The design process can be complex so a wise course of action is to consult sources such as Marvin Jacobs and Linda I. Studer, *Forms Design II: The Course for Paper and Electronic Forms* (Cleveland: Ameritype & Art, 1991). The authors cover all aspects of forms management and design, the design of electronic forms, and the conversion of paper-based forms to electronic forms.

8. Shires and Olszak do a nice job of presenting the principles for designing computer screen templates. Their article brings together a variety of relevant design principles. They also cite a number of other sources that can be consulted. Nancy Lee Shires and Lydia P. Olszak, "What Our Screens Should Look Like: an Introduction to Effective OPAC Screens," *RQ* (Spring 1992): 357-69.

9. Don't forget that the design principles that apply to forms and templates also apply to the design of most questionnaires.

Section Four
How Much Time It Takes

Chapter Ten

Tracking Systems: Throughput/Delay Analysis

Scope note: This short chapter presents techniques that can be used to analyze steps of a process that occur over a period of time. This tool is particularly useful in identifying blockages in complicated processes. Two case studies are presented to illustrate the necessary techniques.

Many processes involve work performed in a sequence of steps that occur at different workstations, different operating units, or in two or more organizations. Performance of the overall process depends on each link in the chain. If one link breaks down, the performance of the overall process is degraded. The receipt, handling, and shelving of returned books in a central building; the delivery of mail from a central public library to its branches; the receipt, routing, and delivery of new issues of journals; the acquisition, purchase, cataloging, and processing of new books are all examples of processes that involve multiple workstations and/or multiple operating units. Federal Express and UPS have been pioneers in developing sophisticated tracking systems. The following two case studies will illustrate how tracking workflows can produce valuable feedback about the performance of a process.

Case Study 1: What Happened to My Request for a New Periodical?

A library that prides itself on responding to faculty requests for new materials, including periodical subscriptions, begins to receive complaints from faculty that it takes too long to process requests for new subscriptions, and more importantly, to get the new issues on the shelf and available for use. The complainers allege that it takes months and months for a request to wend its way through the system.

The library initially suggested that faculty submit their requests via the Web to avoid delays, but some faculty countered that they wanted to continue submitting their requests in person using the existing new subscription request form. Others pointed out that they had submitted their recommendations via Web and the results had been the same—a long wait. When the library investigated the situation informally by checking some files and databases they discovered that up to a one-year delay could occur. But what were the reasons? Where in the process did the delays occur?

A tracking form was devised. It listed all of the key, potentially time-consuming steps in the process. The form was attached to all new subscription requests. The form required each person to indicate the date that the form was passed on to the next step in the review process. It was also possible to keep track of dates in the appropriate serials database.

It didn't take long to discover that numerous delays occurred because there were so many different persons involved in the review process; moreover, several individuals were required to authorize a request. The fact that all requests had to be reviewed by a Materials Selection Committee that only met once every few weeks also contributed to the long delays.

It turned out that there were a number of explanations why the review process took so long. Among those reasons were the decision to hold requests until all branches were informed and had responded and the Selection committee had reviewed the request and had resolved any budgetary issues that might have been raised. There was a reasonable rationale for what the library did, but the library didn't share that rationale with faculty because it knew from experience that faculty would view such explanations as excuses about which they weren't interested.

What happened as a result of the analysis was that the review process was completely revamped, and steps were taken to inform all faculty members about how to submit their requests via the Web-based system. Faculty were also assured that decisions on their requests would be communicated to them expeditiously, i.e., they would be informed quickly whether or not the subscription was approved.

It was a simple tracking analysis that identified the points in the review process where delays occurred, and once the bottlenecks were identified, it was possible to learn from the staff involved the causes of the delays. Among the lessons to be learned from this analysis are that reviews, inspections, and delays should always send up large red flags.

Case Study 2: What Happened to Our New Books?

Frequent or persistent delays in the delivery of new books to a branch library eventually triggered frustration and dissatisfaction among branch staff and library patrons. Too often it was the "messenger" who was blamed, that is, the unit responsible for delivering materials. The delay could have been due to an inefficient delivery system, but there were other, more likely candidates to explain why delays occurred. To silence complaints, the library's director requested the head of technical services to track a series of new book requests from the time they were submitted until the new books were delivered to their destinations.

The library's integrated system made it relatively easy to track the progress of requests. Most requests were submitted directly via the Web, but there was still a significant number of paper request forms for which the relevant information from the requests was added to the library's database. The objective of the analysis was to determine the time required for each new book order and each new book to work its way through the processing system. Once these data were collected, it was possible to compare the observed performance against what was considered to be an acceptable norm.

The head of technical services consulted with his colleagues and they decided that the key links in the process chain were: 1) date the library received the request; 2) date the library submitted its order to a vendor; 3) date the book arrived in library; and 4) date processed book was forwarded to circulation department for delivery. The data could be collected simply by updating the processing database in the integrated library system. The key links in the chain are shown in Figure 10-1.

Acquisition/Cataloging Tracking Study

Date	Activity (Checkpoint)
_____	Request received
_____	Order (submitted to vendor)
_____	Received in acquisitions
_____	Received in cataloging
_____	Delivered to Central Distribution
_____	Shelved _____
	_____

Please return form to Systems Office _____

Figure 10-1 Sample data gathering slip.

The tracking study produced the following data:

Order Request to Order Placed	Order Placed to Book Received	Book Received to Book Cataloged	Central Distribution to Books Delivered	Total Processing Time
7 days	28 days	15 days	2 days	52 days

The results triggered questions about vendor performance, and whether or not new titles, particularly the "hot" titles, could be cataloged and delivered more quickly. There were also questions about whether a local bookstore might be used to speed up the acquisition of popular titles. You can be assured that the delivery staff members were delighted to be vindicated. They were no longer viewed by staff as the villains.

Deciding how much data needs to be collected is an important consideration. The key question is how many transactions need to be tracked in order to be confident that the results will be valid. In the type of tracking described in the first case study, one might only have to track a couple of dozen requests before a pattern emerges. With the second case study, a larger number of observations would probably be required. I've found that a sample of two to three hundred requests is likely to be more than sufficient. The key is to keep collecting data until a distinct pattern emerges. But those who desire to achieve statistical precision should consult a statistics book that addresses such issues as sample size and reliability.[1] The essential point is to achieve agreement that the observed pattern is reasonable. If there isn't agreement then the proper response is to continue collecting data.

In both cases tracking the flow of requests and books through a series of steps in complicated processes produced valuable data. Tracking techniques can and have been used quite successfully as well to analyze the flow of interlibrary lending and borrowing requests. One notable example is the Information Delivery Services (IDS) Project created by the staff at SUNY Geneseo. The IDS Project is a cooperative resource sharing system that not only incorporates delivery performance standards but also tracks actual performance of the participating libraries. Since performance statistics are available real-time, assessment of operations at local libraries is facilitated.[2]

Final Thoughts

Tracking studies can bring to light some really surprising results. Who would have thought that boxes of new books would stand around for several weeks before being opened, or that a library using an integrated library system still took three months to get monographs to the shelves. These were both real examples that were uncovered by conducting a simple tracking study.

Notes

1. Random number tables are readily available on the Web. One site that includes a discussion of sampling is info@surveysystem.com (17 May 2007). Similar questions about sample sizes arise in connection with other tools designed to collect time data, i.e., diary studies, work sampling, and studies that involve direct time observations. One excellent source for determining sample sizes is an industrial engineering text authored by Benjamin Niebel and Andris Freivalds, *Methods, Standards, and Work Design,* 11th ed. (New York: McGraw-Hill, 2003).

2. The IDS project is described in some detail at the following Web site: http://www.idsproject.org/ (11 December 2007).

Chapter Eleven

Staff-Administered Diary Studies

Scope note: Most library cost studies have been conducted using some form of a self-administered diary study. This technique is not designed to collect precise time data, but if carefully administered, diary studies can produce useful time data. This chapter discusses how to conduct diary studies and what steps can be taken to keep errors that are associated with diary studies at an acceptable level. The techniques are also illustrated.

A diary study is a technique that allows staff members to record how they spend their workdays. The vast majority of time and cost studies that have appeared in library literature in recent years are based on data collected via some form of diary study.[1] The best approach to collecting data using self-administered instruments (diaries) is to provide staff participants with detailed instructions on how the diaries should be completed throughout each workday.

Collecting time data using diary study techniques is most effective when the tasks observed exhibit considerable variability in time spent from cycle to cycle. For example, it might take only five minutes to catalog one book but 15 minutes for the next one.[2] The same variability is likely to be observed in activities such as bibliographic searching, Internet searching, and answering reference questions. Direct observation using a timing device is not the best choice for observing activities that exhibit considerable variability from cycle to cycle because the variability will require such a large number of cycles to be observed in order to establish a reliable average time. A carefully crafted diary story can serve as a satisfactory substitute for direct observation techniques when significant variability is involved.

Self-administered diary studies are also particularly useful in determining how administrators spend their time. Here the activities are usually noncyclic in nature, e.g., oral presentations, and activities that span relatively long periods such as meetings and interviews. Blocks of time are also consumed in handling email, writing and editing reports and memos. These are also not the type of activities that lend themselves to direct observation.

While diary-study techniques lend themselves to documenting administrative activities, administrators will frequently point out that some of their activities require confidentiality, and observation by outsiders is not acceptable. Finally, it is my experience that while administrators may consent to keep a diary and carry out this responsibility conscientiously, they will stubbornly resist the idea of being closely watched, especially by someone in a subordinate position, or by a person from outside the organization.

Defining Tasks

One of the most important steps in preparing for a diary study is to decide what tasks will be included in the study, and then to define each task very clearly.[3] An excellent way to identify what tasks need to be observed is to prepare a block diagram or a flow diagram of the relevant workflows. The block chart shown in Figure 6-1 page 54, which depicts the flow of an interlibrary borrowing procedure, illustrates this step very nicely. Overview charts are an effective way of determining what needs to be included and what can be excluded.

Once the tasks are identified, the next step is to define each of them. The definitions of a group of selected tasks are shown in Figure 11-1. They provide some useful examples of how different investigators defined specific technical services-related activities.

It would be nice if tasks were defined alike by different investigators, but the literature reveals that tasks are rarely defined identically from study to study. That is one reason why benchmarking technical services activities among libraries is so difficult.[4] The essential point is that once a task is defined, all staff involved in the study need to have a common understanding of the definition. Without clear and commonly understood definitions, one is almost guaranteed inconsistencies in the data collected.

Conducting a Diary Study

Before undertaking the data collection phase of a study, it is worth repeating that the staff members who will record data need to be thoroughly briefed on how tasks are defined, and given specific directions on how to complete the data collection forms. I place special emphasis on making sure that everyone is informed in advance because there is nothing more frustrating than to learn after data collection has begun, or even worse, after the data collection phase has ended, that the data were recorded inconsistently. One way to minimize this predicament is to conduct a trial run so that there will be one last opportunity to resolve any lingering questions. But no matter how thorough the preparations, there should always be someone readily available who can answer questions as they occur.

In addition to providing thorough instructions, it is also essential to take into account what I'll term as the "human element." What I mean is that some staff will not want to participate in the study. Some are simply uncomfortable when they believe they are being observed, while others view the effort to collect data as a personal affront; some might even feel that they aren't trusted. The reasons for such attitudes, which almost always surface when a study is undertaken, underscore the

Searching orders/new titles received with ordering:[5]

Includes—all pre-order searching and search of new titles received automatically through approvals, standing orders, subscriptions, membership, government publications, gifts and exchanges, as well as not duplicated on approval processing.

Copy Cataloging:[6]

Verification and modification (description and classification) of an existing catalog record, including adding call numbers and subject headings. Does not include re-cataloging of a local record.

Item record-creation and bar-coding, if done as a part of cataloging task.

Verification of call numbers, if done as part of cataloging task.

Passing records into the local system, if done as part of cataloging task.

Pre-order processes and order-record creation:[7]

Pre-order tasks—Includes all pre-order sorting and problem solving, searching, vendor assignments, and creating and submitting orders.

Order maintenance tasks—Includes claiming, updating records, cancellations, and resolving problems prior to receipt.

Out-of-print tasks—Includes initiating searches for books that are out-of-print but still desired.

Receiving-related tasks—Includes opening boxes, checking receipts, moving book trucks, and solving problems related to receipt of new books.

Payment and account tasks—Includes keying payment information into ILS, and resolving invoice-related problems.

Figure 11-1 Illustrative examples of definitions for a series of technical service tasks.

need to make absolutely sure that staff who are to be involved with data collection understand what is going on, and what will be the purpose of the study outcomes; we don't want staff to feel threatened.

Once the study is underway, data should be tabulated as the study proceeds; don't wait until the data collection phase is completed. Reviewing and tabulating data on an ongoing basis provides yet another opportunity to discover flaws in the data-gathering methodology—better to discover flaws early rather than late.

Tabulation entails totaling the times recorded for each task, and dividing by the number of units produced. The total equals the time per unit. Figure 11-2 depicts a typical data-collection form. The form was used to record the activities of an acquisitions assistant during the course of a workday. The information included the time spent on each task and the number of units produced. The data summarized in Figure 11-3 provide a typical summary of a day's activities. The summary form displays the number of items produced and the time/unit produced during the day.

Daily Time —

Library _State College_

Department _Acquisitions_

Minutes	Task	Number Items Handled	Task	Number Items Handled	Task	Number Items Handled	Task	Number Items Handled
Hour	8:00		9:00		10:00		11:00	

Pre-Order

05

28 titles

10

Order Maintenance

15

Break

Out of Print

20

25

23 titles

30

35

20 titles

40

45

50

55

60

Record in the appropriate time space the number of items handled or processed while performing one task.

Figure 11-2 Typical data collection form.

— **Function Record**

Date _____

Name J. Jones

Position Acquisitions Assistant _____

Task	Number Items Handled	Task	Number Items Handled	Task	Number Items Handled	Task	Number Items Handled
1:00		2:00		3:00		4:00	

New Books

Payment

12 invoices

175 titles

35 titles

Pre-Order

Break

If work schedule is other than 8:00am − 5:00pm, consider the columns as first through eighth hour of work.

The same type of data can be recorded on a spreadsheet for the entire data collection period.

	Task	Time in Minutes	Items Processed (Titles, Books, Invoices)	Time/Unit
8:00 – 9:10	Pre-order	69	28	2.5 min/title
9:10 – 10:00	Order maintenance (cancellations)	52	20	2.6 min/title
10:00 – 10:15	Break			
10:15 – 12:00	Out-of-print	75	23	3.3 min/title
12:00 – 1:00	Lunch			
1:00 – 2:45	Receipt of new books	105	175	36 sec/title
2:45 – 3:00	Break			
3:00 – 3:40	Payment of invoices	40	12	3.3 min/title
3:40 – 5:00	Pre-order	80	35	2.9 min/title

Figure 11-3 Summary of activities and items processed by an acquisition assistant.

How Many Observations Are Required?

One needs to exercise judgment when answering the questions of how many observations should be made, and over what period of time. Some studies involve data collection over a one- or two-week period; others involve data collection over a series of weeks during the course of a year, e.g., winter, spring, summer, and fall. It is important to decide what is the appropriate period for the study under consideration. I do suggest that peak and slack periods of activity be avoided. If a slack period is selected, one is likely to discover that more time is spent on a typical task than during periods of peak activity. This occurs because there isn't the same pressure to produce during slack periods. For example, contrast the intensity of activity during the summer months in an academic library with the beginning weeks of a new semester.

One can use sampling techniques to determine how many observations should be taken, and over what duration of time, but for most library studies, rigorous statistical measures are really not necessary. It will be sufficient to continue data collection until the data clearly fit into consistent patterns. And as already mentioned, another way to increase the reliability of the data is to collect it over two or more periods of time with lapses in between. If the data collected during the different periods are consistent, it is safe to assume the data are reliable.

Accuracy Concerns

While self-administered diary studies can produce useful results, keep in mind that they are not precise instruments, and if one is not careful, errors can skew the results. Since each person is responsible for recording his or her own times, it is easy to understand why accuracy can be compromised if participants interpret definitions differently. I've found over time that this factor alone is responsible for a major share of the errors that occur in studies.

There are also other sources of error. Subjects on occasion may forget to record times. In such cases they are likely to complete the data collection form at the end of the day, attempting to recall how much time they spent on each task and how much work they produced. One way to guard against this problem is to make occasional spot checks to ensure that the data collection is proceeding as planned. Another technique is to conduct a few direct time observations at the beginning of the study to gain a sense of what range of times are likely to be reasonable. (See Chapter 13.)

Final Thoughts

In reviewing the published literature of time and cost studies, I was surprised by how often the investigators acknowledged that their methods of collecting data were imprecise. For example, it wasn't uncommon to encounter statements such as: "staff are asked to estimate daily the time spent on tasks." Or, "We interviewed staff to get a thoughtful estimate of the time spent on each activity."

The literature also reveals that it is common practice with diary-type studies for investigators to simply interview staff members in order to collect data. This approach might be the easiest way to gather time data, but it is also the approach that is most likely to produce unreliable data. While staff may be willing and able to give their opinions and impressions, as pointed out previously, people can't remember accurately how much time they spent on a particular set of tasks yesterday, last week, or last month. Time data collected via questionnaires and/or staff interviews will always be of questionable validity.

While I am always skeptical about data collection methods reported in the literature, I also recognize that the methods employed might produce a level of precision that was adequate for the intended purposes. One impression I gained from my review was that most library studies don't require a high degree of precision. That is fine so long as the results from such studies aren't reported in the literature in a way that appears to make the results more precise than is justified.[8]

Notes

1. A series of time and cost studies based on staff keeping track of their workdays was conducted by technical services staff in the Library at Iowa State University over a period of almost ten years. This team was led by Dilys E. Morris who was assistant director of technical services at Iowa State University Library. The team included Pamela Rebarcak, Lori Osmus, Gregory Wool, and Colin B. Hobert among others. Two of the studies that were published are: Dilys E. Morris, "Staff Time and

Costs for Cataloging," *Library Resources & Technical Services* 36, no. 1 (January 1992): 79-92, and Dilys E. Morris, Pamela Rebarcak, and Gordon Rowley, "Monographs Acquisitions: Staffing Costs and the Impact of Automation," *Library Resources & Technical Services* 40, no. 4 (October 1996): 301-18. The methodologies developed by this group have been more recently applied at the library by Fowler and Arcand. *See* David C. Fowler and Janet Arcand, "A Serials Acquisitions Cost Study: Presenting a Case for Standard Serials Acquisitions Data Elements," *Library Resources & Technical Services* 49, no. 2 (April 2005): 107, 109-22. The methodologies developed by Dilys Morris have been further refined in an extensive time and cost study that included Notre Dame and Vanderbilt University libraries. *See* Dilys E. Morris, Joanne M. Bessler, Flo Wilson, and Jennifer A. Younger, "Where Does the Time Go?: The Staff Allocations Project," *Library Administration & Management* 20, no. 4 (Fall 2006): 177-88.

2. Procedures in circulation such as collecting fines, checking out or discharging circulated items, or activities associated with new book ordering routines are all highly repetitive and are illustrations of tasks and procedures that lend themselves to direct time observations. Another group of procedures associated with preparing books for circulation, including labeling and inserting security tags, are also tasks that lend themselves to direct observation. We will discuss how to conduct detailed direct observation time studies in Chapter 13.

3. It is important to define the activities to be observed in all types of studies designed to collect time data, and not just diary studies. This includes work sampling, and direct observation using a timing device.

4. There is nothing wrong with adopting definitions that are idiosyncratic to a single environment so long as one doesn't plan to generalize the study results beyond the local environment.

5. Pam Zager Rebarcak and Dilys E. Morris, "The Economics of Monographs Acquisitions: A Time/cost Study Conducted at Iowa State University," *Library Acquisitions: Practice & Theory*, 40, no. 1 (1996): 65-76.

6. Dilys E. Morris, Colin B. Hobert, Lori Osmus, and Gregory Wool, "Cataloging Staff Costs Revisited," *Library Resources & Technical Services* 44, no. 2 (2000): 70-83.

7. The definitions for the pre-order activities were ones that I used in a study of an ordering procedure.

8. I found numerous examples of this in the literature. I didn't cite any particular study because there didn't seem to be any necessity to single out one or two studies when there are so many from which to select.

Chapter Twelve

Work Sampling

Scope note: Work sampling is a statistical tool that permits one to ana-lyze activities that occur at service areas. Although this technique has rarely been applied in library settings, it will prove to be extremely valu-able during periods of significant change at service desks. This chapter explains how to conduct a work sampling study. The principles and tech-niques are illustrated with a case study. Also included is a discussion of how work sampling techniques can be used to analyze activities in reference service areas.

Work sampling is a technique for gathering data about activities performed in a well-defined work area such as a circulation desk or a reference area. As the name implies, work sampling involves making observations at intervals. Each observa-tion is instantaneous, like taking a photograph of the scene. This type of analysis is particularly useful in answering questions about what is actually occurring in the area under study. Work sampling has not been widely applied by library managers, which I find surprising, since so many important activities occur in well-defined service areas.

The rapid growth of digital and remote reference services raises many ques-tions that can be examined by applying this tool: What is really going on at the reference desk? What kinds of questions are being asked? What proportion of questions are submitted by patrons who are remote from the desk? What informa-tion sources are consulted? How busy are staff workers? This is only a partial list of possibilities.

Similar questions can also be raised about what occurs at busy circulation/ information desks. What activities occur? What types of patron inquiries are re-ceived? At what times of the day is the desk busiest? How many staff are required to handle the volume of business? Again, this is only a partial list. The answers to such questions can be very helpful in determining how service desks should be staffed, the category of staff necessary to carry out the assigned tasks, and the type and level of training staff should receive.

A work sampling study can be designed either to determine how much time is spent on each of the activities under study, or the amount of time each staff worker spends on specified activities. In the first instance the focus of the study is on the activities performed, and in the second case, the focus is on what time of the work-day that specific activities occur. Figures 12-5 and 12-7 highlight the differences. In Figure 12-5 the activities are being observed, and in Figure 12-7, the chart is organized so that one can capture the time of day an activity is performed.

Roots of Work Sampling

Work sampling as a tool has been around for a long time. It is based on a statistical method identified by H. C. Tippett in 1934. He developed the technique for use in the English textile industry to measure operator and machine errors. In 1966 Ralph E. Barnes, a well-known industrial engineer of that era, authored a text devoted entirely to the subject.[1] Among his many illustrations was one I found particularly interesting. Barnes studied a group of large presses to determine what proportion of time a press was productive, and when and how often it was down for repairs. His illustration reminded me of the early days of OCLC and RLG's RLIN when computer-based networks were notoriously unstable. I still remember staff just sitting at their terminals waiting for the system to come back alive. How productive were they really and how often were they "down"?

John Goodall conducted and published a seminal study on how work sampling techniques could be applied to activities at a circulation desk. The principles identified by Goodall still apply. What has changed are the tools that one is likely to use to collect and analyze the data.[2]

Both Barnes and Goodall present the statistical principles on which work sampling methodologies are based. For example, concepts such as random-ness, confidence level and interval, sampling errors, and the normal distribu-tion curve are discussed. Another source of easy-to-understand information about basic statistics can be found in a short report produced by the University of Wisconsin's Cooperative Extension. The report does an excellent job of de-scribing concepts such as probability and non-probability sampling, different types of samples, and also concepts such as sampling errors, confidence levels and intervals.[3]

One's tolerance for errors and the degree of assurance that errors will not ex-ceed a certain level will, in the final analysis, dictate the methodology one adopts. I singled out these authors because if one decides to explore the statistical prin-ciples upon which work sampling is based, these three works can serve as excellent sources to consult.

Getting Staff on Board

On several occasions I've referred to the importance of getting staff on board. I believe this point can't be overstressed. Getting staff on board is likely to be even more crucial with a work sampling study than with other types of time study tech-niques. The reason is that instead of involving only one or two staff members, entire groups of staff are likely to be directly involved in a study, and thus the likelihood that someone will feel threatened is heightened because work study techniques are designed to bring to light instances when staff aren't performing productive work, and/or are absent from their work area. This reality can be quite unsettling to some staff. Again, staff need to be assured of the purpose of the study. Furthermore, it is my recommendation that this technique *not* be used for purposes that staff will view as negative, e.g., to "prove" that staff workers are idle and thus a service desk is overstaffed. On the flip side, if staff workers complain about being overworked, a work sampling study can be very helpful in determining peak loads of activity, and in answering questions about appropriate staffing levels.

Organizing the Study

Like the self-administered diary study, the activities to be observed in a work-sampling study need to be identified and carefully defined so that there is a common understanding among all those involved in the study. The activities must also be defined so that each activity (task) is mutually exclusive; that is, there should be no question about which category each activity belongs to, e.g., charging out a book and handling a reserve request are quite distinct. Steps should also be taken to ensure that the entire range of activities is covered, including personal time or being absent from the work area. One way to account for unusual activities is to provide an "other" category.

It is also good practice to establish subcategories for activities that are more complicated than initially anticipated. For example, if one wants detailed information about the nature of telephone inquiries that are received at a service desk, using a single "on the telephone" category won't generate sufficiently detailed information. Keep in mind it is always possible to aggregate data from smaller categories into larger more general categories, but it is not possible to break down a general category into more specific ones.

Forms

Observation forms should be designed to meet the specific needs of each study, but most forms will follow similar patterns. The objective is always to keep the forms as simple as possible. The data to be collected should dictate the design of the observation sheet. First of all, the form should list activities to be observed. Space should be provided to tally each observation, the totals for each day, and the cumulated totals from the beginning of the study. If space permits, it is also helpful to include the definition of each activity to be observed, e.g., what is meant by patron contact, charging out a book, etc? If space doesn't permit the inclusion of definitions, then each study participant should be supplied with a separate list of definitions. The observation sheets used in the case study and shown in Figures 12-5 and 12-6 are typical illustrations of data collection forms for which the definitions are not included.

Basic Statistical Concepts

Before going any further, I want to introduce a few basic statistical concepts. I don't intend to delve deeply into the statistics on which work sampling is based, but I do want to introduce briefly the concepts of a random sample, confidence interval, confidence level, and sample size.

Random sample—means, in the context of work sampling, that each minute of the time period under study (workday) has the same chance as any other minute of being selected for the sample.

Confidence interval—is the range of the estimates that one is making; that is, it is the plus-or-minus figures that are used when someone says that a sample has an error factor of plus or minus a certain percent. For example, if one were to query a random sample of patrons whether or not they had ever submitted a question via email or chat reference, and 23 percent of the sample responded "yes," and if it had been decided before the sample was drawn to use a 4 percent confidence interval, and had a 95 percent confidence level (see below) been selected, one could then say that we were 95 percent confident that the true average would have fallen between 19 percent and 27 percent had the same question been posed to the entire population of eligible patrons.

Confidence level—tells us how sure we can be that our sample estimate will actually fall within our confidence interval. In the previous example a 95 percent confidence level would mean that we could be 95 percent confident that the actual percentage of the total population from which we had drawn our sample would fall within our confidence interval of 19 percent and 27 percent.

I used a 95 percent confidence level, but I could have also used other confidence levels, for example, 90 or 99 percent. Most analysts select a 95 percent confidence level as providing a satisfactory level of precision.

Of course, the confidence interval calculations assume that a truly random sample of the relevant population has been drawn. If the sample is not really random, one cannot rely on the results of the sampled data. Non-random samples usually result from some flaw in the sampling procedure. For instance, if one were trying to ascertain the reading habits of adults, and conducted a telephone survey during the day, and included only land line phones at residences, not only would everyone who works during the day be missed, but so would those who only use cell phones. The sampling results would certainly not represent the reading habits of the adult population.

Sample size—becomes an issue whenever the purpose is to generalize or show representativeness. How many observations should be made to ensure that the sample provides an adequate representation? The larger the sample, the more one can be sure that the characteristic one wishes to measure truly reflects the same characteristic in the entire population. Larger sample sizes yield tighter confidence intervals. In the previous example, a smaller confidence interval such as plus or minus three instead of four would have resulted in a confidence interval of between

10807	99858	53171	25467	11653	90073	31035	36551	99587	28474	11131
43461	82421	36624	43087	46402	73059	27409	16545	60017	27152	27913
98231	24479	33925	16613	73644	81861	25494	82248	33136	10133	73367
33100	94635	79696	53559	88576	63011	96271	94065	92305	96626	88416
48779	31425	86552	25117	45941	20496	71787	42958	72129	97162	74107
50312	21896	31481	77269	75837	71875	13496	27130	30258	72125	81473
56238	53572	53284	95419	75895	82564	69082	81500	26602	96905	69078
99271	57808	83652	83966	80525	82096	86498	72346	93949	82563	80206
57681	50394	34899	60847	52827	67337	89054	63303	78195	52062	19555
31021	58552	64316	14290	99583	93103	77827	50295	26128	70359	29919
21520	51805	93789	39447	61660	55316	48427	43283	88970	46979	56796
64403	97070	32281	31037	37517	52189	22712	30965	59485	52103	96368
84504	66750	89491	49356	84090	81123	79279	92953	24982	67096	81065
86310	72519	25591	20792	33248	80092	44406	12935	93471	80897	14459
33342	90306	77373	58066	93422	36687	72622	82918	17028	73687	61513
27861	49280	69564	89869	45703	82428	21561	35800	70044	89299	45115
97488	19736	45127	61902	29983	83458	37744	28910	29828	94823	81434
95385	58923	35670	46385	95365	95142	23543	92026	22829	40898	75849
99909	69724	51094	32027	53092	32116	77152	42298	36987	80105	28842
94629	27977	97752	19944	54215	21382	63190	42495	88081	13980	88897
74538	11219	49378	70875	46369	46786	13469	97931	16516	28850	21951
53155	27249	91420	12193	86329	59587	58873	34454	99387	53378	36710
46268	19215	42379	93588	85058	17754	91421	45795	24861	61436	85019
75828	96827	58718	32901	44094	92474	86001	10784	85034	85741	18917
64121	81751	70113	69370	53573	93289	75745	79325	30337	67004	33429
53934	62697	63177	48991	89145	80037	15733	26356	17161	52196	61623
22683	64457	81952	67393	88674	73713	79087	59635	87263	22826	95598
39123	39129	72164	26099	41853	99320	46619	27447	41429	69142	66520
17154	84535	29658	73761	48449	67949	47994	58228	43662	57056	39811
21086	75910	40321	41635	23364	24221	61183	41394	17495	53405	46309

Figure 12-1 Table of random numbers.

20 and 26 percent instead of between 19 and 27 percent. For readers who would like a fuller discussion of these terms, again, I recommend the short work by Ellen Taylor-Powell.[4]

Making the Observations

The availability of Web resources has made selecting random observations much easier than it used to be. In the past it would have been necessary to draw laboriously a sample of random times from a table of random numbers such as the random-number table shown in Figure 12-1. In our case these data would be used to compile the times at which activity at the desk would be observed. To illustrate how the process would work, begin at the upper left-hand corner (10807), and examine the last three digits, which are 807, but since there are only 780 minutes in the workday (780 is the number of minutes between 9 A.M. and 10 P.M., the hours of opening in the library), the 807 would be discarded, and the second group numbers (43461) would be selected. Since the last three integers are less than 780, this group of numbers would be recorded, and then we would move on to the next group of numbers. This process would be continued until enough times had been identified to meet the study requirements for sample size.

But instead of this laborious process it is now possible to consult a Web resource that provides tables of random numbers, and select the number of needed observations along with the number and size of digit groupings required. (See Figure 12-2.) Instead of working with groups of five integers, a sufficient number of random groups all between zero and 780 can easily be generated.[5] Of course it will still be necessary to convert the values for each group into times of the day. But that process too has been greatly simplified. It is no longer necessary to convert each group of random numbers into the corresponding clock time, e.g., 461 minutes added to 9:00 A.M. equals 4:41 P.M. Now a spreadsheet can be set so that one simply plugs in the groups of random numbers and presto, the observation times are quickly calculated.

671	336	226	562	427
536	752	239	272	287
583	390	259	672	60
556	169	343	153	317
66	755	184	399	527
723	78	775	587	777
430	655	501	702	435
765	49	623	117	652

Figure 12-2 Forty random times selected from www.random.org.

In the case study that is presented in this chapter, we decided to make 30 observations each day for a period of 15 workdays; therefore, a list of 450 random times is created.[6]

The process I've described is straightforward, but there is another option. If one wishes to avoid creating a list of random times, a pre-programmed Random Access Mechanism (RAM) can be used. These devices can be either rented or purchased.[7] RAM devices are also particularly useful when there are so many staff being observed that one person can't realistically observe all involved in the study at the same time. RAM devices also make it easier for study participants to record their own times. (See Figure 12-3.)

Finally, if the activities of individual staff workers and what they are doing is the focus of the study, the times that correspond with a staff member's lunch or break period would be thrown out, but if our objective was to analyze the *activities* that were occurring at the service desk itself, then all times from opening in the morning to closing time in the evening would be recorded.

There are basically three ways to make observations. First, assign to one individual the responsibility to observe and record the data at each designated time. Second, design a study that can be self-administered by the involved staff members

Figure 12-3 Pre-programmed random access mechanism. (Permission granted by Divilbiss Electronics.)

themselves. Third, take a snap shot of the work area using a camera with a wide-angle lens or a digital camcorder. The method one selects will depend on the individual circumstances.

Observations should be tallied according to activity throughout the day. At the close of each workday, the data collected are totaled, and the cumulative average time for each activity is computed. After day one the daily totals are also added to the cumulative totals.

The formula for calculating the daily percentage is:

$$\frac{\text{Number of observations for the given category on the given day}}{\text{Total number of observations for all categories on the given day}} \times 100 = \begin{array}{l} \text{Percent of time spent} \\ \text{on the category on the} \\ \text{given day} \end{array}$$

The formula for calculating the cumulative percentages is:

$$\frac{\text{Number of observations for the given category on all days of the study}}{\text{Total number of observations for all categories on all days of the study}} \times 100 = \begin{array}{l} \text{Cumulative percent of time} \\ \text{spent on given category on} \\ \text{all days of the study} \end{array}$$

Number of Readings

For how many days should observations be taken? There are really two approaches to answering this question. The first is what I call the "commonsense approach not based on traditional statistics." With this approach one exercises reasonable judgment, and continues collecting data until distinct patterns emerge. In our circulation case study we observe that the frequency of *patron interactions* soon begins to reflect a pattern of approximately 20 percent per day. (See Figure 12-4.) At this point, it is reasonable to ask whether or not it would make any real difference if the true average fell anywhere between 20 percent and 25 percent? The answer is "probably not."

The second approach it to employ a statistically oriented methodology. This option requires that one first establish an acceptable confidence level and confidence interval. Once agreement on these two measures has been achieved, the next step is to determine the size of sample that will be required. As already mentioned, there are Web resources that greatly simplify this process.[8]

Even though most library-oriented studies will not demand a high level of statistical precision, always keep in mind that with my commonsensical approach, no matter how distinct the patterns that emerge, the results will have no statistical validity.

Estimating the Reliability of Data

One technique we can use to gauge the reliability of the data we collect is to create a simple control chart. The control chart identifies clusters of observations that can't be explained by statistical variations alone, e.g., the telephone system was down for four hours or the circulation server was down, etc. Using the data collected in the circulation case study, the concept of the control chart is illustrated in Figure 12-4. In this illustration there were two possible outliers: one exceptionally high (31 percent) and one low (9 percent). To clarify such occurrences I recommend querying the staff members who are knowledgeable about the situation. What might have caused outliers? Have the possible causes skewed the data so that it is different from other days in the study? If the answer is yes, then the data ought to be discarded.

Case Study: What's Happening at the Circulation Desk?

Let's illustrate the use of work sampling with a real life case study. The circulation supervisor has expressed concerns lately about the increasing number of information inquiries that must be fielded by her staff at the desk. Previously the general

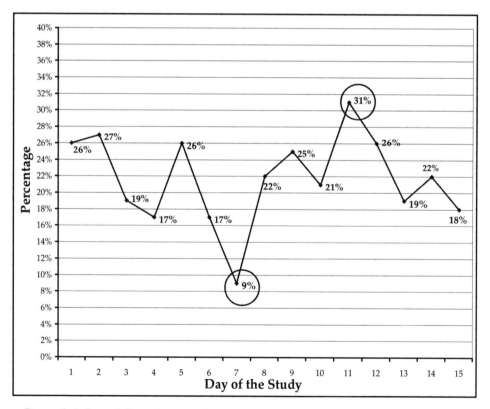

Figure 12-4 Control Chart: A method for estimating the reliability of data for "patron interactions."

information desk handled most of these questions, but that desk was disbanded in a recent budget action. This trend, she says, is increasing her staff's workload at exactly the same time that her budget is being cut back. She isn't objecting to the changing roles of her staff, but she is concerned that these expanded activities are difficult to perform at acceptable levels of patron service. She would like to have her staff budget increased.

What is the actual situation? Do patron contacts consume a significant percentage of the staff's time? To gain a better sense of what is actually going on at the circulation desk, with the consent of the circulation supervisor and the circulation staff, we decide to design and conduct a work sampling study.

The library's hours of opening are 9 A.M. to 10 P.M. Although different staff members are assigned throughout the day, only one person is on duty at the desk until 4 P.M. whereupon two staff members are assigned until the library closes at 10 P.M.

We decide to make 30 observations each day for 15 workdays; therefore, we plan to make 450 separate observations.[9] For the purposes of our case study, only the first 60 random times are shown in Figures 12-5 and 12-6. We decide against using pre-programmed RAM devices so we manually translate the random numbers into the times of the day that the observations will be made.

Since the staff are on board, and we have designed the data collection forms, we are ready to begin making observations. Although we decide to make 30 observations each day, since there are two staff members working between 4 P.M. and 10 P.M., we will actually be able to observe what staff are doing more than 30 times each day.[10] At the end of each workday, the data collected are totaled, and the average percent time for each activity is computed. After day one the daily totals are also added to the cumulative totals. (See Figures 12-5 and 12-6.)

We continue to collect data for 15 days, but we could have made the case, based on the data shown in Figure 12-4, that distinct patterns for patron interactions had already emerged by the tenth day. We found after 14 days of observation, that *patron interactions* accounted for an average of 22 percent, but after only 10 days the average daily percentage of this category hovered around 21 percent, and if we had thrown out the seventh day's reading of nine, the average would have been 23 percent. This figure certainly satisfies my definition of what constitutes as a distinct pattern.

The data for *patron interactions* summarized in Figure 12-5 shows that at the end of day one of our study, this category accounted for 26 percent of the total desk activity each day. However, we also noticed that on the seventh day the number of *patron interactions* declined precipitously to 9 percent. Was this a statistical blip, or was the data collected that day different from the data collected during the other days? To clarify the situation, we talked with the supervisor and her staff. We learned that this day coincided with the campus celebration of a football victory when many faculty and students were otherwise engaged. The library was not on

Work Sampling Data Sheet

Work area studies: Circulation desk Date:______

Number of persons observed: 2 Day of Study 1 of proposed 15 Days

Observed Times	Element	Tally	Total	%	Total Observations: Prior	Total Observations: Today	Cumulative ±%
9:05, 9:07, 9:10, 9:17, 9:43	Charging materials	卌 卌 III	13	31	—	13	31
10:30, 10:46, 10:58	Discharging materials	卌	5	12	—	5	12
11:05, 11:37, 11:59	Patron interactions	卌 卌 I	11	26	—	11	26
12:08, 1:11, 1:33	Telephone interactions	卌 I	6	14	—	6	14
2:08, 3:17, 3:31, 3:44	Idle	IIII	4	10	—	4	10
4:04, 4:14, 4:28, 5:13, 5:49	Absent from desk	II	2	5	—	2	5
6:18, 6:18, 7:51, 8:06	Other (related but minor in nature)	I	1	3	—	1	3
9:18, 9:36, 9:37			42	101	—	42	101

Figure 12-5 Work Sampling Data Sheet: Day one.

their study schedule that day. As a result, the 9 percent total was dropped out of study totals, and thus the accumulated average for *patron interactions* rose at that point from 20 percent to 22 percent.

We also observed that there was another possible statistical blip. It occurred on the eleventh day when the activity level rose to a high of 31 percent. (Again, see Figure 12-4.) Was this a reasonable level? Staff members were queried, and they indicated that for some reason the "place was jumping" that day. We decided, therefore, to retain that day's total in the final analysis.

Work Sampling Data Sheet

Work area studies: Circulation desk   Date:_____

Number of persons observed:_2_   Day of Study ___2___ of proposed ___15___ Days

Observed Times	Element	Tally	Total Observations				
			Total	%	Prior	Today	Cumulative ±%
9:12 9:51	Charging materials	ⅢⅠ ⅢⅠ ‖‖	14	33	13	27	32
10:03 10:05 10:31 10:45 10:48 10:50	Discharging materials	‖‖	4	9	5	9	11
	Patron interactions						
11:53		ⅢⅠ ⅢⅠ ‖	12	28	11	23	27
12:16 12:45 12:50	Telephone interactions						
2:22 2:42		ⅢⅠ	5	12	6	11	13
3:16 3:32 3:34	Idle	‖‖	3	7	4	7	8
4:00 4:09 4:23	Absent from desk	‖‖	3	7	2	5	6
5:28 5:37 5:49 7:16 7:32 7:40	Other (related but minor in nature)	‖	2	5	1	3	4
8:31 8:51 8:59 9:01			43	101	42	85	101

Figure 12-6 Work Sampling Data Sheet: Day two.

Comments on the Case Study

What can we conclude from the study? The question that prompted the study in the first place has been answered. Yes, the circulation desk staff does spend a significant amount of time interacting with patrons outside of charging out books. If we were to factor in the time spent on the telephone, the frequency of this type of activity may approach 30 percent. It also appears that staff members are performing productive work most of the time.

Management might have wanted to learn more about when staff were idle and when peak levels of activity occurred. This information could have been obtained

Work Sampling Data Sheet							
	Description of Activities						
Hours of Opening	Charging materials	Discharging materials	Patron interactions	Telephone interactions	Idle	Absent from desk area	Other
8:00							
8:30							
9:00							
9:30							
10:00							
10:30							
11:00							
11:30							
12:00							
12:30							
1:00							
1:30							
2:00							
2:30							
3:00							
3:30							
4:00							
4:30							
5:00							
5:30							
6:00							
6:30							
7:00							
7:30							
8:00							
8:30							
9:00							
9:30							
10:00							

Figure 12-7 Work Sampling Data Sheet: Time and Activities.

easily by simply reconfiguring the data so that the times of the day were highlighted along with the activities performed. (See Figure 12-7.)

Management might have also wanted to learn more about the nature of patron interactions. What type of inquiries occurred? Were they directional questions? Were they inquiries about hours of opening, upcoming events, meeting room availability, etc.? What else?

The data collected in our case study didn't require the observer to interact with the staff, but it would have been possible to categorize each observation by simply viewing what the staff worker(s) were doing when the observation was made. However, if we wanted to learn more about the nature of the *patron interactions* and *telephone transactions,* it would have been necessary to speak with staff workers at the time observations were taken. Another option would have been to interview staff for their impressions regarding the nature of the transactions. At the very least the staff input might have provided guidance on how to develop a more detailed data collection form.

Work Sampling to Help Organize Reference Service

Since the dawn of the digital age, there have been countless discussions about the future of reference service. More specifically there are discussions about how databases and other digital resources, and most particularly, the availability of search engines such as Google, have transformed reference and information services.[11] I won't pretend to know what lies ahead for reference and information services, but I am confident in asserting that work sampling can be employed to learn more about what is actually happening at reference desks and reference service areas.

Let us say that the reference staff allege that they are still providing a great deal of face-to-face reference service, and that remote reference service users are still less important than those standing at the desk. Moreover, the staff continue to argue that the desk is still understaffed. If the principal question is the amount of time spent providing face-to-face service as contrasted to remote services, then the simple data collection form displayed in Figure 12-8 could be used to provide important answers. But if one wants to learn more about the range and frequency of the reference services provided to patrons, it would be necessary to develop a much more detailed form. The list of reference functions shown in Figure 12-9 could serve as the basis for a more detailed study of activities.

The increased level of detail would require the observer(s) to consult with individual reference staff members to determine what category of activity is involved, e.g., ready-reference, Web instruction, etc.

In a large reference department, it also might be desirable to employ more than one observer to monitor activities. If the number of workers being analyzed exceeds the number that one observer can survey, then it might be better to use a self-administered methodology; that is, each staff member is responsible for recording his/her own activities. Of course, like we discussed in the Diary Study chapter, this would require that all staff be very clear as to the definition of each activity, and trained to record their own activities. If this approach were employed, I recommend that each study participant be supplied with a pre-programmed RAM device that can be set to vibrate at the designated times so as not to be intrusive. It might also be possible to supply only the person in charge with a RAM device. This person simply informs all staff participants when it is time to record what they are doing.

Finally, it is important to remember that when a self-administered methodology is used, the same types of errors associated with self-administered diary studies can creep into the data-collection process. And like the diary study, if busy staff batch their observations at the end of their desk assignment, errors are likely to creep into the study because very few people will remember accurately what occurred earlier.

Work Sampling Work Sheet

Work area studies: Reference desk   Date:_____

Number of persons observed:__**2-4**__   Day of Study _____ of proposed _____ Days

Hours of Opening	Description of Activity	Tally	Daily Total	%	Total Observations		Cumulative %
					Prior	Today	
8:05 8:20 8:40 9:30 9:45 10:20 11:10 11:40 12:15 12:35 1:00 1:15 1:25 2:05 2:45 3:00 3:35 4:05 5:00 5:40 6:25 7:00 7:20 7:40 8:00 8:20 8:35 9:05 9:35 9:50	Remote interations with users Face-to-face interactions Other (including other duties plus reading professional literature) Absent (includes attending meetings, breaks)						

Figure 12-8 Work Sampling Data Sheet: Reference work area. Random times for the first day plus the activities observed.

Final Thoughts

I hope it is apparent how work sampling can be used to resolve debates about what really goes on at service desks. More importantly, work sampling can provide valuable assistance to management in structuring service desks so that resources are used most effectively while also offering services that provide the greatest value to patrons.

Notes

1. Ralph M. Barnes, *Work Sampling*, 2nd ed. (New York: John Wiley and Sons, 1966).

2. John S. Goodall, *Libraries and Work Sampling*, ed. by Robert E. Kemper (Littleton, Colo.: Libraries Unlimited, 1975).

Remote information services
    Telephone
    Chat
    Email
    Instant messaging
 	
Face-to-face interactions
    Direction
    Ready
    In-depth
    Web instruction
    Information literacy
	Collection development
	    Print
	    Electronic
	
	Idle (including reading
	    professional literature)
	
	Absent (includes attending
	    meetings, breaks)
	
	Other duties and activities
	    (e.g., vertical files, ICB request, etc.)

Figure 12-9 List of typical reference activities.

3. The report is not only readable but also eminently understandable. Ellen Taylor-Powell, *Sampling,* Program Development and Evaluation Series, G3658-3 (Madison, Wis.: University of Wisconsin-Extension Division, 1998). The organization's URL is: http://learningstore.uwex.edu (26 May 2007). Once on the Web site, search under Taylor-Powell and a list of her publications will appear. Select the report entitled *Sampling.*

4. Taylor-Powell, *Sampling,* 5.

5. One useful site that provides random numbers for different size samples can be found at http://www.random.org (26 May 2007).

6. As is described in the case study, two staff members are on duty at the desk part of the workday so while we will be observing desk activities 30 times each day, it will be possible to record tasks 40 times.

7. Divilbiss Electronics is a firm that either leases or sells various types of pre-programmable RAM devices. Their Web site is: http://www.divilbiss.com/New/selfadmin.htm (26 May 2007).

8. There are Web sites available that assist in quickly calculating sample sizes, confidence levels, and confidence intervals. One site I found to be particularly useful was located at http://home.clara.net/sisa/ (20 October 2006).

9. Had we decided to employ a statistical approach and had we consulted http://home.clara.net/sisa/ we would have discovered that in order to achieve a confidence interval of plus or minus 3 with a 95% confidence level, a sample size of 470 would have been required.

10. The number of readings in excess of 30 will depend on how many of the random times occur between the hours of 4 P.M. and 10 P.M.

11. One could make the case that a series of workshops entitled Rethinking Reference sparked widespread interest in evaluating current reference services and charting future courses of action. *See Rethinking Reference in Academic Libraries: the Proceeding and Process of Library Solutions Institute, no. 2* (Berkeley, Calif.: Library Solutions Press, 1993). Studies continue to appear underscoring how changes occurring in reference require new approaches to evaluating and costing reference services. One study reported by a group of researchers who have gained considerable experience in evaluating reference services provides a great deal of information about how one might evaluate digital reference services. *See* R. David Lankes, Melissa Gross, and Charles R. McClure, "Cost, Statistics, Measures, and Standards for Digital Reference Services: A Preliminary View," *Library Trends* 51, no. 3 (Winter 2003): 401-13.

Chapter Thirteen

Direct Time Study

Scope note: Direct time studies are rarely conducted in libraries today because so many library processes have been automated. Moreover, most library processes aren't performed frequently enough to justify the cost and effort of a study that involves direct observation with a timing device. There are, however, a few activities that might justify a detailed study, e.g., digitizing and scanning activities. This chapter explains how to conduct a study when precise time data are desired. A case study of an actual digitization process is presented to illustrate the principles and techniques.

Direct time study can be defined as the systematic study of work procedures to determine how much time it takes for a qualified, properly trained worker to perform a given series of tasks. Time study techniques have been traditionally used in industry to analyze frequently performed jobs. They can be traced back to the work of Frederick Taylor in the early years of the twentieth century. But it was the rise of the machine tool industry, and the introduction of assembly lines to mass produce products that motivated managers to take a closer look at how much time was required to perform work. Of course, the rationale of managers was easy to understand. Reductions in the time necessary to perform jobs that were repeated thousands of times could quickly be translated into increased profits.

The techniques are still relevant today. One only has to think about workers in clean rooms assembling electronic devices such as personal computers to understand just how relevant. The principles of direct time study have remained constant over the years. It is the tools one uses to observe and record times that have changed.[1]

When I entered the profession the use of direct time study techniques was fairly common, but today, if the published literature is any indicator, direct time study techniques are rarely employed by librarians to analyze work.[2] As noted earlier, this decline can be directly correlated to the adoption of automated systems as managers seemingly concluded that automation had negated the need for detailed time and motion studies. For example, before circulation systems were automated, circulation activities consumed a great deal of staff time. Automation made staff tasks quicker and easier to perform, and more importantly, automated systems enhanced patron service by reducing the time necessary to check out materials.

The need for direct time studies was also greatly diminished as many frequently performed manual tasks in technical services were eliminated and sophisticated integrated library systems were adopted, e.g., maintaining manual files, filing catalog cards, preparing book labels are only a few illustrations. And, of course, each generation of integrated systems becomes increasingly sophisticated enabling more and more operations to be streamlined, e.g., the handling of authority control work.

Although there are relatively few manually performed procedures that justify a detailed time study using direct observation, there are exceptions. For example, activities such as charging out and checking in books, preparing books for circulation, microfilming processes, book preservation and repair routines, and cataloging books with copy are procedures that might still benefit from a detailed analysis.

Another activity that is increasingly performed in libraries is scanning page images and digitizing texts. This is definitely a candidate for analysis. Scanning of entire books is labor intensive, repetitive, and involves a considerable investment of staff time. The development of a "best method" might well justify the additional time and effort of conducting a direct time study.

How to Conduct a Time Study

Develop a Standard Method

Before timing begins, a standard procedure needs to be established; that is, the procedure to be timed must be performed the same way each cycle. If a standard sequence of tasks isn't established, and the work is performed differently each cycle, the times won't be comparable. It is also highly recommended that the procedure to be timed has already been streamlined. There is really no point in timing a procedure that will subsequently be further improved. In fact, one reason why a procedure is studied is to determine what is done before time data is collected. The procedure should be as efficient as possible before it is timed. This process is sometimes termed "developing a standard procedure."

Divide into Elements

The standard procedure should be divided into observable elements that can be easily timed. Job elements that take longer than 30 seconds tend to become inaccurate. One needs to be conscious of this problem because numerous library procedures consist of elements that are most conveniently timed in increments of several minutes duration. Whenever possible, however, it is advisable to keep each element as close to 30 seconds as possible.

Constant elements that do not involve time fluctuations from cycle to cycle should be separated from those that do. Many industrial procedures consist mostly of constant elements; the opposite may be true for many library procedures. Moreover, library routines often involve two or more individuals—for example, registering a new reader or collecting a fine. Such interactions inevitably produce cyclical variations. This is not a serious problem, so long as one remembers that additional observations may be needed to compensate for the variations.

Selecting the Person to Be Observed

There may be two or more people performing the same tasks either simultaneously or at different times of the day. For example, several staff members may insert RFID tags into new books, or the staff member charging out books in the evening may not be the same person who worked the afternoon shift. In our book scanning case study that is presented later in this chapter, the operator is a part-time employee who is only one of several staff who regularly scans page images.

When selecting the person to be timed, every effort should be made to select an individual who is thoroughly trained and works at an average pace rather than selecting a person who works unusually fast or slow. If a time study is based on the work of an unusually fast worker, the study will produce unrealistic results, which in turn is likely to generate employee skepticism and fears of what is called a "speedup"; if the observations are based on an unusually slow worker, the results will produce skepticism among managers. How to convert observed times to normal times is discussed later in the chapter.

Recording Observations

In the "good old" days most time studies were conducted using a stopwatch, and in fact electronic stopwatches are still used in some industrial settings. But with the easy availability of affordable digital camcorders, and software that facilitates careful analysis, the stopwatch for library studies should now be a museum piece only. Digital camcorders have greatly simplified the process of making observations. A camcorder can also be used to film the existing procedure, and this information used to assist efforts to improve the procedure and develop the standard method that will be analyzed.

Once the standard method has been established, and the person to be observed selected, the analyst can begin to make observations. Once a sufficient number of cycles have been recorded, the data can be downloaded into a software package such as IMovie where the film clips can be analyzed, if necessary, frame by frame. Camcorders provide a time scale that permits such a frame-by-frame analysis.

Deciding How Many Observations Are Necessary

The same type of questions that were raised in connection with work sampling are germane to direct time studies. One has to decide how many observations should be made. Too few observations may render the data unreliable; too many will unnecessarily inflate study costs. Therefore, one needs to decide the minimum number of observations necessary to generate data with sufficient reliability to satisfy the requirements of the study.

The number of cycles that need to be recorded increases with the variation in the elemental times observed from cycle to cycle. For example, if, over ten cycles, the times recorded for inserting RFID tags proved to be (in minutes) .55, 1.22, .32, 1.13, 1.30, .44, .72, .43, .82, and .62, the analyst could not report with confidence that the average of .75 minutes was truly representative. The spread between the fastest (.32) and slowest (1.22) is too great for reliability. There is no definite pattern or no cluster about the average. In this case additional readings would be advised.

But if the times had been .69, .81, .75, .85, .68, .72, .76, .84, .64, and .89, which also yield the same average, .75, but have a maximum spread of .21, the analyst might have more confidence that .75 minutes was representative, even without knowing the exact number of readings that ought to have been taken.

The General Electric Company has established a guide to assist in approximately the number of cycles to observe. This table is shown in Figure 13-1.

In most cases a pattern will quickly emerge, and one will intuitively know when additional observations are not necessary. But if a high level of precision is desired, it is not difficult to determine the needed sample size to achieve a specified confidence level and confidence interval by consulting a standard text on statistics or consulting an appropriate Web resource. [3]

Cycle time in minutes	Recommended number of cycles
0.10	200
0.25	100
0.50	60
0.75	40
1.00	30
2.00	20
2.00-5.00	15
5.00-10.00	10
10.00-20.00	8
20.00-40.00	5
40.00-above	3

Source: *Information taken from the Time Study Manual of the Erie Works of the General Electric Company, developed under the guidance of Albert E. Shaw, manager of wage administration.*

Figure 13-1 Recommended number of observation cycles.

Case Study: Scanning Books

More and more libraries are scanning materials or actually creating digital images of the content of books and journals. Scanning library materials became popular once several private foundations and government agencies began to underwrite the costs of many projects. While creating digital images of pages also enhances the preservation of valuable collections, the real motivation behind foundation support is the promise of being able to enhance the access of specialized collections to scholars and researchers worldwide.

Since I know that scanning books is a labor-intensive operation I decided to visit a library to observe its scanning operation. I watched the operator for a couple of hours and interviewed the staff worker and supervisor. I decided that the library had enough experience and that the current method could be legitimately described as a standard procedure. I also discovered that not only is the scanning itself expensive and labor intensive, but significant costs can also be incurred during the selection and preparation steps, prior to the actual scanning.

Once a volume is ready for scanning, the operator places the opened book face-up in the target area of the scanner. In our study the library uses a top-down scanner manufactured by Zeutschel. It is a model 0S7000.[4] (See Figure 13-2.) Using the software interface, the operator adjusts the tonal properties to ensure that the image will be as sharp as possible; the operator also selects settings that adjust for the skew of a bound volume lying open. The necessary bibliographic information is usually recorded on a work sheet inside the cover, if not, a brief record is created by the operator. The object is to link the scanned volume to its bibliographic record in the library's database. The operator lowers the glass cover that flattens the title page

Figure 13-2 Scanning a book.

and the title page is scanned. The scanning process proceeds with two-page images captured with each exposure. After the last page is scanned, the bibliographic information that accompanied the book is scanned. There are also some additional post-scanning tasks. First the operator uses a special software program to check to see that all pages were scanned. The scanned material will also be burned onto a CD-R. Once the process is completed, the volume is returned to a book truck.

Figure 13-3 depicts a typical Time Study Observation Sheet. Figure 13-4 depicts the first ten cycles of the page scanning procedure in our study. While I was observing the operator, I noticed that he had developed an excellent work rhythm, and the time necessary to capture each two pages didn't vary much from cycle to cycle. In fact, the data in Figure 13-4 reflect the work performed to scan a monograph with no illustrations. (Scanning an illustration or a table represents what is called an infrequent element. Whenever such material is involved, the operator's rhythm was disrupted and the material required special attention.) The observed times for each element in the cycle are recorded as well as the average time for the ten cycles—22 seconds.

Developing reliable times for the pre-scanning activities required a different approach because I soon discovered that the set-up times varied a great deal from volume to volume. When volumes included illustrations, foldouts, or tabular material that required special attention, the set-up time could exceed eight minutes. As a result I decided to observe the set-up activities separately from the actual page scanning. I also chose to observe and record times for the post-scanning steps separately.

The form shown in Figure 13-5 was specially created to accommodate the special needs of this case study. It describes in detail the variety of set-up tasks that can occur.

When the set-up, scanning, and post-scanning elements were totaled, I found that the average observed time to produce a scanned volume was 59.8 minutes or 60 minutes per volume.

Comments on the Case Study

The direct time study analysis produced a number of positive outcomes. First, the staff were able to make several recommendations regarding how to increase productivity further as well as smooth out the workflow without working harder.[5] For example, a volume with tables and/or illustrations should be handled differently than a volume without special materials. Instead of scanning the pages and special materials during a single cycle, staff recommended two cycles. The pages without illustrations or tabular material would be scanned in the first cycle; the illustrative material would be scanned in a second cycle. This suggestion helped the operator to maintain a smoother work rhythm.

Staff also suggested that the post-scan check using special software to ensure that all pages had been scanned be performed by a second operator, and that the

Time Study Observation Sheet

	Operation: Scanning page images								Average Observed Time per cycle				
	Time started:			Time Ended:									
	Observer:			Date:					Adjusted time/cycle				
									Units/hour				

	Elements	1	2	3	4	5	6	7	8	9	10	Σ T	±
1	Places book on scanner opened to title page												
2	Verifies image grayscale												
3	Writes target verification on slip												
4	Places verification slip in source book												
5	Closes glass cover												
6	Captures image (hits F1 key)												
7	Opens cover												
8	Removes verification slip												
9	Turns page												
10	Closes glass cover												
11	Captures image (hits F1 key)												

Figure 13-3 Sample time observation sheet.

post-scans be batched. This change improved both the efficiency and effectiveness of the procedure.

One of the unanticipated benefits from the analysis was a gradual recognition by management of how important it was to provide the scanning machine operators with intensive training. The use of the supporting software can be complicated. Management also realized that staff selected to scan materials need to be individuals who enjoy detailed and repetitious type jobs.

Time Study Observation Sheet														
Operation: Scanning page images										Average Observed Time per cycle			21.6	
Time Started:			**Time Ended:**											
Observer:			**Date:**							Adjusted time/cycle				
										Units/hour				
Elements		**1**	**2**	**3**	**4**	**5**	**6**	**7**	**8**	**9**	**10**	Σ T	±	
1	Opens cover		4	3	5	3	4	6	3	4	3			
2	Removes verification slip		4	3	4	4	3	3	4	3	4			
3	Turns page		5	4	3	4	5	4	5	6	4			
4	Closes glass cover		3	4	3	3	4	3	4	5	3			
5	Captures image (hits F2 key)		6	6	7	6	7	6	5	7	6			
	Total time/cycle		22	20	22	20	23	22	21	25	20	195	22	

Figure 13-4 Time Study Observations: Digitizing a monograph.

And probably most importantly, management finally recognized that among the most expensive and time-consuming aspects of scanning were the activities that occurred before the scanning actually began, particularly when the books to be scanned were selected on a title-by-title basis, or if every book needs to be inspected for missing pages, etc. This realization was one of the reasons why the library eventually decided to outsource a sizeable portion of its scanning and digitizing work to a commercial vendor.

Start Adjusting for Worker Allowances

I began the chapter by pointing out that the objective of direct time study was to determine how much time it takes a qualified, properly trained worker to perform a given series of tasks. What I want to emphasize as I conclude this description of direct time study is to underscore the importance of selecting a staff member who is able to work at a normal pace. As noted previously, if time

Time Study Observation Sheet

Operation: Scanning page images		Average Observed Time per cycle
Time Started:	Time Ended:	
Observer:	Date:	Adjusted time/cycle
		Units/hour

Elements	1	2	3	4	5	6	7	8	9	10	ΣT	±
Set-up Description	The set-up phase can involve a variety of tasks. The operator examines the printout of MARC record to verify the book's identity and to determine the number of pages to be scanned. The record also ties the book to the library's database. The operator needs to get the volume as straight horizontally as possible in the target viewing area. The automatic crop boxes need to be adjusted. The software settings displayed on the monitor are checked in order to produce the best image considering the type of paper, paper color, and font involved. Covers and end sheets usually require their own set-up. So typically with a new volume, there will be a set-up for the front cover and front endpapers. The text block set-up follows. At the end of the text block another set-up for the endpapers that are connected to the back cover are necessary. When illustrations and other special materials are involved the operator will have to select the black and white or the grayscale, whichever is most appropriate and will produce the best results. For some older texts extra work may be required to clean up a page that is smudged with dirt or has yellowed with age.											
Tme/bk (minutes)	2.39	5.06	2.60	3.42	6.03	8.00	7.24	2.48	3.54	7.45	51.39	5.2 min

Scanning (seconds)	1	2	3	4	5	6	7	8	9	10	Total	
1 Opens cover	4	4	3	5	3	4	6	3	4	3	39	
2 Turns page	5	4	3	4	4	3	3	4	3	4	37	
3 Checks Alignment	2	3	4	6	2	3	4	6	3	2	35	
4 Closes glass lid	4	3	4	3	3	4	3	4	5	3	36	
5 Captures image (hits F2 key)	7	6	6	7	6	7	6	5	7	6	63	

Total: 21.0 sec/image

Post Scan tasks	1	2	3	4	5	6	7	8	9	10		
1 Inspection (min/bk)	2.00	1.48	2.12	3.06	2.48	2.00	3.12	2.24	2.18	1.54	23.42	2.34 min
2 Burn CD (sec/bk)	3	2	3	2	2	3	2	2	3	4	2.8	2.8 sec

Summary		
Set up	5	= 5.2 min
Scan 21 x 300p	150 images @ 21 sec/image	= 52.2 min
Post scan	2.38	= 2.4 min
		Total: 59.8 min

Figure 13-5 Example of a customized time study observation form.

study data are based on the times of an unusually fast or slow worker, the study will generate unreliable data.

In the industrial work environment, an analyst would not simply accept the times we observed in our case study. Instead the analyst would make a judgment as to whether or not the staff member was working at what is called a "normal" pace. A normal pace is defined as the time it takes a qualified person working at his or her regular pace, using a standard method to perform a job. Industrial engineers have devised elaborate methods and formulas to convert observed times into normal times. Although the rating systems can be very sophisticated, they all require the analyst to exercise judgment so in reality rating a staff worker always involves a certain degree of subjectivity. Accuracy depends almost entirely upon the skill and judgment of the rater, and on what appears to be fair to the employee who was observed. However, I don't believe a special rating system is necessary to produce acceptable results in library settings.[6]

Even though we have omitted the step of converting observed times to a normal pace, there is a need to adjust the observed times to take into account factors such as fatigue, personal time, and when appropriate, official rest breaks.

If staff workers functioned without interruption throughout the workday, the observed times could be used without further adjustments, but staff workers take rest breaks and are given time off to take care of personal needs. To account for such "allowances" it is necessary to adjust the observed time to calculate a more reasonable adjusted time. The times recorded in Figures 13-4 and 13-5 are observed times only.

As an illustration of how observed times are adjusted, we will return to our book scanning case study. Let's assume that the library grants two rest periods of 20 minutes each and 20 minutes personal time per eight-hour day. The normal workday consists of 480 minutes (8 hours x 60 minutes/hour). Thus the total work allowances are:

$$\text{Personal needs allowance} = 20/480 \text{ minutes/day} = 4.1\%$$

– – – – – – – – – – – – – – – – – –

$$\text{Rest allowance} = 40/480 \text{ minutes/day} = 8.3\%$$
$$\text{Percentage of total working day permitted for allowances} = 12.4\%$$

The adjusted time can now be computed by substitution into the following formula:

$$A_T = O_T \times 100/100\text{-A where}$$
$$(A_T = \text{standard time}; O_T = \text{normal time}; A = \text{allowances})$$

$$A_T = 59.8 \times 100/100\text{-A}$$
$$A_T = 68.26$$

– – – – – – – – – – – – – – – – –

Including the average set-up time, observed time for scanning a 300-page book is 59.8 minutes. But after the time for staff allowances are factored in, the scanning time per volume increases to 68.3 minutes. The adjusted time is much more realistic than the unadjusted observed time. The difference could make a sizeable difference in long-range production projections and expectations. In fact in our case study, we also observed a third factor that would need to be factored into the final figures. The staff worker we observed frequently took short "fatigue" breaks because the job was very repetitive. As a result we would have added in an additional 5 percent worker allowance; and therefore, in this situation a realistic production figure for a 300-page volume would not be 59.8 minutes but 71.4 minutes per volume.

Final Thoughts

The case study highlighted an activity that amply underscores the potential benefits of conducting direct time studies. Scanning activities can consume significant staff resources. If managers had realized when scanning began how expensive this activity was going to prove to be, it's possible many more libraries would have opted to outsource the work rather than establish in-house production units.

Notes

1. When I came into the field one of the most frequently cited industrial engineering texts was Ralph M. Barnes, *Motion and Time Study: Design and Measurement of Work*, 7th ed. (New York: John Wiley, 1968). In preparing this new edition, I found two titles to be useful. See Benjamin Niebel and Andris Freivalds, *Methods, Standards, and Work Design*, 11th ed. (New York: McGraw-Hill, 2003) and Lawrence S. Aft, *Work Measurement and Methods Improvement* (New York: Wiley-Interscience, 2000).

2. Richard Logsden, "Time and Motion Studies in Libraries," *Library Trends* 2 (1954): 401-9.

3. Benjamin Niebel and Andris Freivalds, *Methods, Standards, and Work Design*, 390-92 was helpful. And, as mentioned in the chapter on work sampling, there are Web sites available that assist in quickly calculating sample sizes, confidence levels, and confidence intervals. One helpful site is http://home.clara.net/sisa/ (26 May 2007).

4. The Zeutschel Web site is located at: http://www.zeutschel.com/produkte/os7000.html (26 May 2007).

5. You will recall that the supervisor and the staff had agreed before timing began that the current procedure was the standard procedure. Our intent was only to time that procedure. The fact that further improvements were identified was a bonus. It is possible that the library might decide to time the modified procedure to collect additional data.

6. A detailed description of a ratings system, along with directions on how such a rating system was used, can be found in Richard M. Dougherty and Fred J. Heinritz, *Scientific Management of Library Operations*, 2nd ed. (Metuchen, N.J.: Scarecrow Press, 1982), 170-72.

Section Five
How Much It Costs

Chapter Fourteen

Costs

Scope note: Well-constructed cost studies, particularly those based on ac-
curate time data, can serve as a powerful management tool. This chapter
explains how cost studies can be used and what are the benefits. Basic
terms and concepts are explained. Directions on how to organize and
build cost studies are presented. All categories of direct and indirect costs
are included. Two depreciation models are presented and their uses dis-
cussed. The chapter also introduces the topics of benchmarking and cost
benefit analysis, which are both related to the general subject of costs.

Previous chapters have focused on how to analyze the work done in libraries and how much time is required. The next important topic is how to calculate
the costs of producing products and/or providing services.[1] The literature is full
of articles that report on costs, but most studies are weak methodologically. One
notable exception is the series of time and cost studies that were conducted by the
technical services staff at Iowa State University Library over a ten-year period beginning in the early 1990s. The authors collected their time data using detailed diary instruments, and although I've expressed reservations about this methodology
(see page 133), I'm confident that the costs reported are reliable; moreover, other
libraries could still adopt the methodologies developed at ISU. I don't think there
is any doubt, at least not in my mind, that the ISU librarians during the time period
of these studies, had a better understanding of costs and the impact of introducing
new technology than most other libraries.[2]

In one sense developing cost studies is a straightforward topic, but in another it
is a very complicated topic because there are so many ways costs can be calculated.
As previously mentioned, even a casual search of the literature reveals that librarians have used all manner of methodologies to conduct cost studies. These studies
run the gamut from those that include only direct costs (labor, supplies, equipment,
etc.) omitting all indirect costs, to those that are detailed and include all costs associated with the operations.

There is also the question of accuracy, that is, the degree to which calculated
costs approximate the real costs of an activity. For the most part, accuracy depends
on the quality of the time data on which the cost study is based. Although almost

without exception, the studies from the literature I examined are not based on precise time data, most of them still have practical application.

The key is to be clear about the purpose(s) of a cost study. The purpose of a study will dictate how its methodology should be constructed. For example, if a group of libraries is trying to make decisions about resource sharing, a study based solely on direct costs will probably suffice, but if the director of a public library is preparing to present a budget to the City Council, and the budget includes a cost analysis of the library's operations, then a full accounting of costs is advisable to ensure credibility among the officials who will evaluate the request. Again, keep in mind that a cost study's methodology, and the precision of data collected should reflect the purpose of the study, and that the real purpose of conducting a cost study is not the gathering of data, but in how the information is used to benefit the organization.

The Uses and Benefits of Cost Studies

It has always surprised me that more libraries do not conduct regular, detailed cost analyses. The availability of accurate cost data provides a powerful management tool that can be used for a variety of purposes. But the paucity of well-constructed cost studies shouldn't really be shocking because, as I have mentioned several times, librarianship is a service profession, not a bottom-line oriented corporation. Costs of an activity aren't normally a top concern of many library staff.

Cost study data can be used in a variety of ways to support rational decision making. What follows is only a sample of possible benefits and uses.

Analyzing and Evaluating Alternative Courses of Action

Should a library outsource its cataloging or a portion of its cataloging? Should it purchase or lease its library vehicle or its computers? Should janitorial services be contracted with an outside firm or performed by the library's in-house staff? In these examples, the library would be basing its decision primarily on costs assuming that performance of the options were comparable. But evaluating alternate methods of ILL and document delivery would immediately add performance (time) to the decision-making process. If the cheapest alternative produced an unsatisfactory performance, a more expensive option might be selected. Just the availability of cost and performance data can serve as an important decision-making tool.

Provide a Better Understanding of a Current Activity

Cost studies can lead to a better understanding of the differences in the costs of operations. For example, why the costs of cataloging a monograph or cataloging a serial may differ markedly, or why original cataloging costs so much more than copy cataloging, or to explain why digitizing and preserving books can be so costly.

Determine the Actual Costs of a New Activity

Cost data can be used to clarify for staff and officials the costs of a new activity, e.g., virtual reference service. Cost data can then be used to explain to officials and customers the rationale behind a fee-for-service proposal.

Explain and/or Justify Budget Requests

The availability of cost data can affect how much money a library receives in its budget. A budget based on solid cost studies can better arm a library's administration in its negotiations with funding officials. The customary approach of using last year's budget plus an increment is less persuasive during periods of budget constraints than a budget based on reliable cost data. A library administrator can use a well-crafted cost study to strengthen requests for additional resources, or to explain why it may be necessary to reduce a service in the absence of additional resources. Or, a library might conduct a Cost Benefit Analysis (CBA) to explain why the library intends to purchase licenses to several databases while canceling a number of paper subscriptions. This analysis would also include the benefits to qualified library users who would be able to access the databases at their own convenience and from remote locations. Providing sound cost data is also likely to increase a library administrator's credibility in the eyes of officials.

If libraries conduct cost studies over a period of time they will be able to provide a historical perspective that may enable them to demonstrate to officials how changes over time have impacted current costs. In recent years the availability of such data would have been particularly useful in documenting how technology has increased productivity in the library.

Finally, library unit heads who strive to justify the need for additional resources in their units can also use the cost data effectively. I generally found that unit heads who buttressed their budget requests with cost data usually fared better than their peers who simply included exhortations to justify their requests.

Provide Management with a Tool for Controlling Costs

A carefully conducted cost study based on reliable time data may go a long way toward raising staff consciousness about the actual costs of an activity. I still vividly recall working with a group of catalogers who simply didn't realize that the cost of original cataloging had become so expensive that it was difficult, if not impossible, to justify the cost of adding additional catalogers. Once they became aware of the actual costs, most became more amenable to efforts to increase cataloging productivity and streamlining their cataloging processes.

Cost data can also be used to justify reorganization of a single unit or of a group of units. In some respects the flattening of technical service units in recent years has been based on mounting administrative costs and efforts to improve operational efficiency.

Comparisons with Other Libraries

The desire to compare operations against other libraries is frequently cited as a goal of cost studies. This type of study is often termed "benchmarking." There are obviously potential benefits of being able to compare oneself against the performance of peers, but such a process can be tricky because there is such a strong likelihood that one will end up comparing apples and oranges. In order to be valid, the activities to be compared must be defined identically in order for the costs to be comparable. For example, if some services are supported by a central agency and are not included as part of the library's operating budget, or if some libraries omit some of their indirect costs, the cost comparisons wouldn't be valid. A bit more will be said about benchmarking later in the chapter (see page 181).

Basic Terms and Concepts

The literature reflects enormous variety in the way cost studies are organized and in the use of terminology. There are a few terms associated with cost studies that are frequently used and seem to be standard. These include cost center(s), direct and indirect costs, and fixed and variable costs.[3]

Cost center—is an area of responsibility in which a manager is accountable for incurring costs. Cost centers may be built around major organizational divisions within the library (e.g., branch libraries), internal management functions (e.g., reference), or services provided to the public (e.g., children services). Oftentimes library processes involve more than one typical cost center. For example, the book-ordering process in a decentralized library system could involve branches, acquisitions, cataloging, and circulation units. The goal is to be sure to include all of the relevant activities when analyzing activities that transcend cost centers.

Direct costs—are those costs readily attributable to a specific activity or cost center. Direct costs include salaries and fringe benefits, equipment, supplies, and library materials.

Indirect costs—are those costs that are not assignable to any one activity. These costs are also commonly known as "overhead" costs. This category can include a variety of costs ranging from administrative costs to janitorial salaries and computer maintenance. Other indirect costs frequently cited are physical space (as measured by the cost of comparable rental space), utilities, insurance, building repairs, marketing, and promotion. A special category of indirect costs is the services that an outside agency performs to the benefit of the library. Such activities might include centralized personnel services, data process, networking services, and accounting.

One particularly important category of indirect costs is the various administrative costs associated with a process or procedure. For example, one might not associate administrative costs with acquisitions and cataloging because the heads of the units are not directly involved with the handling of items, but these costs need to be included in order to develop a realistic picture of costs. These costs can turn out to be quite high. I've encountered studies that note up to 30 percent of the total costs could be attributed to various forms of administrative costs. Keep in mind that by not including indirect costs, there is a considerable likelihood that the costs of an existing or proposed new service are going to be underestimated, and as a result the budget request will understate the real needs of the activity.

Variable costs—are those costs that fluctuate in relationship to the total activity or volume, such as use of the library or the number of reference questions answered.

Fixed costs—are those costs that remain constant regardless of changes in the activity level. Rent is an example of a fixed cost; it remains the same regardless of how the space is utilized. Another example would be the computers used in providing virtual reference services; the cost of the computers remains the same regardless of the number of questions processed.

Activity costs—are costs that are not directly associated with production or units produced. For example if a staff member works 35 hours per week at a rate of $16 per hour, then the labor expense per week is 35 x $16, or $660 (plus benefits such as FICA). This type of information provides a manager with data on overall organizational costs, but these figures do not offer any guidance concerning expenses in relation to useful work produced. Hourly salary rates cannot measure the impact of such variables on production. This leads us to the concept of unit cost.

Unit costs—relate costs with the production of a unit of work. In a catalog department a reasonable unit is a cataloged book; in the circulation department, a book circulated; in the reference department, a reference question asked or answered. The unit cost is an average obtained by dividing the total cost of producing a given number of units by the number of units produced (N):

$$\text{Unit Cost} = \frac{\text{Cost of Producing N Units of Work}}{N}$$

The unit cost is the basis of cost accounting. It allows an organization to compare its own performance with others engaged in similar work, and to compare its own performance for one time period with another time period. Unit costs also allow for a certain measure of prediction. For example, a university library is expected to support several new research programs the following year. The university administration promises the library that it will support these programs with additional resources, but the university administrator fails to consider the costs of acquiring and organizing the additional resources. The library director realizes that unless steps are taken quickly, the needed processing monies will not be forthcoming. She asks her assistant director for processing to gather data that can be presented to the campus administration. Fortunately, the assistant director is a cost-conscious person who has kept track of unit costs for acquiring paper and digital resources. He knows that the cost of ordering an item is $A; license fees for databases $L, for cataloging, $C; and for binding and shelving, $B. The average purchase price of an item for this library is known to be $D. The university has said that it will increase the resources budget by $I. Armed with these figures, the library director can demonstrate that acquiring and processing the additional resources will cost $I = (A + B + L + C)(I/D)$.

Organizing a Cost Study

I've already mentioned that even a casual perusal of the literature of cost studies reveals that there are many ways to organize a cost study, and which approach one adopts should be governed by the purpose of the study. The methodology recommended in the PLA Cost Finding Project, and the modifications of that approach adopted by Virgo, provide a straightforward way to organize cost studies.[4] There is also a very useful guide to structuring cost studies for technical services. It was prepared by the ALCTS Technical Services Costs Committee in 1991, and it is still relevant to those designing a cost study.[5] Chapter 4 also includes material about organizing studies because there are many parallels between organizing a management study and organizing a cost study.

Determine the Cost Center

Typically a cost center, as previously defined, is a grouping of activities or an area of responsibility for which costs can be reasonably brought together, and are related to the products or services produced. A cost center might involve a formal unit or product or service, e.g., circulating a book (unit), acquiring a book (product), answering a reference question (service).

Determine the Activities and Tasks Related to the Cost Center

As an example this could be: ordering process (cost center) →establish bibliographic entry (activity) →confirm price (task). The following chart depicts the relationships among a group of activities associated with a reference services unit.[6] (See Figure 14-1.)

Select the Unit Cost Measures Appropriate to the Cost Center, Activity, or Task Being Examined

In most cases, selecting the unit cost measurement involves identifying the product produced or service provided. For example, number of books cataloged, number of books digitized, number of reference questions answered, etc. The specific activity is related to the total direct and indirect costs expended divided by the number of units produced to determine the cost per unit.

Collect the Necessary Data

Data may be derived from existing records, collected via questionnaires, diary studies, or direct time study observations. Regardless of the source, the purpose is to determine how much time is spent performing a defined set of activities.

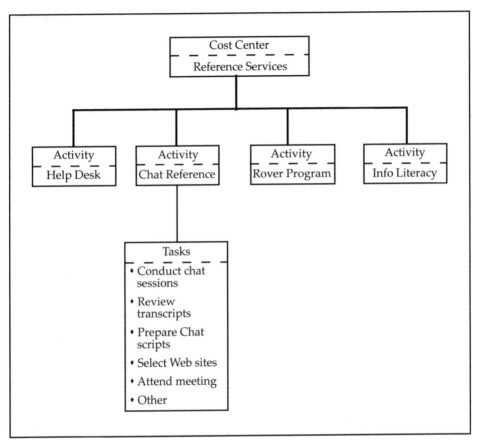

Figure 14-1 Block Chart: Designed to organize activities so that times and costs can be
properly allocated.

Determine the Categories of Direct Cost

This will include all categories of direct costs, e.g., labor costs (salaries and benefits), supplies, equipment, travel, etc.

Determine Indirect Costs (Overhead)

The challenge when calculating indirect costs is to decide what proportion of the costs should be assigned to the total cost of the process or procedure being studied. Normally indirect costs are associated with services, products, or departments, e.g., preservation of a book or the preservation unit, reference service, etc.[7]

Analyze the Collected Data

This step is discussed in great detail in Chapter 15, *Assessing Current Activities.*

Building a Cost Model

All relevant costs that one might want to include in a cost study need to be kept in mind. The reliability of any cost study will be directly dependent on the accuracy of the time data on which the times are based.

Direct Salary Costs

Although the purchase and maintenance costs of automated systems can consume a significant percentage of a library's budget, salaries normally still comprise the largest single expense item. Most library cost studies calculate the annual costs by simply aggregating the base salary plus all fringe benefits and dividing by the total hours paid for all staff involved with the activity during the period under study. For example, a small circulation department's staff budget is $45,000 plus $15,000 in fringe benefits. Therefore the total salary budget is $60,000. But in order to make the number more meaningful, the salary cost must be tied to some measure of activity. In this case the library circulated 250,000 items so that during the year the cost/item circulated was .26 cents.

This basic calculation figures the average cost per item produced or activity under measure. In some cases this degree of precision will suffice, but there may be occasions in which it is necessary to be more precise when calculating labor costs. It will also be helpful to anyone who is charged with conducting a cost study to understand what is actually involved with salary costs.

Right from the outset it is necessary to recognize that salary costs per productive hour do not merely equal time on the job x hourly wage. Libraries routinely contribute to fringe benefit packages, such as retirement plans, Social Security payments, and health insurance plans. Also, staff do not work all the time for which they are paid; they take vacations, enjoy holidays, require sick leave, are granted personal-leave days, and permitted rest periods (breaks) during the workday. The formula for deriving the actual salary cost per hour is calculated as follows:

$$\frac{\text{Salary Cost per}}{\text{Productive Hour}} = \frac{\text{Annual Salary Cost} + \text{Annual Additional Costs}}{\text{Annual Number of Hours Actually Devoted to Work}}$$

$$= \frac{\text{Annual Salary Cost} + \text{Annual Additional Costs}}{[365 - (W + H + V + S + P)]\,[1 - A]\,[D]}$$

where

    W = the number of weekend days per year

    H = the number of paid holidays per year

    V = the number of paid vacation days per year

    S = the number of paid sick-leave days taken per year

P = the number of paid personal-leave days taken per year

A = the percent of a working day allowed for coffee breaks and personal needs (worker allowances)

D = the number of hours in a working day

Let's illustrate how such detailed information might prove useful to the head of a reference department who has a vacancy and must decide whether to recruit a full-time or a part-time staff member. Since the head of public services has provided the reference department with a staff budget, and granted the unit full discretion as to how the budget may be spent, there is a real incentive to stretch dollars as far as possible. The part-time employee would cost the library $15 per hour. (Part-timers who work less than 20 hours per week usually are not granted fringe benefits other than Social Security. They may or may not get rest breaks, depending on the number of hours they work and on local policies. For this example, we will assume that a $20 figure covers all labor costs.)

The full-time candidate would work five seven-hour days (Monday through Friday, 8:30 A.M. to 4:30 P.M., with an hour off for lunch), at a salary of $37,000 per year. Let's assume that the fringe benefits will add 30 percent to the base salary. This will add $11,100 to the base salary of $37,000.

The full-time candidate would receive ten paid holidays and fifteen days vacation per year. Full-time employees use an average of five days of sick leave and one day of personal leave per year; they are allowed two 20-minute coffee breaks and 20 minutes for personal needs each working day.

Substituting into the formula produces:

$$\text{Labor Cost per Productive Hour} \quad \frac{37{,}000 + 11{,}000}{[365 - (104 + 10 + 15 + 5 + 1)]\,[1 - 1/7]\,[7]} = \$34.78$$

So in this case the employment of the part-time worker makes a great deal of sense. Of course in a real situation, cost is not the only criterion that would be used in making such a hiring decision, but if all other factors were equal, the real costs could become a telling consideration. In this case the reference department might even be able to employ a second part-timer who possessed a different type of needed expertise.

Individuals and groups who are paid at different rates often carry out the same activities. In such situations it may be necessary to calculate the weighted mean in order to arrive at a unit labor cost. The first step is to determine the productive hour cost for each staff member involved, and the percentage of the total operation time each person represents. These two factors are multiplied for each person. The products are summed to arrive at an answer. (If the percentages are not expressed as decimals or fractions, it will be necessary to divide the products by 100.)

As an example, suppose that three employees are involved with an activity under study.

	Labor Cost per Productive Hour	Percent of Total Operation Time
Staff 1	15.00	22
Staff 2	12.00	14
Staff 3	8.00	64

The computation is:

$$\text{Average Labor Cost per Productive Hour} = \frac{(22 \times \$15.00) + (14 \times \$12.00) + (64 \times \$8.00)}{100} = \$10.10$$

Indirect Costs (Salary)

In a cost study the most obvious salary costs are those directly associated with the processes under study, there is also a second important category, the indirect salary costs. These include general salary expenses that legitimately should be assigned to the total costs. For example, the head of an acquisition department whose salary is $55,000 per year spends on the average 20 percent of a workday on activities associated with order unit procedures. In such a case the indirect salary charge is (.20 x $55,000), or $11,000. Furthermore, the head of the technical services division whose salary is $75,000 devotes 5 percent of her time to activities that can be legitimately assigned to the ordering unit activities (.05 x $75,000) or $3,750. There are occasions when the indirect salary costs can comprise a significant proportion of the total labor costs.

Cost of Supplies

For most libraries, calculating supply costs is reasonably straightforward. Drawing either from the experience of one's own institution, or by checking with colleagues at other institutions, it should be relatively easy to estimate the number of units that will be used during a given period. The cost of the item for a given period is:

Cost of Supply = Unit Cost x Number of Units

Suppose that we wish to order a supply of paper for our printers. We know that each box contains 10 reams, and the regular cost of each box is $45.00 or $4.50 per ream. Based on last year's level of usage of 400 boxes, and factoring in a 10 percent increase in usage for the current year, we decide to purchase a one month supply. The cost is:

Boxes of printing paper = $45.00 x 37 boxes = $1,665.00

However, buying supplies in quantity will often produce a worthwhile discount. In the above illustration, had the library decided to purchase a six-month supply, the cost would have been reduced to $29.95 per box or $2.95 per ream. This would have resulted in a savings for a twelve-month period of $3,311. Ordering in smaller quantities also costs more in other ways, as multiple orders have to be placed, received, and processed.

However, discount or not, it is not always advisable to order in large batches. The money tied up in stored supplies might have been spent in more productive ways, and storage space itself may be in demand. Moreover, some supplies age, others dry up or their chemical constituents break down. Sometimes a better product becomes available, or a process that required the item may be altered so that the item is no longer needed, e.g., multiple order forms went the way of the dodo bird when the library began to order new books online. Clearly, a library should use common sense to balance discount savings against these other factors.

Capital Expenditures

Capital outlays provide benefits that extend over several years. For example, the purchase of chairs, tables, desks, delivery trucks, shelving, cabinets, book trucks, elevators and conveyers, microform readers, audiovisual equipment, and photocopiers, if purchased, are all examples of capital expenditures. But of course terminals, network servers and software and other components of an integrated system are likely to represent one of a library's major capital expenditure. The value of capital expenditures needs to be determined and figured into the study, and properly allocated in order to determine the full costs of an activity.

If a library uses debt financing to purchase the capital item, the interest component of debt service payment is a current period cost, and is not included in the depreciation calculation. The issue of debt financing raises some other possibly relevant issues. Today libraries may be forced to make sizeable investments in computer hardware and software. Some libraries borrow funds from their parent organization, and pay back the loan over a period of years or over the course of the useful life of the equipment. In some instances libraries have purchased hardware and software by reallocating existing funds from the operating budget.

Oftentimes hardware and software are leased and not purchased. For example, a library might lease PCs or laptops for three years, and at the end of the lease, trade them in for the current models. Leased equipment would be expensed and not depreciated.

Depreciation

Depreciation is used to calculate capital expenses. This includes all equipment and software that is purchased, and which has a life expectancy of more than one year. Depreciation is the portion of a capital expense that is expensed during a given period of time. Or stated similarly, depreciation is the allowance made for decrease in value of capital expenditures due to obsolescence and wear.

Libraries and other nonprofit organizations traditionally haven't paid as much attention to depreciation as have for-profit organizations. The reason is simple;

there are no tax implications for nonprofit organizations. But in order to gain a full picture of the costs of workflows and activities, capital expenditures associated with the process(es) should be included in the cost calculations.

Calculating Depreciation—There are different methods for calculating depreciation. The simplest depreciation model is the "straight-line" method. The name derives from the fact that when dollars are plotted against years, the resultant graph is a straight line (see Figure 14-2). In this method the cost of the equipment minus its salvage value is deducted in equal annual amounts over the period of its estimated usual life.

Annual   Purchase Price – Salvage Value of Item at Time of Replacement
Depreciation   Number of Years between Purchase and Replacement

$$\text{Annual Depreciation} = \frac{\text{Purchase Price} - \text{Salvage Value of Item at Time of Replacement}}{\text{Number of Years between Purchase and Replacement}}$$

An example of the straight-line method: A library purchases a photocopying machine for $2,000. Due to rapid technological advance in the field, and its experience with such equipment, the library estimates that it will need to buy a new model in about four years, at which time the old machine will probably have a trade-in value of about $400. Thus the annual depreciation is:

$$\text{Amount of Depreciation per Year} = \frac{\$2,000 - \$400}{4} = \$400$$

Once the amount of depreciation to allow per year is known, it is then possible to prepare a depreciation schedule. For our example this schedule is:

Year	Book Value at Beginning of Year	Annual Depreciation	Book Value at End of Year
1st	$2,000	$400	$1,600
2nd	1,600	400	1,200
3rd	1,200	400	800
4th	800	400	400

As a check, the remainder should (within rounding errors) equal the salvage value and the sum of the Annual Depreciation column should (within rounding errors) equal (Purchase Price - Salvage Value).

Some managers are reluctant to use the straight-line depreciation model on the grounds that it is not sufficiently consonant with reality. Straight-line assumes the same rate of depreciation each year that depreciation is deducted. The actual rate, however, tends to be higher during the initial years. Various alternative depreciation models have been developed in an attempt to overcome this limitation. One of the most common is the "sum-of-years" method. Figure 14-2 shows the differences between the straight-line and sum-of-years models. To make comparison easier in Figure 14-2, the data used with the straight-line method is repeated. The depreciation schedule for the sum-of-years model is shown along with the comparable year-end balances calculated in the straight-line method:

The step-by-step procedure for constructing the sum-of-years depreciation table is as follows:

1. Estimate the number of years between purchase and need for replacement—4 years, in the example—and write the figures from 1 to this number in a column in ascending order ("Year" column of schedule).

2. Write these same numbers in reverse or descending order in the next column and add them. In the example the sum is 10. For a larger number of years the sum could be found by use of the formula N (N+1)/2 where N is the number of years. Thus 4 (4+1)/2 =10 ("Reversed Year" column).

3. For each year divide the "Reversed Year" value by the sum of the years to obtain either a common or a decimal fraction ("Reversed Year/Sum" column). Note that for each succeeding year the fraction has a smaller value.

4. Subtract the Salvage Value from the Purchase Price. In the example this value is $1,600 ($2,000 – $400 = $1,600). For each year multiply this value by the "Reversed Year/Sum" fraction for that year. This will yield the amount of depreciation to be allowed for that year ("Annual Depreciation" column). The depreciation for the first year would be $1,600 x 4/10, or $640; for the second year, $1,600 x 3/10, or $480; and so on. The general formula is: Depreciation for Year = (Purchase Price – Salvage Value) x ("Reversed" Value for Year/Sum of Years). You can check the arithmetic by adding all the values in the "Depreciation" column. The sum should (within rounding errors) equal (Purchase Price – Salvage).

5. Complete the "Book Value" columns by means of subtraction. Thus for the first year $2,000 – $640 = $1,360, for the second year $1,360 – $480 = $880, and so on. The final subtraction should (within rounding errors) yield a remainder equal to the salvage value.

In summary, the straight-line model is easier to use, and is acceptable for most library studies. The sum-of-years model and others of this type usually present a more realistic picture, but are a little more difficult to calculate. The choice between the two methods will depend on the circumstances and purposes of a particular study.

Estimating the Useful Life of Equipment—The duration of a capital expenditure's useful life needs to be approximated in order to develop a depreciation schedule. More than likely the categories of capital expenditures that need to be considered are computer hardware and software. How long will the hardware last? When will the software have to be upgraded or replaced? The IRS provides manuals to guide corporations in making such decisions, but I believe the best guide for librarians is

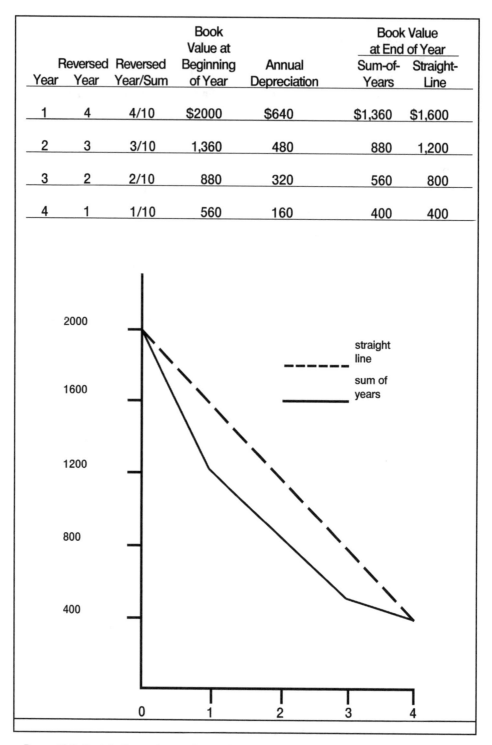

Year	Reversed Year	Reversed Year/Sum	Book Value at Beginning of Year	Annual Depreciation	Book Value at End of Year	
					Sum-of-Years	Straight-Line
1	4	4/10	$2000	$640	$1,360	$1,600
2	3	3/10	1,360	480	880	1,200
3	2	2/10	880	320	560	800
4	1	1/10	560	160	400	400

Figure 14-2 Straight-line and sum-of-years depreciation schedules for a photocopying machine.

previous experience. If the appropriate data cannot be determined locally, another option is to consult other libraries that are using the same equipment and software.

Final Thoughts about Depreciation—In addition to cost-study applications, depreciation data, if skillfully employed, can serve as a useful resource for library administrators who need to justify expenditures for equipment to officials. It is still not unusual for libraries, or the agencies to which libraries report, to consider equipment purchases as current expenditures. This practice creates a false impression. To carry equipment as a current expenditure implies that its usefulness will end with the current fiscal period, and of course, that is not the case. Budget officials need to be reminded that significant capital purchases, particularly computer hardware and software, will occur from time to time. Calculating depreciation on a regular basis is one way to keep officials informed about necessary future capital expenditures.

Finally, there will be occasions when depreciation rates can be omitted from a cost study without doing undue harm to the study results. For example, when one is striving to calculate current costs, and the capital assets have useful lives that extend well beyond the period under study, the depreciation would have a minimal impact on the total direct cost of an activity. An integrated library system however, might be viewed as supporting overall library operations, and therefore considered to indirectly support the provision of the various individual activities. This omission would have little effect on an internally oriented study, but if the audience for the cost study is external, my belief is that depreciation schedules for capital assets need to be recognized.

Cost of Equipment Maintenance

Maintenance of equipment, particularly sophisticated computer-related hardware and software, can become a substantial additional expense, and therefore should be included in cost calculations. With integrated library systems, the annual maintenance costs can involve tens of thousands of dollars. I've seen reports that suggest that $100,000 would not be far out of line.

When complex and essential pieces of equipment are involved, it usually pays for the library to procure annual service contracts with either the manufacturer or with some other firm to guarantee that the equipment can be kept operational with preventive maintenance. Of course, software that supports library integrated systems is a mandatory maintenance expense.

Indirect or Overhead Costs

A cost study should not ignore overhead when costing a particular function. Rather, it should chart a fair proportion to each activity. The general formula is:

Overhead cost to be charged to the function being studied $=$ Total overhead cost x Percentage of overhead cost properly chargeable to the function being studied

Overhead expenses vary relatively little with the amount of work done. It should cost about the same to illuminate a library with only a few patrons occupying it as when it is filled to capacity. In contrast, direct costs tend to vary in direct proportion to the volume of activity. For example if the number of reference questions increases when a new chat reference service is introduced, salary costs will increase if the reference staff must be augmented to handle the increased volume.

What needs to be done is to develop a list of indirect costs that are associated with a particular process or procedure. The PLA Project cited earlier does a very nice job of categorizing three different types of indirect costs. It distinguishes between indirect support services and indirect operating costs.[8]

There are two major categories of indirect costs. The first is indirect support services and the second is indirect operating expenses. The following presents examples of each.

Support Services	**Operating Expenses**
Administration	Utilities
Clerical support	Telephone Insurance
Finance/bookkeeping	Equipment and supplies
Maintenance	Furnishings
Acquisitions	Postage
Cataloging Mending/Bindery	Rent Depreciation
Security/custodial services	Computer system support
Computer system support	

The PLA Project also identifies a third category of indirect costs: governmental or outside costs. These costs pertain to situations such as a local government or campus administration providing centralized services such as accounting, data processing, or personnel services.

Allocating Indirect Costs—It will be necessary to select a method for connecting the range of costs that have been identified with the activity under study. The traditional approach is to allocate indirect costs based on the percentage of labor costs in a unit(s) that are associated with the activity under study, i.e., if 60 percent of the unit's salaries are directly associated with the activity, then 60 percent of the unit's indirect costs would be assigned to the total cost. Today, with the extensive employment of integrated library systems, it may be necessary to determine, to the extent possible, what proportion of the hardware and software costs can be attributed to a given set of activities under study.

Paradoxically computer systems and applications software may be categorized either as a direct or an indirect cost. If the transactions of an integrated system can be associated with the activities under review, the costs can be categorized as direct, but if the integrated system is designed to support activities that transcend technical and public services, and the transactions can't be associated with particular activities, the costs will have to be categorized as indirect.

Another possible approach is to approximate the allocation of costs by using the number of PCs associated with the workflows and activities under review. Some systems provide the ability to allocate the transactions to different activities regardless of where they occurred. When this is the case, it is relatively easy to allocate the appropriate costs to the workflows or activities under study.

Total Costs

Once cost components have been identified—labor (direct and indirect), equipment depreciation and maintenance, supply, and overhead—they should be summed up in order to achieve a total cost. In many library situations it may be sufficient to use simplified calculations in estimating the total cost. For example, suppose that in a study of a library's circulation system we find that the annual labor and supply costs (direct costs) are about $150,000. We know from experience that these two costs should amount to about 80 percent of the total. If precision is not required, we could estimate the total annual cost as follows:

$$(0.80)\ (\$150,000) = \$120,000$$

Thus we are able to account for the overhead and depreciation within reasonably accurate limits without having to calculate them. It is certainly better to estimate them than to pretend that they do not exist. Keep in mind that estimations done with care, and when reasonably applied, can be a most useful tool.

The following formula is one handy technique to ensure that all cost factors have been taken into consideration:

1) Labor cost, both direct and indirect (Ld and Li)

2) Depreciation expenses (D)

3) Maintenance expenses (M)

4) Supply or material costs (S)

5) Overhead or fixed costs (O)

The algorithm for finding the total cost (TC) is:

$$TC = Ld + Li + D + M + S + O$$

Benchmarking

The literature reflects a considerable interest in wanting to compare one organization's activities against those of other organizations. This process is termed "benchmarking." Benchmarking is a process that involves an organization comparing itself against the "best-in-class" libraries and then using that information improve one's own performance. There are many potential benefits to benchmarking. Morris et al have succinctly summarized these in their report of an extensive time and cost study. They noted that "existence of data across libraries, collected in a standardized manner, supports library benchmarking and identification of best practices, which, in turn, is one was of identifying high-payback areas for further exploration."[9]

Numerous writers have called for greater efforts to benchmark activities in technical services. While the benefits could be enormously helpful to libraries that are concerned about the costs and efficiency of their technical services, benchmarking of technical service activities in a meaningful way is difficult because there are so many variables involved.

One significant barrier to benchmarking has been that libraries rarely define tasks in ways that are comparable. For example, one library defines copy cataloging so that professional involvement is excluded; another defines copy cataloging in a way that requires professional involvement. When differences in definitions exist, meaningful benchmarking isn't possible.[10]

Still another barrier to benchmarking of technical services activities is that libraries rarely collect time and cost data using standardized methodologies. One of the contributions of ARL's LibQUAL+ methodology is that it employs a standardized methodology about library activities and facilities. Benchmarking among libraries using the LibQUAL+ methodology is possible.[11]

While benchmarking of technical services activities has not proven to be very successful, efforts to benchmark interlibrary lending and document delivery have produced better results. The studies conducted by Mary Jackson and her colleagues at ARL laid the groundwork so that legitimate benchmarking became possible.[12] One study reported by the New Mexico State University reports on how local procedures might be improved as a result of its benchmarking study.[13] Even more impressive is the study conducted by the Interlending Services at the National Library of Australia. Using the methodology developed by Jackson and her colleagues, over 100 libraries reported data. The investigators identified "high performing" libraries and offered a number of suggestions for improving performance based on the study.[14]

Cost Benefit Analysis

Cost Benefit Analysis (CBA) can be defined as a measure that helps determine how the benefits of a product or service compares to its costs. CBA techniques can be used to determine whether, or to what extent, a project is worthwhile. This type of analysis seeks to identify both tangible and intangible benefits and to compare benefits to costs. For example, one might want to compare the benefits of electronic resources purchased through an academic library consortium to the costs of licensing the resources individually. Such a study would not only include the tangible benefits such as increased access but also ease of use. The intangible benefits might include increased research output that occurs after the new resources are made available.[15]

Unfortunately determining the benefit of many library activities is not easy to do. In 1989 Martin Cummings, a former Director of the National Library of Medicine who was serving as a consultant to the Council on Library and Information Resources, addressed the topic of cost benefits in the context of library services.

Cummings advice is as relevant today as it was then when he observed:

> Cost-benefit analyses that quantify benefits that accrue to society from library services are difficult, if not impossible, to perform. How can one measure the benefits of browsing, comfortable reading space, or even reference service? The public good that results from library service can only be judged in the context of other public services—such as schools, police, and fire protection—that are shared communal costs. The best that one can do is measure performance in the pursuit of objectives. Thus, circulation statistics may be used to reflect the library's objective to increase readership, but there is no way of knowing what real benefit this may lead to. Some aspects of librarianship are simply assumed to be a "public good."[16]

Circulation and reference may no longer be the key statistics, but how does one demonstrate the benefits of chat reference services or campus or community information literacy programs in economic terms? Yes, the same challenges are at play today as when Cummings pointed out the difficulties.

While it is true that many social organizations have trouble documenting cost benefits, there has been a flurry of activity among higher education officials to demonstrate conclusively that the benefits of a college education are significant in economic terms for those who graduate from college compared to those who don't attend college. The objective is to demonstrate that the cost of a college education continues to be a sound investment. Their analyses employ the methodology of cost benefit analysis. It has been extremely important for colleges to demonstrate their benefits in terms of dollars and cents because many politicians and parents continue to express deep concerns about the escalating costs of higher education. The demands for greater accountability grow louder each year.

I'm afraid that many libraries have not been exempted from pressures to document the contributions of library resources and services to the quality of an undergraduate student's experience. I'm familiar with quite a few college librarians who are scrambling to document their library's impact. I'm not suggesting that such analyses are impossible, only that they are very difficult to carry out to the point of having meaningful results. It might be possible to document a library's contributions, but I don't see how those contributions can be meaningfully translated into dollars.

Notes

1. One of the better studies I identified was conducted by Poll. *See* Roswitha Poll, "Analyzing Costs in Libraries," *Bottom Line* 14, no. 3 (2001): 185-91.

2. In Chapter 11 (see end note 1) I acknowledged the contributions of a group of Iowa State University Library technical services staff who developed detailed diary study techniques to collect time and cost data. There is probably no academic library that has conducted more time and cost studies than the ISU Library. Fowler and Arcand have built upon the earlier work to produce yet another study from ISU. For those interested in technical service time and cost studies, I recommend the sources that Fowler and Arcand cite in their article. David C. Fowler and Janet Arcand, "A Serials Acquisitions Cost Study: Presenting a Case for Standard Serials Acquisitions Data Elements," *Library Resources & Technical Services* 49, no. 2 (April 2005): 107, 109-22.

3. Snyder and Davenport did a nice job of defining basic terms in their book. *See* Herbert Snyder and Elisabeth Davenport, *Costing and Pricing in the Digital Age: A Practical Guide for Informa-

tion Services (New York: Neal-Schuman, 1997). Another excellent source for definitions to basic terms can be found in Rosenberg's report. *See* Phillip Rosenberg, *Cost Finding for Public Libraries: A Manager's Hand Book* (Chicago: American Library Association, 1985), 9.

4. The following four publications provide detailed information on how to develop a cost study methodology. *See* Phillip Rosenberg, *Cost Finding for Public Libraries: A Manager's Hand Book* (Chicago: American Library Association, 1985). *See also* Julie Virgo, "Costing and Pricing Information Services," *Drexel Library Quarterly* 21, no. 3 (Summer 1985): 75-98. *See also* Mary E. Jackson, *Measuring the Performance of Interlibrary Loan Operations in North American Research and College Libraries* (Washington, D.C.: Association of Research Libraries, 1998). *See also* Snyder and Davenport, *Costing and Pricing in the Digital Age.*

5. ALCTS Technical Services Costs Committee, "Guide to Costs Analysis of Acquisitions and Cataloging in Libraries" (1991).

6. This figure is modeled after a figure in Rosenberg's *Cost Finding for Public Libraries: A Manager's Hand Book*, 15.

7. Snyder and Davenport provide useful guidelines on assigning indirect costs. *See* Herbert Snyder and Elisabeth Davenport, "What Does It Really Cost? Allocating Indirect Costs," *Bottom Line* 10, no. 4 (1997): 158-64.

8. Rosenberg, *Cost Finding for Public Libraries: A Manager's Hand Book*, 47.

9. Dilys B. Morris, Joanne M. Bessler, Flo Wilson, and Jennifer A. Younger, "Where Does the Time Go?" *Library Administration & Management* 20, no. 4 (Fall 2006): 187.

10. Cheryl McCain and Jay Shorten, "Cataloging Efficiency and Effectiveness," *Library Resources & Technical Services* 46, 1 (Jan. 2002): 23-31. The authors report on a survey of academic libraries that was conducted to supplement findings of cost studies by providing measures of efficiency and effectiveness for cataloging departments based on reported productivity, number of staff, task distribution, and quality measures including backlogs, authority control, and database maintenance. The authors identify benchmark productivity levels for libraries with best practices, but fundamental concerns regarding definitional problems still exist. *See also* Slight-Gibney and Grenci report efforts to create a foundation for benchmarking serial operations. The work on which this workshop was based was solid, but it also demonstrates just how difficult it is to meaningfully benchmark technical service operations. *See* Nancy Slight-Gibney and Mary Grenci, "Starting with an Empty Map: Benchmarking Time and Costs for Serials Operations," *The Serials Librarian* 46, no. 3/4 (2004): 287-93.

11. Association of Research Libraries, *Welcome to LibQUAL+™*, http://www.libqual.org (27 May 2007).

12. Mary E. Jackson, *Measuring the Performance of Interlibrary Loan Operations in North American Research and College Libraries* (Washington, D.C.: Association of Research Libraries, 1998).

13. Karen Stabler, "Benchmarking Interlibrary Loan and Document Delivery Services: Lessons Learned at New Mexico State University, *Journal of Interlibrary Loan, Document Delivery & Information Supply* 12, no. 3 (2002): 57-73.

14. Tom Ruthven and Susan Magnay, "Top Performing Interlending Operations: Results of the Australian Benchmarking Study," *Interlending & Document Supply* 30, no. 2 (2002): 73-79.

15. Glen Holt and Donald Elliott, "Cost Benefit Analysis: a Summary of the Methodology," *The Bottom Line* 15, no. 4 (2002): 154-58. *See also* Gary W. White and Gregory A. Crawford, "Cost-benefit Analysis of Electronic Information: A Case Study," *College & Research Libraries* 59, no. 6 (November 1998): 503-10. These authors present methodologies and illustrations on how to employ CBA principles. Gary White notes: "Librarians can use the results of CBA studies to justify budgets and acquisitions and to provide insight into the true costs of providing library services," 503. Another useful study was reported by Scigliano who showed how cost-benefit techniques could be used to justify consortium purchases. *See* Marisa Scigliano, "Consortium Purchases: Case Study for a Cost-Benefit Analysis," *Journal of Academic Librarianship* 28, no. 6 (November 2002): 393-99.

16. Martin M. Cummings, "Cost Analysis: Methods and Realities," *Library Administration and Management* (Fall 1989): 181-83.

Section Six
Post-Study Activities

Chapter Fifteen

Assessing Current Activities

Scope note: Once the analysis of an activity has been completed, the next step is to assess the study results in order to identify ways to improve the activity. This chapter provides guidance on how to proceed. Because the results of a study and the recommendations it spawns so often must undergo administrative review, this chapter also provides guidance on how to prepare graphics that can enhance the quality of study reports.

Introduction

Once the data are gathered one should be able to describe the activities studied in great detail, and be able to understand how the various elements relate to each other and to other processes and procedures. The data collected will usually describe the work that each staff member performs or the flow of materials or forms as they proceed from one workstation to another.

At one time the analysis of the data collected was performed by trained analysts who specialized in workflow analysis, but today it is more common to involve a group of staff in the analysis. This has a distinct advantage: their involvement permits an analysis of data from a variety of perspectives. Examining data from different perspectives is more likely to generate a greater range of ideas than if only the analyst(s) were involved. The richness of ideas generated is particularly important because the analysis of the data collected can set the stage for actions later that will lead to streamlined and improved workflows.

There will also be occasions when quantitative time and cost data will need to be analyzed. Yesterday's number crunching could be a real chore, but today, with the existence of easy-to-use and powerful spreadsheet packages, this chore has been greatly simplified. But I do want to inject this caveat: The power of the spreadsheet will not improve the accuracy of the data. The principle of "garbage in, garbage out" still applies.

Assessing the Present Situation

Once the documentation and data have been organized, it is time to get staff involved. One way to do that is to organize sessions with staff. These meetings should be designed to encourage participants to think about and respond to a series of questions regarding the data that have been collected. My preference has always been to pose questions that begin with the words *what, where, when, who,* and *how.*

Questions to Pose

What—is the purpose of the activity in relation to the objectives of the library? What does the activity contribute to the process, or what does the activity contribute to the overall system? Or, possibly an even more fundamental question is, why is the procedure or process performed at all? Is it really necessary? For example, is it necessary to inspect each newly cataloged book to ensure that it has been properly Cuttered? Is Cuttering still essential?[1]

Where—is the work performed? Where else could it be performed? Where is the best place in the sequence of operations? For example, if workstations could be grouped together, would time-consuming problems of transportation be reduced or eliminated?

When—is the work performed? Why is it done at this time? Is there a better time? For example, could part or all of cataloging be performed at the time a book is ordered if cataloging copy is available? Would such a rearrangement of tasks save time and get new books into the hands of customers more quickly?

Who—is the best person to perform the work? Why does this person do it? Is he/she the best qualified person? Who possesses the best combination of qualifications? Can a person with fewer qualifications perform the work? The *who* question can involve the separation of duties among personnel classifications, and between people and machines. For example, could a support staff handle reference questions? Could the library's ILS handle a series of tasks that are currently performed manually?

How—is the work performed? Is there a better way? Is there an easier way? For example, how can the library's Web site be modified so that customers can interact with staff directly without visiting the library? Or how can books be delivered directly to a customer's office or home address?

In years past I used to believe that the most effective approach was to lead off a discussion by asking "why" a task or procedure was performed. If one couldn't provide a sound rationale, it was very possible the work being performed was unnecessary. And it had always been my belief that staff members didn't want to think they were performing work that wasn't contributing to the library's goals and objectives.

Over the years, however, I began to realize that by asking the "why" question first, I was inviting a defensive reaction, particularly among staff who had been performing or supervising the work for a long time. I think too many of us have painful memories of people using a series of "why" questions to build a case against us. As a result if one isn't careful to be tactful, the response to a "why" question is likely to be defensive with the person shutting down, thus ending the discussion.

Instead of asking "why," a better approach is to begin by asking "what" or "how" questions. Questions phrased in this manner will generally produce multiple responses which usually lead to the best solution. Also, keep asking "what else?" to keep the conversation flowing, or at least until the person(s) begins to feel uncomfortable.

On occasions I've achieved excellent results by asking questions such as "How can this work be done more easily?" The person felt comfortable offering suggestions because he/she didn't feel attacked. Responses, however, often opened doors to further exploration when replies included observations such as "Oh, the easiest way to get the job done is to stop doing it altogether." With such a lead in, it is much easier to explore the "whys" of the situation.

The What, Where, When, Who, and How questions can be used to examine almost any situation. A list of prompts can also stimulate further thinking and discussion. (See Figure 15-1.) I recall once listening to a group of staff members who were talking about ways to reduce the time required to get new books into the hands of patrons. One suggestion was to purchase more books from local bookstores. This suggestion led an acquisitions assistant to ask: "Why can't we catalog a book when OCLC copy is available at the time of ordering so that the book is ready to go as soon as it arrives?" Another person chimed in: "If we are going to buy books from the local Borders, why can't we alter the way bestsell-

---

- Can any of the tasks (or the entire process) be eliminated?
- Can any tasks be subdivided?
- Can the sequence in which the tasks are performed be altered?
- Can transportations be reduced or eliminated?
- Can another person do the job better?
- Can the task or process be automated?
- Can peak loads of activity be eliminated?
- Can another unit perform the task in order to save time and/or money?
- Can sampling techniques be used to eliminate 100% quality checks?
- Can improved training eliminate unproductive quality checks?
- Can a process be outsourced?
- Is the work performed being duplicated elsewhere in the library?

Figure 15-1 Prompts: Have you considered the following?

ers are selected?" The outcome of this session was modified selection, ordering, and cataloging processes. These improvements were achieved as a result of a staff brainstorming session.

Creating a meeting environment that encourages a questioning attitude and the free flow of ideas is a great way to get staff involved and positively contributing their ideas. Brainstorming is one way to create such a positive atmosphere. (See the Rules of Brainstorming in Chapter 4, page 27). A meeting that encourages staff contributions is more likely to develop a staff perspective that focuses on the big picture, and how changes might benefit the entire library, than a meeting at which discussions tend to focus on how changes are likely to impact individual jobs or units.

Another way to invite staff comment is to invite members to the meeting who may not have been directly involved in the study. Staff members who have no immediate vested stake in the outcome are less likely to harbor unusual biases. And those staff who have no vested stake, but who possess an understanding of the present activity, may be in a particularly advantageous position to offer cogent ideas for improvement.

Creating a supportive attitude among managers is also important if one is to generate ideas on how workflows can be streamlined or even completely eliminated. I know it is difficult, but if a staff member offers a suggestion, others, particularly supervisors, should resist the temptation to reply with knee jerk reactions such as "we tried that once and it didn't work" or "that is the way we have always done that here." Each time I hear such statements, I'm reminded of a story I heard years ago.

> The mother of a friend was preparing a large ham for an Easter dinner. Instead of sticking the entire ham into a baking dish, she cut off both ends and stuck them in a second baking pan. Her daughters asked why she did that and her reply was "This is the way my mother did it." Nothing more was said, but at the next Christmas celebration, the daughters retold the story to their grandmother and asked her why she had cut off both ends. The daughters were convinced that they must have been missing something important. But Granny simply replied: "That's the way my mother did it." Since their great grandmother was arriving for the holiday the next day, they knew they would finally get an answer. But when their great grandmother was asked the question, she looked at the girls with a very straight face and said: "I only had one baking pan. I could never get the whole ham in the pan."

All right, it is probably an apocryphal story, but I believe it offers a moral worth remembering. Keep in mind that just because we have been doing something one way for a long time doesn't mean it was the right way.

Presenting the Data

There will be occasions when those who analyze the activity will be asked to present their findings to the library's administration or to a staff group. On such occasions presentations can be in the form of a report, oral presentation, or a combination of the two. Some people prefer written reports to oral presentations, while others prefer just the opposite—another example of how people learn differently.

Graphics can prove to be very effective. Bar charts, pie charts, illustrations, and photographs can amplify and clarify complex information. For example compare the data shown in Figures 15-2 and 15-3. The growth in the volume of activity is much more striking when the tabular data are displayed as data points along a line graph. Graphics can not only be used to serve as attention getters, they can also highlight key points, and help readers or listeners to figure out what is really going on.

Months	Transactions Current Year	Transactions Last Year	Monthly % Difference	Cumulative Difference %
January	1,186	1,143	4%	4%
February	1,170	988	16%	10%
March	1,144	849	26%	15%
April	1,298	1,109	15%	15%
May	1,120	1,182	-6%	11%
June	743	937	-26%	7%
July	1,395	1,331	5%	6%
August	1,616	870	46%	13%
September	1,377	1,220	11%	13%
October	1,311	1,137	13%	13%
November	1,674	1,077	36%	16%
December	1,701	998	41%	18%
Total	15,735	12,841		18%

Figure 15-2 Table: Comparing the number of ILL transactions for the last two years.

The purpose here is to underscore the potential value of using graphics to present data, and to illustrate some of the most commonly used types of graphics. It is certainly not my intent to provide detailed instructions on how to create graphics. Most libraries will use software programs such as Excel to manage their data. Fortunately this software as well as other packages enables one to transform a spreadsheet full of data into colorful graphics that may reveal patterns and trends that otherwise might be difficult to discern.[2]

The use of color without question greatly enhances the message. Today colorful graphics to accompany oral presentations can be prepared painlessly. And finally, graphical data can now be easily incorporated into presentations using PowerPoint software.

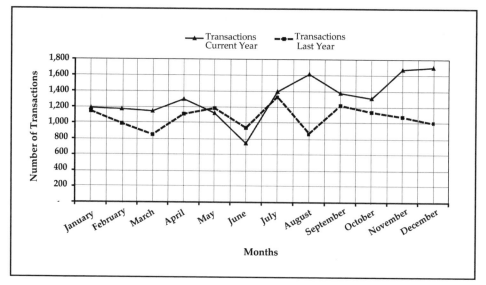

Figure 15-3 Line Graph: Comparing the number of ILL transactions for the last two years.

While available software has greatly simplified the preparation of graphics, a great deal of thought, nevertheless, should go into their preparation. Consider: Who is the audience you will be addressing? Are you addressing administrators who might be more interested in the big picture items rather than the details? What is the purpose of the graphic? What message do you want to convey? Is the graphic appropriate to that message? Will the text or oral presentation clarify the message, or is the graphic clear enough to stand on its own?

One should certainly strive to produce graphics that are easy to understand. One way to find out is to ask a colleague who was not directly involved with the material to offer an interpretation before making a presentation to administrators. Does the graphic fairly reflect the data that has been collected? Don't forget the old cliché, "Statistics lie, and liars use statistics."

Graphical Options

Among the most commonly used types of graphics in library circles are line graphs, bar charts, pie charts, and histograms. While charts can be used in almost any type of presentation, the type of chart selected is important because using the appropriate graphic can greatly enhance a presentation, e.g., a line graph is better at depicting data over time than is a pie chart or bar chart.

Line Graphs—Line graphs are groups of charts that display quantitative information using lines. A line graph displays data over time to highlight trends. A simple line graph displays a single series of data. For example, the two line graphs shown in Figure 15-4 depict the difference in incremental and transformational changes that have occurred in ILL over the last 20 years.

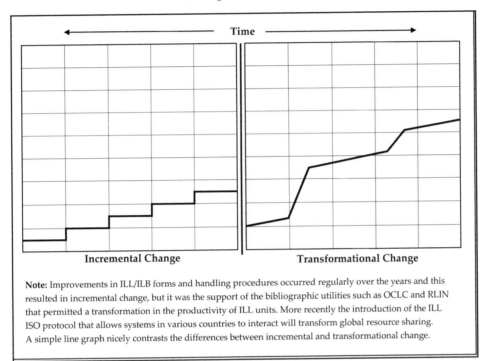

Time

Incremental Change | Transformational Change

Note: Improvements in ILL/ILB forms and handling procedures occurred regularly over the years and this resulted in incremental change, but it was the support of the bibliographic utilities such as OCLC and RLIN that permitted a transformation in the productivity of ILL units. More recently the introduction of the ILL ISO protocol that allows systems in various countries to interact will transform global resource sharing. A simple line graph nicely contrasts the differences between incremental and transformational change.

Figure 15-4 Line Graph: Patterns of change reflecting the difference between incremental and transformational organizational change.

A simple line chart can also be used to examine the growth in the number of chat questions that a reference department receives over time. (See Figure 15-5.) Such a graphic could be used to explain to officials how a new service is taking hold, or it could be used by a reference department to underscore and justify the need for additional staff. Of course, one could also add more detail such as the actual number of questions received to further strengthen the case.

A line graph can also be stratified to analyze data. Stratification can help to analyze cases in which

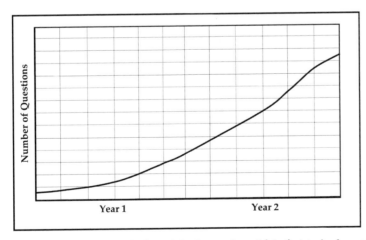

Figure 15-5 Line Graph: Growth in the number of (chat) virtual reference questions.

the data reported could actually mask the real facts. Let's return to an illustration I have used previously, namely the study of an ILL unit. In this instance, the library's administration gained a valuable lesson about statistics as a result of the study of its interlibrary lending activities. It was a busy operation, and its fill rate varied between 40 percent and 60 percent. This rate appeared to be typical of its type of operation. But during the analysis, we discovered that the published fill rate was misleading because of the way the data were presented. In Figure 15-6 the total fill rate is reported, but the information is misleading because it masks the fact that the library was recycling unsuccessful searches through a second round of searching. In point of fact the second search was contributing 15 to 20 percent to the overall reported fill rate. The

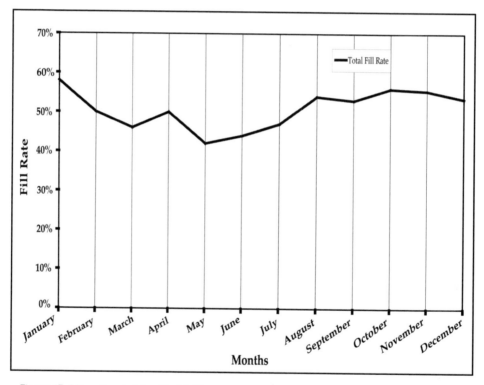

Figure 15-6 Line Graph: Monthly ILL fill rates.

chart was modified to show that it was a combination of two searches that produced the overall fill rate. (See Figure 15-7.)

In this instance when the additional information was revealed, concerns were raised about the need for a second search because this practice materially increased the time and cost of processing interlibrary loan requests. Once management became aware of the problem, actions were introduced to reduce the need for second searches.

Bar Charts—This type of chart is particularly useful in comparing and contrasting discrete values that occur at different times or different locations. Bars

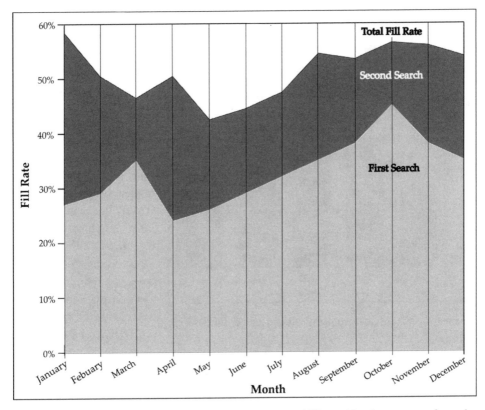

Figure 15-7 Line Graph: ILL fill rates highlighting portions of fills resulting from a second search.

make it easier to recognize small differences in quantities or frequencies and compare one category with another. A simple bar chart could be used to depict the growth of an in-house digitization project. Figure 15-8 not only shows the rapid growth that has taken place, but also a significant decrease in year five. The library had conducted a detailed cost study in year four, and discovered that it made a great deal of sense to begin outsourcing some of its digitizing work to a commercial firm—thus the decrease.

A multiple column bar chart can effectively depict the dramatic changes that occur over a period of time. Figure 15-9 reveals changes in the mix of reference desk activities that took place over the last four years as chat and email reference coupled with instructional questions came to dominate work performed at the reference desk. The casualty of this transformation was face-to-face reference question activity.

Pie Charts—Pie charts show proportions of a whole. Their major purpose is to display the magnitude of components relative to one another and to the whole. A pie chart consists of a circle divided into wedge-shaped segments. The areas of each segment should be the same percent of the total area of the circle as the data

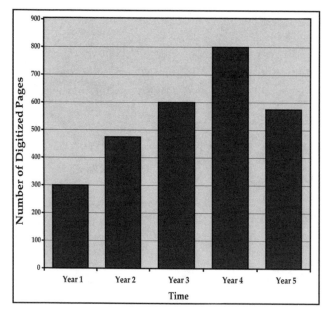

Figure 15-8 Bar Chart: Number of pages digitized in-house over a five-year period.

element it represents in relation to the total number of the data set, e.g., if the proportion of remote reference questions recorded in year one represents 10 percent of the total activity at the desk, the wedge-segment in the pie chart should also represent 10 percent. Figure 15-10 illustrates the use of a pie chart. Note that in this application the two charts focus on a mix of activities. The second pie chart reflects the changes that have occurred over a period of time, but the pie chart is

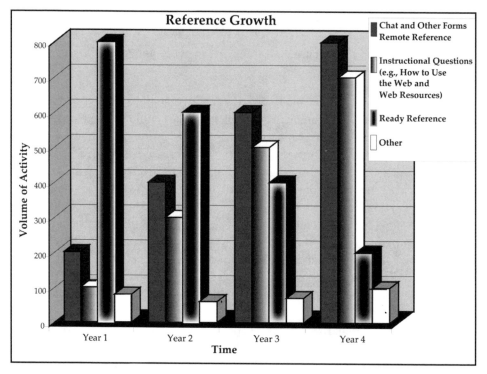

Figure 15-9 Bar Chart: Depicting changes in reference activity over a four-year period.

not as effective in showing trends as is the line graph. Note how in Figure 15-11 we have partially removed one of the segments to highlight a single activity—in this case how much face-to-face ready reference has declined in recent years.

Histograms—The histogram is a type of data distribution graph. It is also sometimes called a frequency distribution. A histogram displays the frequency

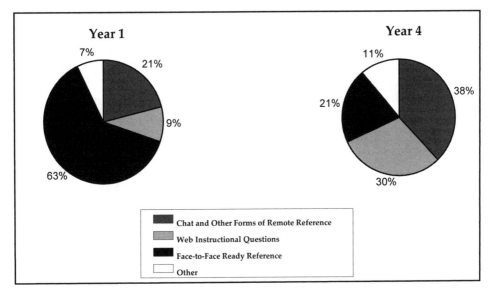

Figure 15-10 Pie Chart: Transformation of reference activities over a four-year period.

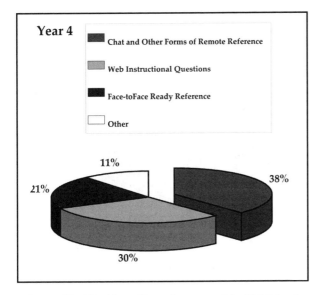

Figure 15-11 Pie Chart: Chat reference activity highlighted.

with which specific values or values within ranges occur in a set of data. The data are represented by a series of bars that are proportional in height to the frequency that the data occur in the data set. A histogram can be combined with a frequency polygon by connecting the midpoints of the columns to produce a smoothed line version of a histogram. A frequency polygon is a segmented or smooth line version of a histogram. A frequency polygon can make the visualization of data easier and is helpful when comparing multiple data series.

The use of histograms and frequency polygrams is illustrated by the data shown in Figures 15-12 and 15-13. These data reflect the results of a simple study a library conducted when it was faced with the question of whether or not it should increase its Interlibrary borrowing of items from libraries that charged fees. The option wasn't clear-cut because the library's existing policy didn't allow the ILL unit to pass on charges to patrons; the costs incurred had to be absorbed. Therefore, the increased operating costs would have to be balanced against the promise of improved delivery performance to patrons. The study involved keeping records for the 100 requests that were submitted to libraries that charged fees. Data were also collected for the next 100 requests that were submitted to libraries that didn't charge. The results, as shown in Figure 15-12, clearly reveal that delivery performance was markedly faster when libraries that charged fees were selected over libraries that didn't charge. The study also revealed that the costs per loan would not be increased significantly. This straight-forward study caused the library to shift its policy, and begin to rely more on libraries that charged fees so long as the fees didn't exceed an agreed-upon limit. The use of the superimposed frequency polygons in Figure 15-13 that compares the two data sets is a particularly effective way of presenting the results of the study to management.

Final Thoughts

The tools that have been presented are undoubtedly the ones most commonly used by librarians, but this sampling of graphics represents only a small taste of the charts and graphs that are available. For example, there are also point, area, vector,

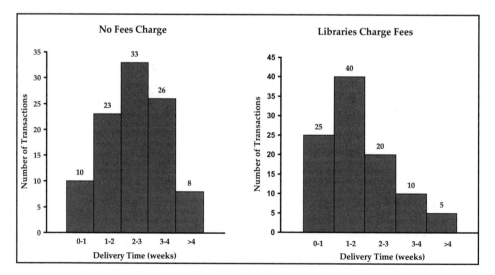

Figure 15-12 Histogram: Comparison of delivery times for items borrowed from libraries that do and do not charge lending fees.

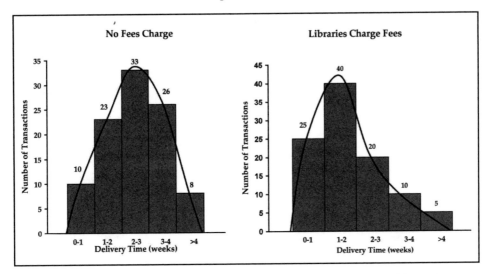

Figure 15-13 Histogram: With a polygram used to highlight the differences in delivery time for libraries.

radar and nomographs—and that is only a start. I found *Information Graphics: A Comprehensive Illustrated Reference* particularly useful in providing information and guidance in the selection and use of graphics.[3] It is a volume worth consulting. The Web, of course, is also a fertile resource for those who are interested in designing and using graphics in their presentations.

End Notes

1. Some have suggested that Cuttering may no longer be necessary because enhanced OPACs and discovery tools have reduced the incidence of patron browsing in some libraries. It is now less of a problem if two books are co-located on the shelf.

2. A number of publications provide instructions and tips on how to prepare various types of graphics. One source that I found particularly helpful is: Ed Minter and Mary Michaud, *Using Graphics to Report Evaluation Results* (Madison, Wis.: University of Wisconsin-Extension Department, 2003). Check Web site: http://learningstore.uwex.edu (26 May 2007). Click on Research Publications and select the article entitled: *Using Graphics to Report Evaluation Results.*

3. For those who are interested in specialized forms of graphs, the following source is highly recommended. Robert L. Harris, *Information Graphics: A Comprehensive Illustrated Reference* (Atlanta, Ga.: Management Graphics, 1996).

Chapter Sixteen

Designing Streamlined Activities

Scope note: There are numerous guidelines a library can apply that will help it develop new and improved workflows and processes. A library that is in the process of preparing for a new integrated system or is about to launch a new service can apply the same guidelines and tips. This chapter also discusses a number of tips that can help libraries avoid common errors when new workflows or activities are introduced.

Introduction

Streamlining an existing workflow or creating a new workflow or even establishing an entirely new activity presents numerous challenges and opportunities. I think this is the fun part of systems work. Improved workflows can enhance a library staff's performance and esteem; they can help stretch dollar resources thus enabling the library to better achieve its service objectives. When I use the terms "streamlining" or "improving" a workflow or a procedure, I'm saying that the goal is to improve the quality of operations by making them more efficient and effective either by simplifying them, or modernizing them through the introduction of technologies.

Checklists such as the one shown in Figure 15-1 (page 189) can be very helpful in stimulating thinking about improved methods, but it is also important to keep in mind that each project presents its own set of unique conditions. Out-of-the-box thinking is often the best way to achieve a breakthrough.

Staff members who are designated to lead efforts to introduce new methods are wise to make conscious and continuous efforts to keep abreast of new tools and techniques. This is not an easy task because developments seem to appear almost daily. Fortunately there are a number of ways to accomplish this objective. Attending professional meetings, and checking out new products at exhibits are traditional methods that are still effective. But today, technology has made it easier to check out new products on the Web, and much easier to network with colleagues by participating in relevant listservs and checking out blogs of professional leaders.

Over the years I've been surprised numerous times by how much I was able to learn by simply paying attention to what others were doing and saying. In other words, keeping my mouth shut and listening, which isn't always easy. As has always been the case, and is still true today, we can learn a great deal from the experiences of others; there is no need to "reinvent a wheel" that is already turning effectively in a comparable environment. There is also no profit from repeating the errors of others.

If a library administration truly wishes to create an organizational climate that will nurture ideas for improvements, and also increase chances that staff buy-in will be achieved, as already discussed in the last chapter, the best approach is to create opportunities for staff members to contribute their ideas. Sure, many ideas staff generate are likely to be impractical, but one can never tell when a "diamond in the rough" idea will be offered. I suspect that many managers don't fully appreciate the impact on staff when such a suggestion from within is adopted. If staff begin to believe that management is really listening, management will gain a great deal of credibility in the eyes of staff. And it is also worth keeping in mind that success often breeds more success. Based on personal experience, I can assure readers that such credibility is worth a great deal. An organizational culture that is known to be receptive to staff ideas is more likely to generate ideas than a culture that is perceived to be top down and unresponsive.

A recent experience I had working with a group of support staff in a technical services unit illustrates the importance of creating a work environment that encourages staff to contribute their ideas. I asked the group for their ideas on how to speed up the flow of books through their units. I was extremely impressed by the number, and the quality, of both labor and cost-saving ideas that were volunteered. After listening to this group, I asked why some of the more obvious ideas hadn't already been implemented. Their reply was that they as clerical staff hadn't been asked, and more importantly, the last time suggestions had been offered, their unit supervisor had made it clear that they were supposed to "just keep doing what you have been told to do." The implied message was even worse: "You are only clerks who couldn't possibly be able to offer any worthwhile suggestions."

Guidelines for Improving Systems and Processes

We all know that the automation of processes and procedures followed by the introduction of integrated systems have transformed many traditional library activities. These new systems have led to enormous increases in staff productivity; they have also enabled libraries to expand and/or enhance most library services.

When one begins to consider how to streamline a library workflow, a logical starting place is to ask whether or not the activity can be folded into an existing automated process, or if a new automated alternative makes sense. But even if the system is to be automated, it still makes sense to streamline the activity before it is automated. So let's now focus on specific guidelines that can be helpful in creating improved workflows and processes.

Eliminating Unnecessary Activities

Even in this era of the integrated systems, many staff, unfortunately, still seem to spend considerable time and energy performing work that doesn't need to be done in the first place. There are a variety of reasons why this occurs. Some staff still check the work of another staff member just to make sure that everything is correct, or actually repeat the task simply because he/she really believes "I can do this better than anyone else." Occasionally staff workers will even keep personal records to cover themselves in case questions or complaints are raised later. And, there are still incidents when staff members perform tasks simply because that is the way they have always done something.

Duplication of effort is still common between branches and the central unit. Even in an integrated library system environment, it is not unusual to discover unofficial files such as on order, periodical check-in, or bookkeeping records that are duplicated somewhere else in the system. Duplicated periodical check-in files have been particularly common. What happens is that a branch librarian maintains an "unofficial" record just to be sure that the records are correct. While a central-ized, unified approach often makes the most sense, if the population of duplicate records can not be extinguished, another approach is to "roll with the flow" and transfer responsibility for maintaining the official record to branch locations. Not only is work eliminated, but public service is improved because periodical issues will be available to patrons more quickly. Nonetheless, transferring the responsi-bility would not be my preferred solution; furthermore, with the growth of digital subscriptions this type of duplication should gradually fade away.

It is true that the benefits of eliminating procedures must be weighed against the risk of incurring the worst-case scenario that could occur if something is eliminated. For example, a library decides that it will not longer require a juvenile to obtain a parent's signature in order to obtain a library card. What risks are involved? What is the worst-case scenario? The juvenile loses a book or keeps books out past the due date. How strict is the library about collecting fines from juveniles? How serious is this potential problem? How often does it occur? Libraries have to make choices.

Combining or Eliminating Files

Prior to the integrated system era, libraries were known as a haven for a variety of files. I've made this point numerous times. The first generation of stand-alone automated acquisition modules made it possible to reduce the number of paper-based files that the department maintained. Not until the introduction of integrated systems however, did it become practical to eliminate most paper-based files in order units and throughout technical services. Nonetheless, there are still some li-braries that continue to rely on paper forms, e.g., multiple-part forms for activities such as ordering materials and processing interlibrary loan requests. And, there are still libraries that maintain paper back-up files even though operations are based on integrated systems.

Some libraries are required to maintain financial and personnel records in order to satisfy local regulations. The crucial point is to maintain no more files than is absolutely required, and to make every effort to avoid the existence of duplicated files. The probability of duplicated files increases when multiple units are involved. For instance an interlibrary lending unit and the accounting office may both maintain a record of paid invoices for document delivery transactions, particularly if the two units are physically separated. I remember once talking with a branch librarian who confided to me that she kept an informal record of books on order along with a file of outstanding encumbrances even though technical service operations were automated. I asked her why and she replied: "The central database isn't always correct, and a couple of years ago, I was criticized by my supervisor when I inadvertently overspent my budget." That type of embarrassment, she assured me, would never happen again.

The prudent course of action I recommend is to conduct periodically a census of all existing files. What types of files are maintained? Are any of them duplicated? Is the information located elsewhere? Can any file be combined—or better yet—eliminated? A particularly appropriate time to review files is just prior to the purchase or upgrade of an integrated system. It is also important to construct a library's databases so that as many paper files as possible can be eliminated. This review is also necessary in order to determine whether or not local programming will be necessary to meet special requirements. Such determinations should be made on a case-by-case basis.

Combining Operations

There may be opportunities to improve operational efficiencies by combining operations or consolidating processes. One particularly common illustration is the closing and/or consolidating of service units. Anyone who has ever been involved with the consolidation of a service unit or a branch library, however, understands that there is much more than gaining efficiencies involved with such actions. One must be very sensitive to the possible campus or community reactions.

As the Web and its resources became ubiquitous, and the number of face-to-face ready-reference questions declined, some libraries decided to combine their central reference desk with the general information desk. The effectiveness of such an organizational change was further enhanced by telephonic devices that made it possible for information desk personnel to communicate directly and easily with reference specialists who were based elsewhere in the building.[1]

Changing the Sequence of Operations

Oftentimes a process can be streamlined by simply rearranging the sequence in which tasks are performed. Probably the most dramatic example of this approach occurred when libraries decided to catalog books as part of the acquisition process. In this instance not only were operational efficiencies achieved, but service to patrons was also enhanced as books were ready for circulation more quickly.

A simple change in the way new order requests were handled resulted in significant benefits for one library. The library in question traditionally verified the accuracy of citations before it checked to determine whether or not the title was already on order or already owned by the library. It finally occurred to one staff member that a lot of time could be saved if the on-order and OPAC databases were checked first. In this way all duplicates would be discovered during the initial check, and immediately discarded or returned to the person who originally submitted the request. Thus, no additional work was necessary by this simple rearrangement of the sequence in which the tasks were performed.

Reducing or Eliminating Inspections

Every effort should be made to reduce the number, or better yet, eliminate unnecessary inspections. Edward Deming[2] always pointed out that inspections were not productive, and that they should be reduced and/or minimized. For example, is it necessary to inspect all books that have been digitized, or all books that have been cataloged by an outside agency? The answer might be yes, it might be no. It is a judgment call. But always keep in mind that inspections are not productive and can consume lots of time, energy, and money.

There is also another type of inspection that is often more difficult to pin down. I'm referring to the unofficial checks that occur as a book, form, or record proceeds from one work area to another. One might have hoped that with the advent of integrated systems with centralized databases that this penchant to check work performed earlier in the process would gradually disappear, but I've found that the tendency to "just check" is unfortunately alive and well.

There is also a relationship between the quality of training, and the need for quality control inspections. For example, cataloging with MARC records is complex, some might even argue overly complex. Thus, there is probably justification in checking the work of a new cataloger, but for how long? And how extensively should the work of a trainee be reviewed?

The real or perceived need for inspections can often be symptomatic of inadequate training programs. For example, if one feels there is a need to check rigorously the work of an assistant who is responsible for locating books in an interlibrary loan unit, is it possible that the assistant's inadequacies are being caused by the absence of a proper training program? It certainly makes sense in the long term to invest more in training programs than to perform time-consuming and repetitious checking on a continuing basis.

Eliminating Unnecessary Movement of Staff and Materials

Jobs that require frequent movement of staff, forms, or equipment should be closely examined. Materials, forms, and equipment should be located in the work areas where they will be used. Related library routines should be organized so they reflect the natural flow of the work, and thereby minimize unnecessary movement. The increase of a few steps for one person might save thousands of steps for others. Years ago it wasn't uncommon to see reference librarians scurrying around the reference room consulting a variety of reference tools. In time some librarians began to conduct studies and discovered that the vast majority of reference questions were derived from a small number of reference tools, e.g., handbooks, general encyclopedias, directories, almanacs. These discoveries led to the rise of the ready-reference desk collections shelved right behind or adjacent to the reference desk.

It is still common to see reference/information commons organized so that there is a lot of unnecessary running around by staff. Of course, I'm not referring to roving staff members who are expected to mingle with patrons.

Lots of staff movement was eliminated when a small public library decided to ask patrons to retrieve their own books from the Hold Shelf instead of requiring a staff member to walk to a Hold Shelf located behind the circulation desk. One reason why this change was introduced was that the staff realized that most patrons actually enjoyed retrieving their own books. Here was an example of a simple change that proved to be win-win.

Over the years I've encountered numerous situations when the reorganization of a process could have resulted in significant increases in productivity and staff job satisfaction. Two personal experiences come to mind. The first concerns a library that offered a document delivery service to faculty and graduate students. This library also operated an extensive ILL operation. Instead of coordinating the book retrieval activities to avoid unnecessary, time-consuming treks through the stacks, each unit maintained its own book retrieval staff. In this case the units were independent, and each supervisor valued his independence. Too bad because a well-trained unified stack retrieval staff would have produced enormous savings in time and money.

The second example involved a library assistant who was responsible for mailing ILL materials. She was required to travel several floors to reach the loading dock area where she prepared books for mailing. Each trip required her to create a workspace. This meant bringing together mailing labels, envelopes, a scale and a postage machine. A great deal of time was saved once the unit head realized that it made much more sense to create a permanent workstation within the ILL unit itself.[3]

The analysis of movement of staff and materials is often closely tied to planning for new or renovated space. This means that library staff should work closely with architects during all space planning activities. Questions that need to be considered are: What is the optimum physical arrangement between acquisitions, cataloging, reference, circulation, public computers, group study rooms, staff room, public café, etc? The goal is to locate key functions in order to minimize unnecessary movement of staff and also reduce inconveniences to patrons.

Selecting the Appropriate Staffing Pattern

It should go without saying that the staff member possessing the most appropriate skills should perform a job. This strikes me as a pretty commonsensical axiom, but it can also prove to be a tricky issue because there might not be agreement on who possesses the most appropriate skills. Let's begin with two classic cases.

First, who was best qualified to catalog books when OCLC cataloging copy became available? Some librarians immediately responded that such work could and should be assigned to a library assistant, but other librarians insisted that such work ought to be performed by an experienced cataloger with educational credentials.

Second, who should staff a reference desk? Can a trained support staff perform this work? Should a professional always back up the support staff, or, should answering questions at the desk be handled by professionals? This debate was rekindled when chat reference gained popularity. I've watched and listened to this issue debated several times on College of DuPage teleconferences that I have hosted.[4] The participants of these debates were all well-known, smart, and successful librarians, but on this issue they simply reflected different philosophies on who is best qualified.

The outcome of debates about what qualifications are necessary to catalog a book or answer reference questions isn't a matter of right or wrong, but a reflection of different values and perceptions. There are enough libraries that have successfully used assistants to catalog books and staff information desks to convince me that libraries ought to consider very carefully whether or not support staff can't be more effectively utilized.

This brings us to a related consideration: money. If library work is assigned to individuals who are overqualified, the library will be paying higher salaries than is necessary. In industry this issue makes headlines because many companies, in an effort to avoid paying no more than is absolutely necessary, have outsourced thousands of jobs to other countries. Haven't we all contacted Help Desks and discovered that we were speaking to a person in the Philippines or India? Even libraries have not been exempt from outsourcing work to save money. Workers who are located in other countries often perform catalog conversion activities.

The use of staff who are blatantly overqualified to perform jobs is not only a questionable managerial practice because overqualified persons will soon become bored, but because it may also be a violation, if not the letter of the law at least in the spirit of equal opportunity legislation. Such a pattern can, and sometimes has, prevented minorities from being considered for jobs they were perfectly capable of performing.

I've worked with supervisors who made a conscious effort to hire new staff who were not only qualified to perform the job for which they were being interviewed, but who were also fully qualified to carry out the job requirements of the next higher classification. Such behavior, at least in my range of experiences, was not intended to be discriminatory, but was an effort to secure staff recruits who didn't require a great deal of training. There are a significant number of library supervisors who really don't like to spend their time training new staff. Nonetheless, this practice ought to be discouraged.

Outsourcing Activities

Outsourcing an activity often merits serious consideration. Many may not realize that outsourcing is not a new phenomenon. For example, binding of periodicals became common over fifty years ago when periodical budgets mushroomed in the growth years following World War II, and the equipment needed to bind periodicals became sophisticated and very expensive. Because it was extremely difficult to justify the capital expenditures necessary to maintain in-house or campus binderies the use of commercial binders became widespread. Initially many librarians resisted moves to outsource binding because of concerns about quality and accessibility of materials while periodicals were in the hands of the binder.[5]

In a few cases the reason for resisting outsourcing was a fear that jobs would be lost locally, and in truth some jobs were lost as local binderies were phased out. Nevertheless, the decision to outsource binding was inevitable because even the largest of libraries could no longer justify the expense of maintaining in-house binderies.

Another long-established form of outsourcing has been the use of processing centers to acquire and prepare books for use. Many public libraries and even some academic libraries have relied on processing centers for years. Some libraries have for years relied on vendors for their cataloging copy. In both cases these are forms of outsourcing. Today, numerous academic libraries receive new titles that are fully processed and ready for the shelf. This trend gained momentum as processing costs mounted, and as it became easier to add vendor catalog records to local integrated library systems.

Outsourcing for some librarians became contentious when several libraries decided to outsource their cataloging in the 1990s.[6] Some argued that outsourcing produced significant savings, and that the savings could be used to improve public services. Others felt that putting cataloging in the hands of a vendor only reduced the quality of records and thus was a disservice to patrons seeking information.

I recall one library launching several extensive time and cost studies to determine whether or not keeping cataloging in house could be justified. This study was partially undertaken for political reasons: The university's Provost had suggested that outsourcing of cataloging would save the campus money. Since the Provost's views couldn't be ignored, the library launched its studies. The studies produced improved workflows, and the resulting increased productivity convinced the Provost that no action was warranted.

There are now many activities that are outsourced on a routine basis. It is now common for libraries to outsource cataloging and to accept vendor catalog copy and shelf-ready books. I've already mentioned that many libraries decided to outsource the conversion of their card catalog records. Another example is the outsourcing of some or all of chat reference services to a vendor or a consortium office. Libraries are also commonly outsourcing the digitization of selected materials to outside vendors.

Although the issue of outsourcing doesn't seem to be as contentious today as once was the case, I would be remiss if I didn't at least mention the potential for political fallout. I'm sure that when the Hawaii State Library in 1996 announced its decision to outsource selection, processing, and cataloging of most materials to the Baker and Taylor Company, the library's administration never anticipated the firestorm of criticism that would erupt. Shortly after the decision was announced, the State Librarian was severely criticized by staff, patrons, and politicians. Later this particular contract was terminated.[7] The moral is: don't forget to consider the political dimension of outsourcing decisions. In general, activities that are considered core, such as selection, are more likely to spark criticism than support activities such as binding, payroll, accounting, etc. In fact it is now common for libraries to outsource a variety of administrative functions such as, accounting, personnel hiring, copying services, janitorial services, and even various computing activities.[8]

The question shouldn't be whether outsourcing is good or bad. It is really a matter of optimizing the use of scarce library resources and balancing costs against quality of library services. Decisions to outsource library activities may make a great deal of sense. It is simply an option that shouldn't be ignored. In fact, it is questions like "Should we outsource an activity?" that may justify the time and energy necessary to conduct a detailed time and cost study.

Simplifying Remaining Operations

Once a library has eliminated all unnecessary steps, combined processes and operations, examined the sequence in which activities are performed, assigned the most appropriate personnel to perform a job, and investigated the option of outsourcing, it is time to begin thinking about whether the remaining aspects of the activity can be simplified. On the one hand such an examination could involve some very simple, straightforward tasks such as deciding how many property markings are stamped on each new book. On the other hand such reviews could involve more complicated activities such as reducing the number of data elements that are keyed into a cataloging record. There are a growing number of librarians who are questioning the need for a bibliographic record that conforms to the complexity of MARC, particularly in this age when more and more people are routinely turning to Google or a Google-like search engine to obtain information. Is the MARC record format becoming obsolete? Is it too complex?

I realize I might be reaching back a bit, but one of the first large-scale integrated systems that became available to libraries was NOTIS. NOTIS represented a significant step forward in handling technical service processes for most libraries, but some of the early NOTIS modules were also pretty cumbersome. One example that stands out in my mind was the serials check-in module. Users of NOTIS registered complaints, and as a result successive revisions streamlined many of the problem procedures. My point in citing NOTIS is not to criticize the designers of

NOTIS, but to remind readers that streamlining processes and procedures should always be kept uppermost in one's mind. Even today, this continuous improvement is evident as each generation of software in integrated systems embodies new features that further streamline operations. The moral: always keep thinking about further simplifications.

Finally, some staff workers may go out of their way to make their jobs more elaborate and complicated than they need to be. This behavior occurs in all types of organizations, not just libraries. The explanations for such behavior are many, but one cause lies in the human desire to expand the importance of their jobs so that they appear to be doing more, and thus contributing more to the organization. Although I've encountered some staff who deliberately strive to complicate their jobs in hopes of achieving a higher job-classification, I believe most staff workers simply want to feel that their jobs are important, and that they are contributing to the organization no matter where they are positioned in the organization chart. One parting thought—never forget the KISS principle of management: Keep It Simple, Stupid.

Other Considerations: External

Up to now we have focused on tactics that can be employed to improve existing processes and procedures that comprise a workflow or system, but there are also other considerations that occasionally come into play. Some issues will be of particular concern to those who are actively involved with streamlining an existing activity or preparing a library to introduce a new system. For example, not confusing means and ends, providing for a smooth transition between the old and new system, balancing costs with service benefits, staffing to avoid peaks of activity, handling variable responses, providing opportunities for design revisions, handling errors, and avoiding unreasonable scheduling.

External considerations may not be top priority to staff who are focused on reviewing a local system, but they definitely ought to be of concern to a library's administration. These matters could include addressing the politics of change, ensuring that new processes and systems conform to professional standards, making certain that new systems and processes reflect a library's service philosophy, and of course, being realistic about resource availability. There is no point in making grandiose plans if the dollars needed to implement and operate a new system aren't available. Let's begin with the big picture issues.

Political Environment

It is very important not to overlook or ignore the local political environment before a new system or activity is introduced. One can encounter difficulties when potential political risks are ignored. I've already cited the controversy that erupted in Hawaii when the State Library administration (see page 209) failed to assess adequately the existing political climate before deciding to outsource its book selection and processing, but lots of other, though less dramatic, illustrations come to mind—a couple I'm afraid from personal experience. Removing and relocating unused and unread esoteric periodical issues to an off-campus shelving area provoked protests from faculty members who were on vacation even though the library's faculty advisory committee had supported the transfer. The second experience occurred when we introduced a campus book/periodical delivery service to faculty. It never occurred to us that faculty would object, yet some were quite vociferous and plaintive with their objections. These faculty members wanted the funds to be spent buying more books and journals. They also argued that they didn't want their colleagues to be spoon-fed. As it was, we went ahead with the service, and ironically the complainers became some of our heaviest users.

There is also the case of a public library system that decided to centralize its book selection system in order to achieve greater processing efficiencies, but in doing so forgot to consult with their branch librarians who strongly objected. As a result several branch librarians began to encourage patrons to complain directly to the library's administration or better yet, to write letters to the editor of the local newspaper. The campaign proved effective, which caused a great deal of unhappiness among the library's senior administrators.

There have also been several widely reported cases of backlashes when metropolitan library systems proposed to eliminate neighborhood branches. The chances are that unless the politics of such situations are handled adroitly, a library is likely to find itself ensnared in a political firestorm. Academic libraries aren't immune either. I'm familiar with a small university library system that decided to improve service and at the same time conserve scarce staff resources by consolidating a series of small branch libraries into a single science library. When the faculty returned from their summer vacations, they were extremely dismayed because they loved their small, but very convenient, departmental libraries. The library administration's logic in launching the centralization project made a great deal of sense, but it failed to adequately factor in the local political climate. By doing this over the summer, and by not involving the faculty in the discussion, the library administration created a lot of unnecessary ill will for itself.

Even changes in procedures that seem logical and minor can produce a backlash. Two examples come to mind. First, the library decides to save the cost of mailing overdue forms by using its new circulation system to send out overdue notices in the form of email. The decision made a great deal of sense, but in reality there were patrons who didn't own a personal computer or have easy access to email. In this case the decision provoked outcries because the segment of the population base that were most likely to be affected adversely were at-risk students and their parents.

Second, a library introduces RFID tags, which also makes a great deal of sense, but the library's administration didn't anticipate that some patrons would raise issues about privacy. While there have been assurances that the use of RFID technology would be accomplished without any intrusions on patron privacy, the fact is that as government has permeated more aspects of our lives, social institutions have had to become more sensitive to the potential public policy implications of library policies. Both of these examples involved only minor procedural changes, but each created major political repercussions.

National Standards

The importance of adhering to nationally accepted standards and protocols has been recognized since the days when the Library of Congress issued such documents as the *Anglo-American Cataloguing Rules, 2nd Edition* (AACR2), Library of Congress subject headings, and the International Standard Bibliographic Description (ISBD). But unfortunately many libraries didn't always pay attention to admonitions that libraries should conform to such standards; the penalty of this disregard became apparent as libraries encountered difficulties and extra expenses as they tried to merge bibliographic records into regional or national databases.[9]

An example of an international protocol that is gaining acceptance among ILMS vendors is ISO 10160/10161. This protocol allows libraries to manage "... interlibrary loans traffic or incorporating existing systems developed by other vendors to enhance the overall functionality of their product."[10] This protocol is also related to standards such as Z39.50, the NISO Circulation Interchange Protocol, and ISO 2146, the international standard for library directories. Another example of a protocol that could play a role in the days ahead is the Open Archives Initiative Protocol for Metadata Harvesting.[11]

As libraries become more and more dependent on Web technology and more tightly networked, the significance of standards and protocols will assume even greater importance to those who are responsible for introducing library systems and processes.

Finally, it is likely that the standards I've cited will either be old hat or have already become obsolete by the time this book appears in print. The point to remember is to be cognizant of existing standards as new systems are being introduced.

Organizational Objectives

It is crucial to emphasize the importance of designing new processes and procedures that reflect an organization's service goals and objectives. Most studies should flow logically from an organization's strategic plan, paying close attention to the intent of the library's overall service objectives. When a process isn't in harmony with the library's service objectives, problems can arise.

A few years ago I was working with a library that really prided itself on being able to respond to faculty requests in a timely manner. It was little wonder that the library's administration became upset when it began to receive angry complaints from faculty about how difficult it was to get a new journal subscription started. The faculty complainers alleged that it took months and months for a request to wend its way through the system. I described this situation in detail on page 123 in Chapter 10. The bottom line was that the procedure did in fact often take months to be completed. Although the staff were happy with the status quo, the old review procedure was scrapped in favor of a streamlined version. The complaints not only disappeared, but the library staff received kudos from the same faculty who had faulted them earlier.

The current interest in resource-sharing systems offers another relevant illustration of the importance of designing processes that adequately reflect a library's organizational service objectives. A public library consortium I'm familiar with recently introduced a new integrated system. The system supports a sophisticated interlibrary lending and borrowing module. The software is flexible and a variety of parameters can be used. The library now needs to decide how to implement the system so that it best reflects its service philosophy.

- What user groups will the system be designed to serve, and what level of service will be provided to each group?

- Will service be available to citizens from neighboring communities? Will some groups be restricted?

- Should the library provide the same level of access to collections for everybody or just to a group of designated libraries?

- Should the library charge for interlibrary-loan transactions? If so, should any institutions receive priority treatment, and if so, what would be the rationale?

- What categories of materials will or will not be lent?

What if the library's administration intended that high school students from communities who are members of the consortium should be eligible to borrow materials, but unbeknownst to administrators, the consortium's ILL librarians currently excluded students from borrowing? Past experience had taught them that ILL didn't serve well the needs of most students. The interlibrary loan staff may well be correct, but the exclusion of students unfortunately could contradict the consortium's service objectives and public commitments. Political problems could lie ahead for all concerned.

Resource Availability

There is absolutely no point in designing new processes, procedures or introducing new systems or services, if the resources necessary to operate and maintain the activity are not available. I've read a number of reports prepared by consultants that seem to be recommending a Rolls Royce system for a library that can afford only a KIA.

When assessing resources, one should consider, in addition to dollars, such factors as availability of trained personnel, accessibility to computers and servers, and physical constraints caused by current facilities. The constraints of older buildings can be particularly frustrating when a library tries to convert traditional reader and stack space into an information commons type of public service area.

Additional Tips and Guidelines

There is a lot to think about when one is preparing to introduce new processes, procedures or introducing new systems or services. After long years of experience I've developed a checklist of issues that I believe needs to be considered.

Provide for a Smooth Transition

The transition from a manual process to an automated system, upgrading from one version of an integrated system to a newer version, or the introduction of a new or upgraded software package will require changes in existing procedures. There will be no exceptions to this rule; therefore, it is essential to carry out careful planning and preparation well in advance. I'm familiar with a library whose staff assumed that the transition to a new ILL software package would be seamless. They failed to realize the new package would bypass the existing ILL module in the library's integrated system. Patron requests would now flow directly to the new ILL module. It soon became apparent that this and other changes would necessitate a number of changes to the current handling procedures; moreover, the statistical packages for the two systems were incompatible. This meant that the library system's staff were forced to create a link between the new system and the existing statistical software package so that the library could continue collecting data about traffic that might impact existing collection development patterns.

Balancing Costs with Service Benefits

This is an issue that often ventures into the political arena. There are probably no clear-cut answers, but it is wise to keep in mind that some public officials will want to know the cost benefit of a service. Legislators and city officials must appear to be concerned with costs of activities because costs of publicly supported organizations seem to escalate each year. But unlike organizations from the for-profit sector that can point to the bottom line as a measure of success, libraries are not bottom line organizations; they are organizations that contribute to the quality of life in a community and help to enrich the human spirit; these are values that stubbornly resist measurement.

Regardless of our lofty objectives, however, accountability has nevertheless become a popular concept among public officials. How can we help officials to understand better the relationship between costs and the social value of a library's service? Like I've already noted, there are no quick or guaranteed strategies. I have found that it is usually necessary to be patient, and work hard to explain the intangible benefits of many of our services and why they are important.

For example, resource-sharing arrangements can often be shown to reduce local operating costs. When this occurs most city officials will be satisfied because their support was rooted on the promise of future savings. But if the resource sharing arrangement doesn't actually reduce local operating costs because the library lends more materials than it borrows, then one has to adopt a different tact. For instance, we know that participation in a successful resource-sharing consortium will greatly enhance the universe of resources available to citizens in our community; moreover, resource sharing has also helped the library to avoid purchasing items that can be quickly obtained through resource-sharing arrangements. There is a good chance that a strong non-monetary argument can be mounted, but again it is wise when introducing a new system or service to remember that it might be necessary to balance costs and benefits in order to justify the new activity.

Avoiding Peaks of Activity

One should avoid staffing to accommodate peak periods of activity. I've observed numerous public service desks with staff standing around talking or reading because there wasn't enough activity to keep them busy. Banks and supermarkets were leaders at staffing only enough checkout stations to meet the current level of demand. When lines begin to form, additional stations are opened up. I believe libraries have gotten much better at assigning staffing levels that are appropriate to the level of demand; nonetheless, it is a consideration to keep in mind.

When we think of peak periods of activity, what comes to mind is usually the workday itself, but one can also think in terms of the time of year. Workloads at most service desks fluctuate not only during the day but also according to the season. Demand for services diminishes significantly during academic vacations. Furthermore, workloads in units such as acquisitions and interlending and borrowing units fluctuate throughout the year. Levels of activity are much heavier in the early fall and spring. A unit head might like to see his/her unit staffed to handle the peaks of activity, but observant managers might find that level a bit too rich.

Balancing Demand and Supply for Services

Companies in the private sector are able to expand their capacity to meet increased demands for products or services, e.g., Burger King simply builds or leases new stores to accommodate increased demand. In fact Burger King is delighted whenever this occurs because growth is one sure sign of success. Unfortunately, organizations in the public sector, including libraries, must accommodate growth within an existing fixed annual budget. This may limit a library's options. Available options usually include: reallocating resources from other activities, rationing the new service, collaborating with other libraries, or introducing a service fee. Of course, there is one less desirable option: Let the service deteriorate until demand levels fall off as more and more people become dissatisfied. Public libraries have employed rationing techniques for years. That is why they limit the number of books or CDs one is allowed to borrow at one time. A number of relevant illustrations are described below.

Database Searching—The failure to plan ahead was particularly painful for some libraries when they introduced database searching in the 1970s. These services proved to be popular, and as demand grew some libraries responded by introducing fees; other libraries continued to offer the service free of charge. The imposition of service fees led to the "fee or free" debate that consumed a great deal of time and energy at professional meetings. Of course the dilemma was never resolved. More recently the introduction of chat reference services sparked similar discussions.

Chat Reference—When virtual or chat reference services were introduced, at first there was concern that the level of demand would not justify its costs, but over time more and more libraries found themselves grappling with increased demands that were stretching existing staff resources. Again, a library's options are limited. Allocate additional staff to the service, allow the service to deteriorate, ration the hours the service is offered, or introduce some sort of service fee. Most libraries have decided to assign additional staff in the short term, but the long-term outcome is less clear. I would be surprised if the next step for many libraries weren't an effort to extend collaborative agreements in order to avoid imposing direct service charges. We shall have to wait to see what develops.

Document Delivery—I first encountered this phenomenon when we introduced a campus delivery service for faculty and graduate students. As we publicized the service, and more and more faculty members tried it, demands for the service went through the roof because faculty loved the service. It wasn't long before the document delivery office was swamped. Since we didn't want the service to deteriorate, and we couldn't assign any additional staff, we found it necessary to impose a modest fee to curtail frivolous requests. The fee produced the desired effect, but we would have been wise to consider the likelihood of charging a fee before the service had been introduced. The fee was not well received. Some faculty felt that we had acted deviously by hooking them with a free service and then socking them with the fee. While that wasn't our motivation, it appeared to be so to some faculty. As a result, our relations with a few faculty members took a temporary hit.

Public Printing—When public access computers became common, many libraries offered free printing, or if not free, a maximum number of free copies. (A form of rationing.) But as the volume of printing from databases and Web resources escalated, many libraries became alarmed as their subsidy for printing went through the roof. Thus, it gradually became the norm to charge patrons for printing. It might have been wise to develop a long-range strategy right from the outset.

All of these illustrations possess one common element. They all involve activities that were successful. In fact it was the success itself that created the dilemma of how to manage the growing demand. The lesson is that one should consider how a library will deal with the demand/supply issue before a crisis occurs.

Ignoring Exceptions to the Rule

Systems designers have traditionally over-designed systems. This frequently means that their designs strive to accommodate every possible exception. One of the reasons why early automated systems were cumbersome was that the designers tried to cover every eventuality. Some vestiges of this tendency can be found in the latest version of some integrated library systems.

As a matter of fact, the complexity of the MARC format itself is a product of over design. This story may be apocryphal, but my boss at the time told me that the Library of Congress brought a group of ARL library directors together to decide what elements needed to be included in a catalog record that was to become the MARC format. The directors didn't know a great deal about cataloging so they consulted with their heads of technical services in advance of the meeting. As a result they brought with them a laundry list of needs as identified by their technical service experts. The problem was that the needs and philosophy toward cataloging differed from library to library. In order to gain widespread support for the new machine-readable format, Library of Congress officials strived to accommodate as many as possible of the special needs that had been identified by the different libraries. Needless to say, the final product became incredibly complex.

Library directors who were reluctant to disregard the wishes of their technical services staff, and the Library of Congress' need to generate widespread support, produced the perfect storm. Were all of the complexities necessary? I'll let others debate that issue. The point here is that the format was designed to cover every possible exception. This is what one wants to avoid when designing a local process or system. Once again, the KISS system should apply.

It is still common to observe processes that are overly complicated. A digitization preparation process that includes preliminary checks to identify quality problems is a case in point. It is common to design the process so that each book is assumed to be a problem when in fact most books are not. Another example is an approval book selection process that requires each book to be checked for relevance before it is added to the collection. If too many books are excluded then the library should quickly review its vendor profile. In either case a lot of time is devoted to checking books that don't require checking.

I've found that one is often better off designing a process to accommodate 90 percent of the activity. Design sub-routines to accommodate exceptions to the rule. Keep in mind that trying to eliminate exceptions may require increased inspections, and inspections are not productive. One need only remember that exceptions should be handled as just that—exceptions to the routine.

Getting Feedback

This should be a commonsense tip, but we often forget to ask users of a new process or service what is working and what is not. This principle applies to internal and external customers. The library's patrons represent one group of customers, but the public staff are also customers when an integrated system is introduced. It is important to learn what problems, if any, are being experienced as a new system or service is introduced.

Most librarians quickly realized that it was important to obtain feedback from patrons after library Web pages were introduced. Some libraries conducted usability studies to discover how patrons were using the library's Web site, and what problems patrons were encountering. This leads nicely into my next tip.

Allow for Iterative Designs

Once customer feedback is obtained, be prepared to modify the design of the system, process, or service. Many of us still remember when we asked patrons what they wanted in an automated catalog, and their responses usually reflected personal experiences in using a card catalog. Most people couldn't visualize what was possible. But once the catalog became available, patrons began to recognize lots of possibilities. It wasn't uncommon to hear complaints about information that couldn't be provided or listings that weren't possible. Of course over the years the OPACs have been greatly enhanced in many ways, e.g., abstracts, links to databases and Web resources. Many of these changes reflected patron feedback, and were made possible because of advances in technology.

As already mentioned, it was necessary to revamp library Web pages as patrons gained experience in using them. Initially it was usually the local Web master who designed most library Web sites. Oftentimes, these designs reflected what the Web master and librarians thought patrons wanted and needed. Unfortunately, these initial homepages often proved to be confusing and unhelpful to patrons, but such problems weren't discovered until libraries began conducting usability studies.

There is a certain irony about all of this. Being willing to redesign new systems, processes, and services, based on customer feedback takes a page directly from the field of market research; that is, marketers seek to learn what are their customers' wants and needs, and then alter their products or services to better satisfy what customers desire. We have been slow to adopt this philosophy; we still tend to cling to the notion that we know best. I believe that in the days ahead librarians will have to become more responsive to the needs and desires of their patrons or run the risk of finding themselves out of the mainstream as patrons abandon libraries for other sources.

Allowing for Variable Responses

Library systems have traditionally been designed to deliver a uniform rate of response. By this I mean all requests for service carry the same sense of urgency, and thus all requests merit the same speed of response. All requests for service are not equally urgent. For example, when customers order documents through interlibrary loan, the need for a quick turnaround varies greatly. Some patrons really do need the document as soon as possible, but others can wait for a couple of weeks without incurring any inconvenience. The borrowing process should be designed to provide variable responses.

Other examples that come to mind are ordering new books and cataloging new acquisitions. Some books are ordered RUSH; others are requested for RUSH cataloging. Should the same procedures be used to catalog or order all new books or should special handling procedures be created for items that merit special handling? I believe an expedited process should be designed to accommodate special needs, but the ability to accommodate variable responses must be accomplished in a way that avoids bogging down the entire system. In Chapter 4 (see page 25) I described a case where the acquisitions department became bogged down because too many faculty were ordering books RUSH in order to speed up the flow of books. But in reality the impact was that very few books could be handled RUSH. The process was bogged down. The strategy adopted was to temporarily put a ceiling on the number of items that could be ordered RUSH. This allowed the acquisitions department to work off its backlog of RUSH items. Then those faculty who had been ordering books RUSH were encouraged to be selective with their requests, but this request was also accompanied by an understanding that those books ordered RUSH would be given special handling.

The principle to keep in mind is that all requests are not equal in urgency. Try to create processes that allow for variable responses.

Avoiding Unrealistic Scheduling

The tendency of people to raise expectations with overly optimistic project schedules has always been one of my pet peeves. Some would argue that this practice is not a tendency but a chronic disease. Systems specialists and programmers have been notorious for underestimating the complexity of projects. Vendors don't seem to be much better. This is particularly true when the vendor is selling a complex software package such as an integrated library system.

Anyone associated with a project would be wise to be cautious with promises. Be realistic, or better yet, be conservative. Unanticipated delays can breed staff frustration and may even make the acceptance of a new system or service more difficult. Those involved in designing and introducing new systems, processes, and services would be wise to remember the wisdom of Murphy: "Anything that can go wrong, will go wrong." Enough said!

Notes

1. The Orlando Public Library introduced the Vocera system software when it reorganized its reference and information services. More information about Vocera can be found at http://www.vocera.com/ (27 May 2007).

2. Terry Mackey and Kitty Mackey, "Think Quality! The Deming Approach Does Work in Libraries," *Total Quality Management in Libraries: A Sourcebook*, ed. Rossana M. O'Neil (Englewood, Colo.: Libraries Unlimited, 1994): 11-12. Deming also talks about inspections extensively in his *Out of Crisis*.

3. The suggestion to create the permanent workstation wasn't made by a supervisor, but rather by two part-time student assistants. Nobody has a monopoly on good ideas.

4. For more information about College of DuPage teleconferences check http://www.cod.edu/teleconf/ (27 May 2007).

5. I've learned that some large libraries are beginning to bring back in-house selected categories of binding because of the high costs of commercial binders and the availability of better machines.

6. A number of monographs on the subject of outsourcing cataloging appeared in the literature in the 1990s. One of the most cited was authored by Hirshon and Winters. *See* Arnold Hirshon and Barbara Winters, *Outsourcing Library Technical Services: A How-to-do-it Manual for Librarians* (New York: Neal-Schuman, 1996). Wilson and Colver presented a broader picture of outsourcing of technical service operations. *See* Karen A. Wilson and Marylou Colver, *Outsourcing Library Technical Services Operations: Practices in Academic, Public, and Special Libraries* (Chicago: American Library Association, 1997).

7. The State Library's decision to outsource activities was extensively covered in the library press. It also generated a number of studies critiquing what happened as a result of the decision. It was a painful political lesson for all concerned. Anyone interested in the details of what happened should consult databases such as ProQuest or InfoTrac OneFile to identify the many news articles and editorials that appeared soon after the decision to outsource was made public.

8. Although somewhat dated, Kascus and Hale have compiled an extensive checklist designed to stimulate thought regarding the advantages and disadvantages of outsourcing activities. This work should help a library select possible services to be outsourced, determine associated in-house concerns and costs, and gather information about potential contractors. *See* Marie A. Kascus and Dawn Hale, eds., *Outsourcing Cataloging, Authority Work, and Physical Processing: A Checklist of Considerations* (Chicago: American Library Association, 1994).

9. Today one of the most important standards that libraries need to pay attention to is MARC-21. A great deal of information about this standard can be found at: http://www.loc.gov/marc/ (27 May 2007).

10. Margarita Moreno and Rob Walls, *When Protocol Works: The State of the ISO ILL Protocol in the Australian Resource Sharing Environment*. Available from: http://www.vala.org.au/vala2002/2002pdf/41MorWal.pdf (27 May 2007).

11. More information about the CDL project, and background information about the OAI Harvesting Infrastructure project is available at: http://www.cdlib.org/inside/projects/harvesting/ (27 May 2007).

Chapter Seventeen

Implementing New Activities

Scope note: Implementing a plan of action is often the most challenging phase of bringing about change. This chapter presents a potpourri of topics that should be considered before, during, or after the study/planning stage is completed, and certainly before implementation is actually undertaken. The topics range from timing the transition, providing back-up capability, to creating an ergonomically friendly and comfortable work environment, to providing necessary training, and dealing with the complicated topic of errors and their acceptance.

Introduction

I've found that implementing a plan of action is often the most challenging phase of bringing about change. There is a lot to think about. I've worked with a number of libraries that were extremely effective at analyzing and planning of either new workflows or a new service, but when it came time to implement their plans, they fell far short of success.

There are many reasons why organizations falter when it comes to implementation. In some cases the administration itself doesn't *really* want to move ahead. In a way it is a case of wanting to "talk the talk" of embracing change without having to take the proverbial walk. Another source of failure is that the library takes on too much, and the staff gradually loses its momentum and gets bogged down in details or putting out brush fires that all organizations encounter. Still another source of failure is that the need for resources was underestimated. While it is important to plan for a new activity, it is equally important to develop implementation strategies that are realistic.

The topics presented here aren't ranked in order of importance or priority. Some may be considered of minor import; whereas others may be of critical importance in some situations. It all depends on the nature of the activity and local circumstances. I'll leave it to readers to decide into which category each topic falls.

Appointing a Transition Team

When introducing new activities, it may be wise to appoint a team that is given specific responsibility for shepherding the implementation effort from beginning to completion. I call this group the transition team. First of all, the team needs to learn how to function as a team, which in some cases may require special training. Skipping the training step is tantamount to courting disaster. One library I worked with appointed a transition team, but was in a hurry and didn't think training was necessary, so they skipped the training step. At the first meeting, the group appointed one of its members as chairperson. This person was one of the most influential staff members and highly regarded by her peers. However, she was totally incapable of serving as a team leader: As chair she routinely cut off discussion and behaved like a mini-dictator. Before long the rest of the team was completely turned off, and soon the team began to spin its wheels and work at cross-purposes. The team had to be disbanded and a new team appointed before implementation could proceed. Also, a lot of hurt feelings had to be assuaged.

Developing an Overall Plan

The specifics of an implementation plan will depend wholly on what type of activity is to be introduced. For example, if the new system, process, or service requires staff to undertake new or different duties, these staff will need to be retrained. If not, productivity and the quality of public services are likely to suffer. The necessary training programs should be put into place early in the implementation process.

In order to anticipate possible contingencies, I suggest developing a checklist of tasks that need to be performed, or tasks that at least need to be considered. Figure 15-1, page 189 is one illustration; it represents a typical list of tasks. Some of these tasks are discussed in greater detail in this chapter.

Timing the Transition

An implementation plan should be timed to avoid distractions that might otherwise interfere with the introduction of activities. A reference staff will not be overjoyed if asked to learn the intricacies of a new federated searching platform during the opening of a new term when many meetings with students are scheduled.

Implementation should be neither pell-mell nor unnecessarily protracted. Excessive delays can cause a staff to lose its momentum and enthusiasm for the new activities. The guiding principle should be to minimize difficulties for those who must alter their behaviors. The next few sections apply mostly to the introduction of new hardware and software, but the principles still apply even if hardware or software aren't involved.

Parallel Systems

Most hardware and software systems provided by vendors today tend to be more stable and reliable than were their locally developed predecessors. As a result, the need to run systems in parallel has somewhat diminished; nevertheless, it is essential that any new platform and software be thoroughly tested before the system is introduced. The key is to test, test, and test some more in order to ensure that the system will perform as expected once it is turned on, and the library becomes dependent on the new system. Even so, there are still reported incidents where systems that were successful in one location didn't work as effectively in a similar environment. Possibly the question to ask is: "What is the worst-case scenario?" I'm familiar with a case in which a new circulation system failed, and the library was forced to enlist staff to handle all circulations manually until the new system could be brought back online. It was a costly backup both in terms of staff costs and loss in public relations.

Backup Systems

We normally think of computer-based systems when we think of backup, and that is certainly understandable, but there is also the critical need to backup the data itself, e.g., financial records, full-text databases, bibliographic records, etc. The need to backup data begins with one's personal computer and extends to the most sophisticated integrated library system. Multiple backups should be the rule.

The need for a backup system also depends on the nature of breakdowns that might be experienced, their duration, and the cost to the staff and patrons. Hardware experts and vendor representatives can provide information about the probability of breakdowns. Management and systems staff should also enquire about the experiences of others who are using the same equipment and software. Inevitably the decision whether to install a backup capacity will revolve about the question of risk versus cost. In general, the larger the investment, or the greater the penalty of a service breakdown, the more comprehensive should be the precautions.

The need for backup extends to non-technical activities as well. For example, a manual operation can become overly dependent upon one staff member who could resign suddenly, be on vacation, or unexpectedly call in sick. In small libraries and branches this problem can be of particular concern to administrators. Therefore, the prudent course of action is to always have another person ready to step in, in case the need arises.

Debugging a New System

The debugging stage can be particularly critical. It is at this point that management must establish staff confidence in a new system, process, or procedure. The systems personnel should have taken precautions during the planning and preparation stages to ensure that possible snags are eliminated, but there is still a chance that unanticipated problems will surface after the system is put into operation. Anyone who has worked in a library technical services division knows that over a period of time a wide variety of exceptional cases can arise.

There are different philosophies on the best way to introduce a new system. The strategy employed should depend upon the system in question and the prevailing local circumstances. If it is reasonably simple, then all subsystems can be introduced simultaneously, but if the activity is composed of several complex subsystems, such as an integrated library system, the new system might best be introduced in phases. This allows one to make sure that each component functions as expected before the next module is introduced. It also allows more time for staff to receive training and to gain confidence in the system's operation.

First Results

This might seem obvious, but even if all of the safeguards discussed earlier, such as testing, training, and system overlap, have been taken, unanticipated problems can still arise. One such occasion occurred when a public library introduced an upgraded circulation module. The circulation staff assumed that the new module would not only provide new capabilities but would also retain the features of its predecessor. In the earlier version, patrons were notified via email three days before a book became overdue. Patrons appreciated this early warning. Unfortunately the new module wasn't programmed to provide this automatic notification. As a result many patrons who depended on this early warning system began to incur fines for overdue books. Staff members remained unaware of the problem until they began to receive complaints, and the library director was even confronted by an irritated patron at a Rotary Club meeting. The new module was quickly modified so that the early warning service was restored. It is smart to pay close attention to what occurs after a new activity is launched.

Inadequate training can also generate a range of problems. I recall a Web-based system that allowed faculty to submit orders for new books online. It wasn't a big deal, but for some reason a couple of key staff in the acquisitions unit weren't briefed by the systems staff so they weren't aware of the new service. When new order requests reached the library via the Web, they simply sat there because the staff never checked the relevant database. This small oversight generated faculty criticism, and several angry acquisition staff members.

I heartily recommend that steps be taken to solicit staff reactions, or when appropriate, patron feedback to a new system or service. What one is looking for is constructive feedback about how the new activity is performing. Is it working as billed? Are patrons experiencing frustrations? If so, for what reasons? I'd also try to identify other features that patrons believe would further enhance the process or service. Earlier I mentioned that many people have a difficult time envisioning the potential of a new process or service if they haven't seen or used it previously. One illustration that comes to mind occurred just before a new virtual reference service was to be introduced into a college library. Staff and students were asked about possible features. It never occurred to anybody that students already in the library itself would be the heavy users of the service. Everyone had assumed that the students would contact the library from their dorms or homes. This behavior pattern resulted in a demand for the service that hadn't been anticipated. This also led to a decision to introduce a wireless network within the library.

The important point is that it is wise for management and staff to pay close attention to a new activity after it has been introduced. What period of time will be required is hard to predict because it will depend on the activity in question. Just be observant until everyone is convinced that the system or service is performing as anticipated.

System Evaluation

In general one should strive to measure the effectiveness of a recently implemented activity against objectives formulated during the design and planning stages. Whenever possible, measurements should be based on quantitative scales placed against a time/cost continuum. Does the system save dollars or improve service? If so, over what period of time? In some cases it is possible to measure productivity or costs saved, but many library activities are difficult to quantify. One can introduce a book-detection system and determine fairly accurately its impact on theft and mutilation, but it is quite another matter to measure, at least with great assurance, the effectiveness of an expanded virtual reference service or an information literacy program.

Whenever possible all persons involved should agree on the evaluation criteria to be used before implementation begins. One approach is to judge the new activity against the original expectations. If the results do not meet those expectations, steps should be taken to ascertain why expectations haven't been met, so that modifications can be introduced.

A number of studies have already been cited. The series of time and cost studies conducted at the Iowa State University Library are examples of attempts to evaluate services on the basis of costs and productivity. Another source of useful information is the publications of professional associations such as the American Library Association (ALA), the Public Library Association (PLA) and the Association of College and Research Libraries (ACRL), which are both divisions of the ALA, and the Association of Research Libraries (ARL). They have all produced guidelines that can be used to evaluate library activities and services. Anyone about to embark on an evaluation project should consult the publications of these organizations.[1]

Evaluation of a new system, process, or service can be a complex and demanding activity. Too often follow-up studies are not undertaken. Or, if undertaken the results rarely find their way into print. While some study results are of local interest only, there are numerous studies that if published would provide helpful guidance to others. The most likely reason for not publishing the results of an evaluation is that the new activity is doing just fine or that the library is too busy to conduct a formal study. These are understandable responses, but also unfortunate as the need to evaluate new systems is growing as demands for greater accountability grow. Much could potentially be gained if the results of evaluation studies were shared more often.

Creating a Supportive Work Environment

There is an extensive body of literature on the topic of what constitutes a high-quality work environment so I won't delve deeply into this topic here. But I do want to stress that those responsible for implementing and operating new activities should make every effort to create a work environment in which staff are willing to help each other. They should not be made to feel that they are pitted against each other so that "one person's gain is another person's loss." The goal should be to create a work environment that inspires staff to look forward to coming to work each day.

There is a set of basic human needs that staff in any organization strives to achieve. A few years ago Peggy Lippitt surveyed a group of sociologists and psychologists to identify characteristics that caused people to function "harmoniously, cooperatively, and productively." Her list includes being liked and respected, accepted, useful, being included, being able to exert influence, being able to grow in skill and autonomy, enjoying a sense of adventure, and being a part of and belonging to something larger than self. [2]

I've known instances in which staff really took great pride in what was going on in their libraries. You almost knew that they were "standing tall and proud." You could tell that they felt that they were the best. Whenever one encounters such a situation, and delves into the reasons why such feelings are evident, one is likely to discover that the characteristics identified by Lippitt are clearly present. One is also likely to discover that the library's top leaders are excellent.

The list of characteristics identified by Lippitt should not raise any eyebrows. The behaviors she cites are pretty much commonsensical, but I've been amazed over the years by the number of managers and supervisors who underestimate the abilities of their staff, and fail to offer them adequate opportunities to develop existing and/or new skills.

I believe a better approach is to assume that an existing staff possesses significant untapped potential. As plans for a new activity are being developed, think about ways to tap that potential, consider tactics that can lead to a happier and more productive staff. Can jobs be created or redesigned to enhance staff feelings of achievement and accomplishment? Specifically can a job be enlarged or designed to extend its range so that the number and variety of activities an employee performs is increased? Can a job be organized so that staff control of what is done is increased in order to enrich the experience? Does the job enable a degree of staff autonomy over what they do? Are there provisions for providing staff with performance feedback about what they are doing well and where improvement is needed? Is the job meaningful? That is, does the staff know how their work really contributes to the objectives of the unit or library? If there isn't such recognition, some staff are likely to jump to the conclusion that their work isn't meaningful. In such cases staff workers won't feel any sense of accomplishment. Other ways to enrich a work experience include:

Scheduling Flexibility

Flexibility can be used to enrich staff members' work experiences or support their family life. For example, a library can adopt flextime scheduling that allows earlier or later starting or ending times. There are also instances when libraries will allow an employee to adopt a compressed schedule, e.g., work ten hours a day for four days instead of working a regular five-day week. There are other variations of both flextime and compressed scheduling.

Job Rotation

This is another way to enrich a staff member's work experience. Many years ago Frank Lundy, who was then Director of Libraries at the University of Nebraska, began to rotate catalogers and reference librarians. Lundy rotated his staff because he was having trouble attracting catalogers, but what he created was, in my judgment, an excellent growth opportunity for his staff.[3] Over the years other libraries adopted this or similar forms of job rotation. I've heard many staff complain about job rotation, but I've never heard any person say that the experience hadn't been valuable.

Job Sharing

Job sharing can be a particularly effective way to create opportunities for people who want to work, but who are also deeply involved with other responsibilities like raising a family. Job sharing also makes it possible to broaden the range of talents and backgrounds that are available to the library.

Training

Training is an important topic that has also generated its own enormous body of literature. Although I don't feel the need to dwell on the details of organizing training programs, I do feel, however, that it is very essential to underscore once again the importance of staff training programs. The extent and quality of training programs can have an enormous effect on how successful the transition will be from the old to the new activity, and how well the new activity will be received by staff and library patrons.[4]

The need for training goes well beyond the implementation of new systems, processes, and services. Today there is a pressing need to keep staff knowledgeable about changes in software and databases that seem to occur on a daily basis. It is equally important that libraries be able to finish the education/training of new graduates from Library and Information Science programs. It isn't possible for LIS programs to instruct students in the details of specific software packages and databases. First of all, there isn't enough to time to accomplish such a goal, and second, the changes in software and databases occur so rapidly that what might be learned last semester would likely be rendered obsolete by the end of the next semester. It is simply now incumbent on libraries, or groups of libraries, to make a commitment to keep their staffs current. Without adequate training, libraries are guaranteeing that their staffs will be unable to make effective use of the latest software innovations.

Before leaving the topic I want to mention again the potential of cross training. This approach to training, which has so many potential benefits, hasn't received much attention in libraries.[5] In a way this is a form of job sharing or job rotation. The intensity of numerous library workflows fluctuates significantly throughout the course of a year. As mentioned previously, the volume of new monograph orders peaks in the fall and in the spring but declines sharply during the early summer months. Why not train acquisitions staff to perform selected cataloging activities, particularly when backlogs exist? The point is that cross training of staff can often achieve real benefits. Like Frank Lundy's staff, they will be better trained and prepared to take on a wider range of duties.

Providing an Ergonomically Sound Work Environment

Ergonomics is the study of individuals and their physical relationship to the work environment. The scope of ergonomics is extremely broad. It ranges from the design of individual workstations and desks that accommodate groups of staff workers to the work environment itself. The literature on the subject of ergonomics has become voluminous in recent years as more and more studies reveal that hundreds of thousands of workers suffer from aching backs, crippled fingers, and sore wrists that can all be traced back to their jobs. Research has also shown that there is a strong relationship between the quality of the work environment and productivity.

Some libraries have organized staff-wide programs to address systematically ergonomic issues that are pertinent to their libraries. Oftentimes a systematic approach may include bringing in outside experts to evaluate the special needs of individual jobs, e.g., the layout of a circulation area where books are constantly being handled.

Many libraries now provide staff with packets of information about ergonomic issues. This could include the causes of repetitive motion injuries and suggestions for stretching exercises that can relieve stress for those who spend hours working at computer terminals. Another approach to providing staff with ergonomic-related information is to create a special purpose Web site.

Staff also need to be trained to take advantage of ergonomically designed equipment. They need to know how to adjust their chairs, and if possible, the height of work surfaces, how to lift and carry books and other objects, and what to do if an injury occurs. Libraries that have started library-wide programs also advise that training sessions should not be one-time affairs. Refresher sessions are necessary not only for new staff, but also for staff members who have been onboard for a while.[6]

I believe all libraries should adopt a formal ergonomics program. And when budgets permit, I'd further suggest engaging outside experts to provide advice. The following paragraphs focus on just a few of the issues that need to be addressed.

Workstations

For many years one could expect a library to equip its work areas with furniture that was designed to accommodate a person of average dimensions. But as more attention has been placed on the importance of providing staff workers with ergonomically sound furniture, libraries have begun to make conscious efforts to improve their work environments. Fortunately most manufacturers of furniture now offer a wide variety of ergonomically designed workstations, chairs, tables, and privacy partitions for individual workers. Some companies now even offer suites of furniture that are designed for specific service areas such as reference. Figure 17-1 represents the layout of a reference desk. The ergonomic principles incorporated into this furniture are based on a cooperative project that involved the Bretford Incorporated and staff from the San Francisco Public Library.

Figure 17-2 depicts the layout of a circulation work area that was developed as a result of this joint effort between Bretford and the library. This workstation not only reflects ergonomic principles; it also reflects efforts to incorporate workflow improvements.

The project was undertaken because soon after San Francisco's new central library was opened, the library's administration began receiving reports of staff suffering from repetitive stress injuries. A board-certified ergonomist and independent consultant was hired. Based on the consultant's recommendations, the library

Figure 17-1 Ergonomically designed reference desk and work area. (Permission granted by the Bretford Incorporated.)

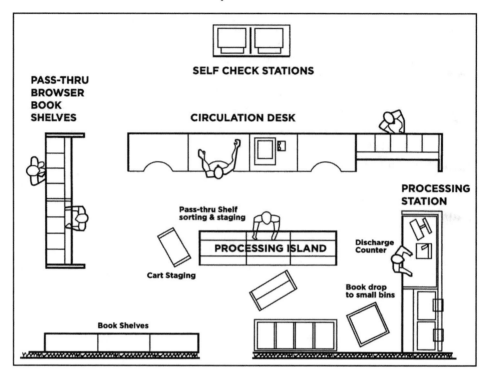

Figure 17-2 Specially designed circulation work area with provisions for processing island and processing station for large libraries. (Permission granted by the Bretford Incorporated.)

approached the Bretford Incorporated to work with the library's administration and branch staff to produce a line of furniture that reflected recommendations of the consultant. But this project went a step further. The library also wanted to create furniture that would facilitate improvements in workflows. To gather information about workflows, a series of workshops was held with branch staff in order to identify problems, and generate ideas and test ergonomic concepts. The result was a line of furniture that embodied a variety of ergonomic principles. For example, the components are designed to make it easy for staff to reach materials comfortably, maximize the staff's ability to slide materials (sliding is much less stressful than lifting), provide for a variety of heights to accommodate people of different stature, and reduce the need to bend and lift materials in order to process them. This is only a sampling of the ergonomic considerations that are reflected in what became known as the San Francisco Collection line of furniture.

Special Workstations

Most library workstations are designed primarily to permit the easy interaction between a computer and associated equipment and an operator. All of the equipment and materials that are used should be located within the normal work area. (See Chapter 8, page 93.) There are occasions when the needs of a job re-

Figure 17-3 Ergonomically designed workstation.

quire specially designed workstations. The workstation shown in Figure 17-3 is just such an illustration. It is an excellent example of a workstation that incorporates the principles of motion economy and ergonomics. It is a workstation used by a staff member who performs a variety of book repairs. All of the tools and materials are located within easy reach. A magnetic strip enables the worker to keep a variety of tools organized so that she can retrieve what is needed without looking. A series of cubby holes were built to store needed materials. (See Figure 17-4.) Cups are used to hold pencils, brushes, and other non-metallic tools. (See Figure 17-5.) Alongside the work area is a rolling cart that is designed to store large-sized supplies, and also to provide easy access to a paper cutter and a press. (See Figure 17-6.) This layout makes it possible for the employee to complete most repair jobs without ever having to leave her workstation. This was a carefully thought out and excellent design.

Work Environment

There is no question but that the design of workstations and service areas is extremely important. However, careful thought should also be given to more general considerations, namely, illumination, noise, thermal comfort, and esthetic appeal.[7]

Illumination

Lighting should be geared to the type of work being performed. One doesn't want to work at a computer where the light is causing a glare on the screen. More light

Figure 17-4 Workstation showing storage cubby holes.

Figure 17-5 Cups for pencils and other small tools.

is not necessarily better. Without question lighting requirements will vary from area to area in the same workplace. The challenge of providing adequate lighting is also complicated by the need to reduce glare on computer displays while providing enough light for paperwork.

One also has to keep in mind that ceilings, floors, and furniture all reflect light depending on material used and its color. While it is preferable to have controls for different work areas, it is advisable to supplement general light sources with lamps or other lighting that may be portable. This allows a staff worker to change the location and angle of the light based on the time of day and the work being performed.

Noise

Libraries traditionally are quiet places, but of course that is no longer strictly true as libraries have adopted more open and receptive service areas. Still, compared to most types of organizations, noise levels are normally manageable. However, one must not forget that noise in certain areas can be disruptive. Printers, photocopiers, and change machines may require special provisions.

Technical service staff and others who share a work area may require partially enclosed cubicles that can reduce noise substantially while providing a sense of privacy and a workspace staff can identify as their own.

Thermal Comfort

I believe most of us have experienced discomfort because our work area was either too warm

Figure 17-6 Rolling cart for large-sized supplies.

or too cold. Moreover, because what is comfortable to one person is uncomfortable to another, the challenge of providing comfortable areas can be formidable. Although temperatures and humidity need to be carefully monitored in areas where computer equipment and rare books are housed, for the most part these do not pose insurmountable problems for libraries.

I do confess that I prefer buildings in which windows can be opened, but this is not possible in buildings that are designed for centralized climate control. Central climate control may save money, but it doesn't always produce staff satisfaction. One just has to hope that a heating and ventilation engineer is right around the corner when the need arises.

Esthetic Appeal

Allowing staff workers to individualize their workspace goes a long way toward creating a positive work environment, but there are still other considerations. To the extent possible each person should have access to windows at least part of the day. And as previously mentioned each staff worker ought to have a well-defined private space. Privacy does lead to greater satisfaction, and one can argue that it also leads to greater productivity.

Summary

A comfortable working environment is a critical component in providing a hospitable workplace. Work conditions have never been as important as they are now. For example, the Americans with Disabilities Act helped organizations to realize they had an obligation to accommodate the special needs of some workers. Libraries were very responsive when this Act became law.

There are also numerous regulations promoting a healthy and safe working environment. The Occupational Safety and Health Agency monitors such regulations.[8] In the final analysis staff at all levels need to recognize that applying the principles of ergonomics can lead to greater staff satisfaction and greater productivity—a classic win-win situation.

Dealing with Errors—Nobody's Perfect

The subject of how to deal with errors is bound to occur at some point in a project. It is a topic that needs to be addressed early on, possibly even before data collection begins. That is the reason I raised the issue of errors in Chapter 5, page 47. Library staff members have traditionally been concerned about the occurrence of errors. As new systems, processes, or procedures are introduced, however, keep in mind that perfection is beyond our reach. Thus, we have no choice but to accept the reality of imperfection.

We do need to learn more about why errors occur, and the penalties for providing erroneous information. We know that librarians love creating high-quality bibliographical records. Enormous amounts of time, money, and energy have been devoted to ensure that errors are kept to a minimum. Some library staff still believe that the only acceptable goal is "bibliographical perfection." In order to achieve perfection, or at least avoid the stigma of producing less-than-perfect work, it is common, even in an integrated system work environment, for a staff member in one unit to inspect routinely the work produced in another unit. For example, bibliographic searchers may check the work of selectors; catalogers check the work of acquisitions personnel; reference personnel review the work of catalogers, and so on. No one knows how extensive such checks might be, but it is a phenomenon that needs to be recognized as a reality in libraries. Most libraries would probably be appalled to find out just how much money, time, and energy are spent on such non-productive operations.

There still seems to be no widespread recognition among librarians that errors are inevitable. No amount of inspection will eliminate all of them. Therefore, a manager would be wise to design appropriate quality control measures for key operations such as a checking procedure designed to ensure that books are correctly reshelved. There are also instances when the need for quality and accuracy warrants an intensive formal inspection program. One doesn't want to key inaccurate URLs, ISBDs, or OCLC numbers on records. And one doesn't want to attach the wrong RFID tag to a book being prepared for circulation.

Even though librarians are so conscious of errors, formal quality control programs are rarely in evidence. At the same time there exists "off-the-book" quality control initiatives which would include the "blacklists" that catalogers created at the dawn of shared cataloging. One of the real ironies of those lists was that almost every library was on somebody else's blacklist. The catalogers' message was that local cataloging was still best. These lists also resulted in higher costs and lower productivity—all with questionable benefits to the information seeker.

One would have thought as shared cataloging became more widely adopted and accepted, such lists would have disappeared from the scene, but that does not seem to be the case. There are still libraries that will not accept the cataloging of others under certain circumstances such as digital texts, videos, or CDs.

Based on personal observations, even in the face of overwhelming evidence to the contrary, I suspect many library staff still cling to the belief that anything short of perfection is unacceptable. The irony is that all this time and energy spent inspecting others' work should have convinced these very same people long ago that "errors are inevitable." The following is a discussion about the causes and consequences of errors, the concept of acceptable level of errors, and the rationale for quality control inspection programs.

Consequential Versus Inconsequential Errors

A consequential error is one that precludes success—say, gives a reader the wrong information or prevents a Web user from locating a desired URL. An inconsequential error is one that detracts from the appearance or aesthetics of a product (book, record, brochure) but does not prevent success—a misspelled publisher's name, such as McGras-Hill instead of McGraw-Hill is an example.

The consequence of errors should be taken into consideration when designing an inspection program. To take a typical example, what should we do with purchase orders that are prepared for distribution to vendors? It is common for a staff member to inspect the data before it is transmitted to the vendor. But several questions might be asked before we decide what to do. These include: Is an inspection warranted at all? If so, why? What kind of errors should we be looking for? Should the goal be an attempt to generate error-free purchase orders, or will the inspection be limited to identifying errors that might prevent or delay the vendor from supplying the proper item, or cause money to be encumbered from the wrong fund? Inspections should be designed to focus on only those errors that will delay or prevent a book's acquisition. These are what I would term the "errors of consequence."

Errors and Their Causes

Errors occur for a variety of reasons. Probably the chief cause of errors is inadequate training and/or poor day-to-day supervision. New employees should have ample opportunities to learn their jobs. Workers who are only half-sure of what is expected of them, or are provided with inadequate guidance are bound to allow errors to pass undetected. Staff who are responsible for training need to be sure that adequate training materials are provided, and that as part of the training, new staff receive comprehensive explanations of how to perform the relevant procedures along with explanations as to why each task is performed, and what types of errors to guard against. For example, why it is so important to have the correct RFID tag adhered to a book.

Some problems can be traced to people who are unqualified for their positions—and this includes both over- and underqualified workers. Staff who are simply over their heads will make errors because they don't know better, but staff who are overqualified are also likely to make errors because they become disinterested or outright bored. Obviously better interviewing and other selection techniques will minimize improper placement of staff.

A substandard working environment, such as poorly lighted, poorly ventilated, or overcrowded offices, can also contribute to the number of errors that occur. Staff workers who are not comfortable or feel cramped will find it more difficult to concentrate on their work.

Acceptable Levels of Error

What is an acceptable level of error? We have already underscored the point that a zero level of errors is unattainable, but what level is acceptable—1 percent? 5 percent? or 10 percent? It is probably true that 1 percent in most cases will be difficult to attain, and more than likely most people would agree that 10 percent is too high.

Most of the studies that I'm familiar with suggest that the occurrence of processing and filing errors in technical services prior to the integrated system era began ran between 2 and 4 percent. Since the adoption of sophisticated integrated systems, many types of processing errors that formerly plagued technical service operations are now under manageable control. That is not to say these errors have completely disappeared or that new types of errors haven't been introduced. Errors will be found, but the level of errors associated with most integrated system working environments is within acceptable limits.

There will be occasions when every effort should be made to keep the number of errors to an irreducible minimum. A couple of illustrations immediately come to mind. The first deals with the scanning or digitizing of books from a library's collection. One should strive to ensure that the book and its bibliographical record are correct, and the book won't be lost after it is digitized. A second illustration, as already cited, is being sure that the correct RFID tag is adhered to a new title.

Reference services create a more problematical area of concern when the question of acceptable level of errors is raised. First of all, what is an error? Hernon and McClure once asserted that reference librarians were achieving only 55 percent accuracy, but many researchers subsequently challenged this level of error, pointing out that their methodology was, if not flawed, seriously limited. Nevertheless, Hernon and McClure raised some legitimate issues, ones that continue to be debated in this era of virtual reference.[9]

For all of its operations and activities, each library will have to decide for itself what are acceptable levels of error. While I don't believe it is appropriate for me to suggest specific thresholds, I feel comfortable in saying that eliminating all errors is impractical, and I will leave it to each library to establish its own threshold of what is acceptable. Each will also have to decide what is an "error" and each library will have to decide what steps it will take in order to achieve levels it judges to be acceptable.

Quality Inspection Programs

There will be occasions when a library is probably justified in spending the time and money to ensure the quality of a product or service. One example would be answers to questions provided via a virtual reference service. It is possible to use the transcripts of questions along with staff input to enable a library to develop what it judges to be an acceptable level of performance. A second example might be cataloging in a special collections library that is accessed by scholars worldwide. Another example might involve the digitization of a unique special collection. Inspection programs should be undertaken only after careful thought that weighs costs against benefits.

An inspection process can take one of two forms. First, all work can be reviewed, in which case all that remains is to decide which errors will be tolerated, and which will be rejected. The second form involves the introduction of acceptance sampling where only a sample of the work is inspected. If the sample meets the predetermined criteria for acceptance, the quality of the work is assumed to be acceptable, If not, enlarging the sample makes sense for additional checks.[10] Lugg and Boese make a persuasive case that libraries could reduce the costs of cataloging while also increasing productivity by adopting a program of acceptance sampling. They discuss in some detail how a program of sampling could be undertaken. The techniques for developing an acceptable-sampling program are discussed thoroughly in many management texts.[11]

Providing Constructive Feedback

There are occasions when complaints about the quality of work arise and follow-up action is warranted. To cite a relevant illustration I'll return to an earlier story. A few years ago I was working with a large university library that was operating a thriving interlibrary lending business. One of the irritating problems the staff encountered was not being able to locate books in the stacks, even though records indicated they should have been available. The problem was sufficiently aggravating that the interlibrary loan supervisor adopted a two-cycle process that required a second person to follow up the first search. Data revealed that the overall success rate of the second search did justify the additional effort. But no one seemed to recognize that the follow-up process also increased overall costs, and no one seemed to realize that the need for the follow-up also suggested that student assistant staff might require additional training to improve their ability to retrieve books. The interlibrary supervisor did recognize that part of the problem was due to student assistants in the circulation department who were responsible for reshelving returned books.

The interlibrary supervisor provided feedback to the circulation supervisor on several occasions but with no apparent effect. That was the reason why the follow-up process had been introduced. Finally the division chiefs of the two units were given the feedback about the situation, and as a result, data were collected and analyzed. What was quickly discovered was that the problem was more complicated than had first been believed. It was certainly true that the student assistant staff in both interlibrary lending and circulation required more training, but it also became apparent that part of the problem was because some shelves were so tightly jammed with books. Patrons were also not able to shelve books, in fact they were also contributing to the overall problem of misshelved books by squeezing books back into the wrong locations.

The problems encountered by the ILL staff should have served as a red flag that something was wrong. These problems could have been addressed more promptly if the interlibrary lending supervisor had provided feedback about the problem to her supervisor instead of going directly to the circulation supervisor. She didn't realize that the circulation supervisor would interpret her feedback as unwanted, and more importantly, unwarranted criticism thus prompting a defensive response.

Here was a case where timely and dispassionate feedback would have been very helpful. While locating and reshelving books are simple procedures, because they impacted the quality of public services as well as the lending processes, these related activities warranted some level of quality control.

The important principle to keep in mind is that if an activity merits a formal inspection, it also merits a formal, dispassionate feedback loop so that constructive feedback can flow unimpeded. In this case additional training was required. But if the problems had persisted, one might have been tempted to conclude that some staff were miscast, and should be reassigned to other duties.

While I have discussed the topic of feedback in the context of discovering errors and taking corrective action, it is the case that providing feedback can also lead to kudos for staff who are performing above and beyond expectations.

Final Thoughts

Whenever new activities are introduced, a host of implementation issues need to be tackled. This is the critical period. One wants the introduction of a new workflow or service, or a transition from one system to another to go smoothly. Some implementations do proceed smoothly, but as I implied at the outset of this chapter, the road to successful implementation is unfortunately littered with near misses and outright failures. I believe the most important ingredients for successful implementation efforts are not technical considerations, but rather the quality of an organization's leadership and the culture it inspires. Does the culture encourage change and experimentation, or is it a rule-bound organization that discourages disagreement and staff dialogue? If the culture is reflected by the latter description, the road to successful implementation of new activities is likely to be rocky.

Notes

1. The Standards for College Libraries issued by the ACRL in 2000 is one source of useful guidelines. Nelson and Fernekes also issued a workbook designed to help college librarians apply the new standards. *See* William Neal Nelson and Robert W. Fernekes, *Standards and Assessment for Academic Libraries: a Workbook* (Chicago: Association of College and Research Libraries, 2002). LibQUAL+™ is another example of an evaluation methodology that is currently available through the Association of Research Libraries. It is a methodology for obtaining feedback from patrons regarding various dimensions of library service. More information about various evaluation strategies can be found at the Web sites of ALA, PLA, ACRL, and ARL.

2. Lawrence L. Lippitt, *Preferred Futuring: Envision the Future You Want and Unleash the Energy to Get There* (San Francisco: Berrett-Koehler Publishers, 1998), 186-89.

3. Frank Lundy, "Dual Assignment: Cataloging and Reference: a Four-Year Review of Cataloging in the Divisional Plan," *Library Resources & Technical Services* 3 (Summer 1959): 167-88.

4. The important topic of training staff to work as productive team members merits special attention. *See* Jerry Spiegel and Cresencio Torres, *Manager's Official Guide to Team Working* (San Diego: Pfeiffer, 1994). Pfeiffer & Co. is a publisher that offers a wide-ranging list of books and practical manuals on subjects such as training, team building, organizational development, facilitating, cross training, and change management. http://www.pfeiffer.com/WileyCDA (27 May 2007).

5. For an interesting account of how support staff were cross trained to provide service at a new location that had been the sole province of reference librarians at a central reference desk, *see* Frada

Mozenter, Bridgette T. Sanders, and Carol Bellamy, "Perspective on Cross-Training Public Service Staff in the Electronic Age: I Have to Learn to Do What?" *The Journal of Academic Librarianship* 28, no. 4 (November 2003): 399-404.

6. Teri R. Switzer, "Ergonomics: An Ounce of Prevention," *C&RL News* (May 1995): 314.

7. The Kroemers have produced a comprehensive treatment of the topic of ergonomics. Among the chapters is one devoted entirely to office computer workstations. There are also extensive discussions on illumination, noise, esthetics, and thermal comfort. The depth and scope of this book is really more than most librarians, even a library space planner, will require but its range of topics provides useful insights as to what is considered under the umbrella of ergonomics. *See* Karl Kroemer, Henike Kroemer, and Katrin Kroemer-Elbert, *Ergonomics: How to Design for Ease and Efficiency* (Englewood Cliffs, N.J.: Prentice-Hall, 1994). Demarco and Lister's book really isn't about ergonomics in the traditional sense, although the authors do include a great deal of practical information and advice. What I found most useful were the authors' efforts to show what can be done to create a healthy, work-conducive environment. While not aimed at librarians, the advice certainly applies to libraries. *See* Tom Demarco, and Timothy Lister, *Peopleware: Productive Projects and Teams.* 2nd ed. (New York: Dorset House, 1999).

8. A great deal of practical information on regulations as well as useful advice on office ergonomics can be found at www.osha.gov (27 May 2007).

9. Andrew Hubbertz does an excellent job of explaining why studies of reference using unobtrusive methods are rarely accurate. *See* Andrew Hubbertz, "The Design and Interpretation of Unobtrusive Evaluations," *Reference & User Services Quarterly* 44, no. 4 (Summer 2005): 327-35.

10. Ruth Lugg and Kent C. Boese, "Cataloging: How to Take a Business Approach," *The Bottom Line* 17, no. 2 (2004): 50.

11. There are numerous texts on the subject of acceptance sampling and quality control. See Edward G. Schilling and Dean V. Neubauer, *Acceptance Sampling in Quality Control.* 2nd ed. (New York: M. Dekker, 2008).

Chapter Eighteen

Managing Organizational Change

Scope note: This chapter focuses on how individuals and groups of staff employees are likely to react to the prospect of change. It also touches on big picture issues relating to organizational change that should be of particular interest to administrators and supervisors. The chapter then introduces the topic of diffusion of innovation and how targeted groups of potential patrons are likely to react when a new or streamlined system or service is introduced. Finally, the chapter offers some tips designed to aid administrators who wish to build a base of support among staff for organizational change.

Introduction

The traditional approach to introducing new systems, workflows, or even a new service is first to bring in a consultant who is asked to identify the problems, and make recommendations about what needs to be done. Based on the recommendations of the consultant, management is likely to begin telling staff how to do their jobs differently, and why the new methods are superior to the old methods.

Then after the implementation process begins, management is likely to find itself devoting considerable time, energy, and money trying to overcome the resistance that their unilateral actions have provoked trying to fit someone else's solution to their situation. No matter how carefully a new activity is planned, as noted in the last chapter, once the implementation process begins, performance and expectations for the new activity are apt to fall short of anticipated objectives, particularly if the library as a whole is not prepared to accept or support the changes.

There is no doubt in my mind that the most important responsibility when introducing new activities is managing the change process, and paying particular attention to how the changes will impact staff. It generally makes no difference whether the activity, i.e., procedure, process, workflow, or system, affects only a few staff and jobs or many staff and jobs, there is bound to be a wide range of reactions. Some staff will embrace the changes, others will question the need, while still others may object and be inclined to find ways to resist the new way of doing things. There are many reasons why staff resist change. For example, they don't understand the purpose of the proposed change and they don't trust management, they are afraid that their status and power will be adversely affected, or they are afraid that they may not be as competent in the new situation as they are at present. Resistance to change is a very normal reaction of staff. Some resistance should always be anticipated.

One shouldn't be too quick to point a finger at others who seem to be objecting or resisting a proposed change. It makes more sense to identify the reasons why a person is resistant, and work with the resister to see if there aren't ways to persuade him/her to "get on board." One won't discover the reason for the objections unless an effort is made to understand why a person objects. I have found a better approach to dealing with staff resistance is not seeking ways to "overcome" the resistance, but in finding ways to "manage" the resistance.

Individuals Reacting to the Prospect of Change

Several years ago I listened to a group of staff griping about the way management was treating them. Their view was that they and their colleagues were being "punished" for being successful. The focus of their gripes was the proposed changes in the way the reference desk was going to be staffed. The rub was that more support staff would be placed on the front line. I'm not sure I agreed with the complainers, but because perceptions can be a person's reality, I suggested to management that they ought to pay greater attention to the concerns of the objecting staff. Although we might not want to acknowledge this reality, it is almost always true that the initial thought of staff, when confronted with the prospect of change, is "what is in it for me?" Such reactions might be interpreted as self-centered or self-serving, and maybe they are, but such reactions also reflect reality. This reaction is not limited to library staff. Everyone who is confronted with the prospect of change will immediately try to figure out how they will be affected.

No matter how extensively staff participate in planning for the introduction of a new activity, if they aren't 100 percent sure how the new activity will affect their status, they will feel concerns about their future. They will want to know if anyone will be displaced and, if so, who it will be? They will also want to know if management has made provisions to transfer and train displaced staff to assume new job responsibilities. The best approach for managers is to be straightforward, and definitely avoid obfuscating the impact of changes. Sooner or later the real impact will become apparent to all.

Fear and suspicion of the unknown are the enemies of proposed organizational changes. If an information vacuum exists, the grapevine will put staff on guard, and if suspicions are allowed to fester, management will have a hard time regaining credibility among affected staff. Human beings exhibit incredible creativity in developing new and subtle forms of resistance when the old ones don't work any more.

Management needs to be sensitive to the concerns of staff. If concerns are ignored, sooner or later staff may begin to undermine or even actively sabotage the new activity. This sabotage may show up in subtle ways, such as reduced effort and energy, sloppy work, complaining to fellow workers, tardiness, missed days, and/or a general lack of commitment. All of these efforts may be designed to "prove" that the new way doesn't work.

Let's examine in greater detail some of the behavioral characteristics that give rise to many forms of resistance. Various forms of resistance can be traced to relatively few causes.

- The perception or reality that one's job may be threatened or eliminated will inevitably raise serious anxieties among employees. This shouldn't come as a surprise during this era when technology is transforming a significant percentage of library jobs. A great many jobs are being eliminated or drastically altered. Whenever a job is likely to be eliminated, management should make every effort to assure employees that they will be retrained and reassigned to suitable positions. Whenever possible the new posts should provide for career growth.

- The fear that inadequate job performance might be exposed can be the real reason for expressed objections to a new activity. The same reactions can be generated when staff learn that their jobs may be analyzed. They secretly harbor fears that the analysis will reveal inadequate performance, which in turn could lead to lowered performance ratings, lowered peer esteem, reassignment, or, in the extreme case, dismissal.

- Loss of status, whether real or perceived, is another cause of resistance. The question is a particularly sensitive one among professional librarians, who have been sensitive about status for years, but such concerns are not confined to professionals only; they pervade the staff from top to bottom. Management needs to be aware that job and/or peer status are real concerns that must be dealt with when new jobs are being designed.

- Habit can be as powerful a source of resistance *to* change as is the fear *of* change. It is human nature to prefer the status quo. It is much easier to function in an environment in which we are familiar and comfortable. This is far from an unmitigated evil, for such behavioral patterns ensure a more orderly, predictable society than might otherwise be the case. However, this natural tendency does increase the complexity of carrying on management studies and introducing change.

- Clashes of values can produce overt or covert resistance. One common library example is how individual reference librarians reacted when various forms of reference services to patrons who were remote from the reference desk began to replace traditional face-to-face reference service.

No one is exempt from resisting something new. As Sara Fine points out, we are all potential resisters to change. She has a nice way of making this point:

> We must never be smug about being progressive. Those of us who are today the staunchest supporters of a proposed change may very well be future front-line

resistance fighters as new inventions make the present obsolete. It is inevitable that time will erode the utility of even the most admirable innovation and that the next generation of change will once again threaten our equilibrium. We might even hypothesize that the more committed we are to a current change, the more likely we are to resist its replacement. We are all — without exception — potential resisters to change.[1]

Again, no one is immune to this. I can recall objecting rather vocally when it was proposed that a document delivery system I had personally implemented was to be eliminated because so many documents could now be retrieved directly over the Web. In the end it didn't take much effort to persuade me that my "baby" was now obsolete, but it was a hard reality for me to swallow.

Strategies for Introducing New Activities

It is my personal belief that the most effective way to introduce a new system or service is to have it recommended in a strategic plan in which staff are deeply involved. Strategic plans prepared by consultants or management without meaningful staff involvement are not as likely to generate enthusiasm as plans in which staff are directly involved. A top-down approach will work sometimes, but the selling job will be tougher.

Another strategy for introducing change is to mount a pilot project to demonstrate the value of a new activity. This is a fairly common approach. At the time database searching and campus document delivery services were first gaining popularity, and even more recently when chat reference services were becoming popular, staff and/or faculty objections were commonly voiced. When such situations arise a pilot project to test the waters often reduces the risk of failure.

Still another strategy, particularly when staff members of a key unit object to a new activity, is to create a separate unit to provide the service. I can recall many libraries establishing special database searching units because reference librarians objected to the new service. I remember creating a separate document delivery unit because my interlibrary lending staff objected to a campus delivery service. Eventually such separate units often can be disbanded as the objectors realize that they have made a mistake and want to be part of a successful service. More recently we have seen a similar trend as chat services invaded traditional references activities, and some reference librarians objected to this new approach. In each case the key is to identify library staff who are committed to the new idea. Make the resources available and unleash these individuals, or as a former boss expressed it: "Let them do their thing and get out of their way."

Offering an incentive is another way to launch a new activity or to stimulate change. An incentive might take one of several forms. It could be a promotion or a salary increase, public recognition, or granting additional funds to a unit. Any one or more of these approaches might get the job done. I recall once the provost with whom I was working suggested that we needed a way to "bribe" faculty in order to introduce a new service. His solution was to provide some incentive subsidies to key departments. There have been several occasions when I found myself suggesting to an academic administrator that if he/she wanted to see change in the library that seed money could serve as a powerful incentive.

Roles of Administrators and Supervisors

Administrators at all levels play a crucial role in implementing organizational change. Implementation plans are less likely to be successful if administrators and supervisors are not receptive and supportive of the proposed changes. Lingering issues and questions should be resolved before the implementation phase begins. Administrators who will be responsible for the new system or service should feel comfortable with it. Procedure manuals that describe the new activities or workflows should provide instructions on what to do under all foreseeable circumstances. The manuals may consist of written narratives, flow process charts, flow charts, or other tools that illustrate the relevant activities. Some organizations use such training aids as video clips or PowerPoint presentations to ensure that a training program appropriate to the situation is available.

Supervisors must be knowledgeable about and supportive of the change before they undertake an implementation process, and especially before they begin to supervise the employees who will be responsible for the day-to-day activities. Supervisors and middle managers have special responsibilities which include:

- Buying into the culture of the new system or process. Lip service support is not acceptable behavior.

- Being willing to tackle tough decisions even if it involves confrontations with others.

- Being committed to the new ways. This particularly refers to supervisors who have been recently appointed or hired.

- Being willing to work with staff who are inflexible and territorial and who don't want to let go of the old ways.

- Supervisors being actively involved in fixing problems, not simply waiting for the boss or his/her consultant to fix things, and if these changes don't work, sitting back and complaining and becoming more cynical.

I should add that middle managers who are effective in the ways suggested should be rewarded for their effort, risk-taking, and contributions.

There are also some special issues associated with organizational change that supervisors need to keep in mind. Particularly important are the existing culture of the library and the political climate in which the library operates. These factors will always affect the course of change. Administrators and supervisors bear a special responsibility to be sensitive to these factors because they are the ones most likely to understand the big picture issues. Most front line staff workers will be focused on their immediate jobs; the big picture issues are of less concern to them unless they are confronted with their consequences.

Political Climate

Management should always take the temperature of the political climate before launching a change that will impact the library's stakeholders.[2] In recent years numerous examples that dramatically illustrate the dangers of underestimating how stakeholders will react have been reported in the literature. Consider the following illustrations:

- A university library digitizes old newspapers that have become extremely fragile. This decision makes a lot of sense, but the library then decides to discard the originals once they have been digitized. When the history faculty learn about this decision they go ballistic.

- A public library decides to weed its collections to make space for additional computers. This seemed to be a no-brainer decision since computers have become so popular, but several influential members of the Friends strenuously object to reducing the book collections. Their objections provoked an outcry in the community.

- A university library decides to consolidate a group of branch libraries in order to save money and improve services by consolidating staff resources, but the changes are made while the faculty are gone for the summer and without their knowledge. When the faculty return from vacations they are incensed because they preferred their small branch libraries to the new divisional library that is not conveniently situated near their offices.

- A college library decides to outsource a large portion of its cataloging. The catalogers object and convince reference librarians that outsourced acquisitions will be poorly cataloged. Soon thereafter management is confronted with a mini-staff rebellion.

- A public library decides to streamline its book selection process by outsourcing some of its selection decisions to a commercial vendor. While the process is streamlined, many staff object, and they make their objections known to library patrons and key politicians. The library is eventually forced to back away from its outsourcing decision.

With all of these illustrations, I am sure the actual situations were much more complicated and contentious than was recorded in the literature. In one or two of the cases I have cited, the rancor and vindictiveness were so intense that one editor was inspired to coin the phrase "guerilla librarianship." In all of these illustrations opponents of the changes leveled charges of mismanagement and myopic visions, while supporters of the embattled administrators continued to argue. These decision makers were visionaries who became victims due in part to bad luck, poor timing, power politics, and to some degree, insubordinate staff.

In each of these cases campus or community politics played a major role. One might wonder to what extent the major stakeholder groups, e.g., staff, patrons of branches, public officials, friends of libraries, etc. were consulted in advance, and if consulted, how many supported the proposed changes? As I mentioned previously, I was personally involved in a situation where a faculty advisory committee officially voted to support a project to move little-used periodical issues into a storage area, but when a few of their faculty colleagues objected to the transfer, they quickly rescinded their support. Unfortunately the volumes had already been transferred to the new location. Clearly I thought I had taken the necessary precautions, but I got blindsided because I had failed to involve a few key stakeholders, which in this case were fewer than five very influential faculty members from History, English, and Classics. It was a lesson that I long remembered.[3]

The message here is that politics is always an important dimension of organizational change. Too often we neglect to fully take into account how affected stakeholder groups are likely to react to a proposed change. It is obviously important that key stakeholders be identified. Who are the people who will view themselves as winners and who will feel they are losers? Administrators not only have to gauge the reactions of various stakeholder groups, but they have to evaluate objectively whether any of the potential objectors have the power to block a change. It is better to know in advance who will be your adversaries and who will challenge a change. Can the adversaries stop you? Can you persuade them to change their minds? If the answer to the second question is yes, you are obviously home free. If the answer is no, then it might be better to decide realistically whether the group or individual has the power to block the change. If they have that power, it may be better to return to square one than to fail. If not, then move ahead and be prepared to deal with the opposition that can be anticipated.

There is also likely to be a group of stakeholders who will question a proposed change, but not necessarily openly oppose it. These stakeholders may be fence sitters who can be convinced to mute their objections or even become supporters of the change. But in order to be persuasive, it will be necessary to work hard to convince them that the change is for the better—maybe they will personally benefit in the long run. Remember years ago, how many people challenged a library's decision to replace their card catalogs and how many objectors eventually became supporters.

So far I haven't said much about the role of staff in the political process. Staff shouldn't be ignored. As noted in a couple of the illustrations, it was staff that helped to rile up faculty and community officials with their "guerilla librarianship." I really don't know whether these staff members were justified, but they made their objections heard, and as a result, these staff objectors made an impact.

The lesson here is to bring staff into the process early on, listen to their concerns and objections. Management may not be able to persuade staff or to squelch their objections, but they will have a better sense of what to expect. Of course staff also have a responsibility to their libraries, and most changes proposed, even those cited above, were justified and if implemented would have led to better service and a better utilization of scare dollar resources.

Organizational Culture and Core Values

Most organizations focus their time, energy, and resources on activities such as strategic planning, improving processes, increasing production, resolving staffing issues, and improving leadership, but paradoxically it is often an organization's culture that is a better predictor of how well an organization will perform, and how its staff are likely to behave, than the customary organizational activities.

Organizational culture can be described as the set of beliefs and expectations shared by members of an organization. An organization's culture reflects what the staff really believes is important, not just what it says is important; that is, the difference between lip service and the values that are really embraced. The culture of an organization has an enormous influence on whether change is likely to occur and be successful. The power of culture was starkly underscored in the aftermath of the shuttle Columbia disaster. Those investigating the disaster brought to light the fact that the Columbia was launched over the objections of several engineers who had serious concerns about the foam that protected the shuttle. Nine requests to delay the flight were ignored, or outrightly rejected by management. But the culture of NASA prevailed; no delays were to be tolerated. Such a culture within NASA seems to persist even today.

Of course, the impact of core values and organizational culture isn't nearly so dramatic in libraries as it was with NASA, but nonetheless, clashes of values within a library can prove to be a major obstacle to efforts to introduce new activities. My first encounter with the power of culture and values occurred many years ago when the idea of using shared cataloging copy was first introduced. I quickly realized that a few senior catalogers thought this was a very bad idea. In fact, some catalogers were openly hostile to the idea. They argued that the acceptance of cataloging by other libraries would produce a degraded local catalog. Of course we pressed forward with the new policy in spite of the objections. What we didn't fully appreciate was the vehemence of the objections. We didn't realize that several catalogers proceeded to work quietly to undermine the policy. They found reasons to introduce "local refinements." Thus, the shared copy was not accepted without a thorough review by an experienced cataloger. Of course this action had the effect of reducing the benefits that had been originally envisioned. I believe that some catalogers felt almost betrayed by the administration. The bottom line was that a sharp clash of values had undermined the program of accepting the cataloging of other libraries.

But I shouldn't be singling out catalogers; there are many other illustrations that can be highlighted. Here are a few others with which I am familiar:

- Branch librarians in a public library system strenuously object when they learn that the library's administration has decided to centralize book selection into the main library. The rationale for the change is that the new process would reduce costs and get books into the library more quickly. Library records had revealed that most branches ordered the same books, but since they didn't order them at the same time, multiple order placements and processing were necessary. Branch librarians were invited to participate in the process, but that meant traveling to the central library. The branch librarians were adamant that they were the only ones who knew the needs and desires of their patrons. The culture of local decision making was very strong.

- Reference librarians allege that the quality of services will be undermined when they learn that support staff and student assistants will now be assigned to the reference desk. Of course, arguments about what level of staff should be assigned to the reference desk have been with us for several generations. The most recent version of this debate is who is best qualified to answer questions received via chat reference systems. As previously noted, some librarians insist that professionals must handle such questions, whereas, other libraries make liberal use of support staff. Objections are most likely to surface in libraries that have had a long tradition of professionals manning the reference desk.

- The attempts to merge libraries with computing centers represents another classic example of how differences in organizational culture and values can impede, if not entirely block, organizational changes. To academic administrators it seemed quite logical to bring together two organizations that dealt with information. In the back of their minds they envisioned such mergers as generating dollar savings by combining overlapping operations such as reference and help desks. Boy, were these officials in for a surprise. Most of these attempted mergers were less successful than anticipated or not successful at all. The greatest obstacle proved to be differences in culture and value systems of the two organizations. For example, librarians tended to be less receptive to change than computing center staff; librarians were much more service oriented than their counterparts from the computing center; librarians placed greater emphasis on educational credentials; computing center staff were more focused on skills. Probably the greatest barrier of all was that computing center staff, often with less impressive educational credentials, made a great deal more money than librarians. All in all this was a recipe for disaster, and as time passed, it became increasingly clear that most of these "shotgun" mergers were not going to be successful.

When exploring the topic of core values, one of the challenges is to find ways to tease apart the deeply held beliefs from behaviors that are triggered by self-interest motives, e.g., a reference librarian who strenuously objects to support staff being assigned to the reference desk. Ostensibly these objections are based on a set of beliefs that services really will be degraded, but although unstated, it is also possible that these objections are *really* based on fears about job security and status. At worst the objector is fearful that his job might be phased out, or at the very least, he will be reassigned to a job that will require a new set of skills.

Managing objections based on core values can be especially difficult. I have found that there are no magic bullets when dealing with situations in which the objections could be traced to real or imagined clashes in core values. It is extremely hard for some staff to shed values that are genuinely deeply held. I've known reference librarians to resign when support staff were assigned to the desk. I've also known catalogers whose greatest job satisfaction is, "the perfectly cataloged book." Such individuals will not be pleased to learn that the source of their satisfaction is going to be lost because of changes in their jobs.

While there are no magic bullets, I have also learned that getting such objections out on the table so that they can be discussed is an important first step. Sometimes acknowledging the contributions of a person, along with explaining once again the rationale for the proposed changes, helps. Occasionally other staff members who are more supportive of the proposed changes may be able to persuade an objector that the need for change is so great that it is time to revise his or her traditional value system. Think back at the number of catalogers who learned to accept cataloging copy produced in a network environment, or the reference librarians who became skillful at handling chat reference transactions. It can happen.

How Groups of Staff React to the Prospect of Change

A few years ago, Myers-Briggs Type Indicators (MBTI®) tests were particularly popular among librarians. In fact, it wasn't uncommon for people to exchange their types. I was introduced to Myers-Briggs while a student in an organizational management program. As those familiar with Myers-Briggs will recall, the MBTI® was developed in the 1940s by the mother-daughter team of Katharine C. Briggs and Isabel Briggs Myers.[4] Their work built on the theories of Swiss psychotherapist Carl Jung from the 1920s. Today it is one of the most widely used psychological tools in the world.

The MBTI® reflects individual preferences for energy, information gathering, decision making, and lifestyle. An important point to keep in mind is that the "key" word is preferences. MBTI® tests have been used to predict behavior of present or potential employees. It has been used as a coaching tool, to assist staff in career development, management training, and organization development. It is important to avoid stereotyping individuals based on their MBTI® type. Remember that MBTI® indicates preferences, *not* predicted behaviors. People can exhibit behaviors that are not based on their actual preferences to adapt to specific situations. For example, ask a person to write his signature and he will automatically select the hand he is accustomed to using. After he has signed using his preferred hand, ask him to sign his name using the other hand. The second effort will be slower, and more awkward, but nevertheless, he will be able to complete the assignment, thus exhibiting a behavior that is not his preference.[5]

The aspect of MBTI® that I find particularly interesting in connection with this book is its use to explain the behavior of groups when they are confronted with the prospect of change. Hirsh suggests that each person's MBTI® type falls into one of the four Quadrants of the type table IS, ES, IN, or EN.[6] (See Figure 18-1.) She points out that the Quadrant lens is a helpful tool in assessing how a team is likely to act when change is in the offing.

I realize that I'm in danger of oversimplifying the situation; nevertheless, I believe one can make some useful interpretations about teams when dealing with change or culture issues.

ISs

Hirsh says that ISs "want to be careful and mindful of details." I've found that a team dominated by ISs will be the group most likely to focus on the traditions of an organization. One might hear statements such as "If it's worked before, it should work again." It is the ISs who are most likely to be labeled as "resisters."

IS TJ	IS FJ	IN FJ	IN TJ
IS TP	IS FP	IN FP	IN TP
ES TP	ES FP	EN FP	EN TP
ES TJ	ES FJ	EN FJ	EN TJ

Figure 18-1 MBTI® Team Member Types: Quadrant lens.

ESs

Hirsh says that ESs "want to see and discuss the practical results." I would add that ESs are less likely to want change than the ENs, but are more willing to change than are the ISs. This is a group that also may include those who say "please don't bother me with details, let's just do it." Later these same people are apt to say "you didn't consult me."

INs

Hirsh says that INs "want to work with ideas and concepts." I've found that INs are much more willing to change than the ISs. Some INs are also good at "talking the talk of change" but continually ask for more data before acting.

ENs

Hirsh says that ENs "want to maximize variety." They are likely to say that they love change. They constantly look for variety and new ways of doing things. They are oriented toward the outside world.

Maureen Sullivan, an experienced library management consultant, has noted that MBTI® can also make a big difference in the process of forming and developing a team. I couldn't agree more with her. Sullivan also points out that the use of MBTI® techniques can lead to the identification of problem areas for a newly formed team and its work. She also injects one note of caution, and again I agree with her. She stresses that MBTI® is most effectively used in team building when it is facilitated by a person who is experienced and knowledgeable about team building and group development.[7]

To me there are several points worth keeping in mind. First, if a team is composed of too many people of a single type, it is likely that the dominant behavior of the group will conform to that MBTI® type. For example, one would be wise to avoid appointing too many ISs to a committee asked to explore the new opportunities in reference work. Second, if a team is composed of a mix of MBTI® types, it is my belief that the chances of success are heightened. And third, and most important, groups will react differently to the prospect of change. Particular care should be taken when teams will be involved in planning for or in implementing new activities. But also keep in mind that all team types have their strengths and weaknesses.

New Services: How Patrons Are Likely to React

"We will be overwhelmed!" "We will need additional staff!" "We won't be able to keep up with our regular duties!" These are all typical reactions whenever a new, innovative service or activity is proposed. I encountered these reactions from staff when we first introduced a campus-wide document delivery program. I could understand the staff's reaction because we would be allowing faculty to simply telephone the library to submit their request, and we were committed to respond. Such a service was going to be a great convenience to faculty. As it turned out, we weren't overwhelmed, although demand for the service grew rapidly as the service proved to be very popular among faculty users. Great service, but the question remains: why weren't we initially overwhelmed?

A similar situation arose when libraries first introduced chat reference services. Some reference staff expressed great angst that they would be overwhelmed, but in fact most libraries weren't overwhelmed initially. Instead what we began hearing were concerns that the demand for the service wasn't sufficient to justify the added costs. But as time passed, the demand for the service grew, and it wasn't long before some libraries began to refer to chat reference services as "basic" services. Again, the question remains: an innovative service, why weren't those libraries overwhelmed right from the outset?

The explanation can be found in the work of Everett Rogers who has thoroughly researched how innovations are diffused throughout social groups. Rogers writes, "'diffusion' is the process by which an innovation spreads. The diffusion process is the dispersion of a new idea from its source of invention or creation to its ultimate users or adopters."[8] What Rogers found is that not every person adopts a new idea at the same rate. Some people, whom he termed "Innovators," are venturesome and are eager to try new ideas. This is the small group that will be the first to try something new.

This group is followed by what he terms the "Early Adopters." Early Adopters often include the opinion leaders in a social group. This can be a particularly important group. In an academic setting this group might include the campus faculty opinion leaders. Rogers notes that this is the group to which other potential adopters look to for advice or information about the innovation. The Early Adopter is the "man to check with" before sampling the new service.

Rogers says that the "Early Majority" adopters are a little ahead of the diffusion curve. They make the commitment before the next identified category, the "Late Majority." Finally, there are the "Laggards" who are the last to adopt an innovation. Rogers says that their point of reference is the past, and their decisions are usually made in terms of what has been done in past years.

Figure 18-2 symbolizes the diffusion and adoption of a new library service. The figure also symbolizes the degree to which the potential population adopts a particular innovation, that is, the rate of market penetration. The rate of penetration rarely if ever achieves 100 percent. There will always be potential custom-

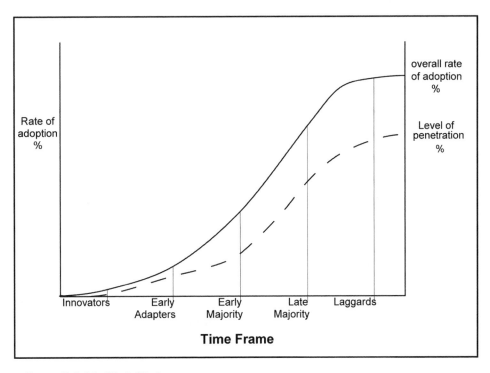

Figure 18-2 Modified diffusion curve.

ers or patrons who, for various reasons, never adopt the innovation. Maybe they never learned of its existence, or if they heard about it, they decided that they didn't need it. There is also the category of users who try a new innovation, and for one reason or another, decide not to use it again in the future. They in effect have rejected the innovation.

Another reason why a new service is not likely to be initially overwhelmed is that not every potential patron will learn about the service at the same time. New products, no matter how desirable, must be marketed and advertised. There is no difference between a new product and a new library service. One has to get the word out to potential customers. This is exactly what happened with virtual reference services. Once the Innovators had tried the service and word began to spread, Early Adopters learned about the new service and were willing to try it, and the demand for the service began to grow. Thus the rate of innovation diffusion can be accelerated by skillful marketing campaigns. What one is trying to achieve is what Rogers terms the "critical mass." (See Figure 18-2.)[9] This is the point at which "a sufficient number of individuals in a system have adopted the innovation so that the innovation's further rate of adoption becomes self-sustaining."

I introduced innovation diffusion in this chapter on change because those planning to introduce new workflows and services should keep firmly in mind that the principles of innovation diffusion will apply, and as a result, they should plan accordingly. Understanding the principles of innovation diffusion will help smooth the introduction of organizational changes.

Building a Base of Support for Change

Managers are likely to view a proposed organizational change quite differently than front-line professional and support staff. As noted earlier, managers are in a better position to see the big picture issues. They are like the officers who stand watch on the bridge of a large cruise ship. They can see out to the horizon. The crew in the engine room, however, has no outside view. They have to be kept informed about the "bigger picture." The same is true with a library's staff who aren't in a position to be aware of the bigger picture issues.

Managers should be more familiar with trends and developments that are driving the profession or are impacting the campus or community. Managers should also have a more realistic sense of the short- and long-term budget prospects. Too often staff members have unrealistic expectations of what is budgetarily possible. In the absence of information to the contrary, this should be no surprise. Managers need to make every effort to keep staff at all levels fully informed about what is going on outside the library.

Nevertheless, when a new activity that will affect staff is in the works, management should take time to consider how staff members are likely to react when they learn about the proposed changes. As previously mentioned, and it bears repeating, most staff will be asking themselves questions such as: How will the changes affect me? What is in it for me? How will my job be affected? Will I lose status? Are these changes a subtle way of saying that I wasn't doing a good job? Staff members' reactions to such questions will have a bearing on how they react to the proposed changes.

If management fails to create an environment that persuades staff that the proposed changes will result in a better situation for not only the organization, but the staff itself, the chances of securing a staff buy-in for change will be lessened. Staff must be given opportunities to change the way they think and interact. This transformation can't be accomplished by increased training, or through command-and-control management approaches. No one person, including a highly charismatic director, can train or command other people to alter their attitudes, beliefs, skills, capabilities, perceptions, or level of commitment.

It should also be abundantly clear by now that staff will react quite differently to the prospect of change. It is almost guaranteed that some staff will embrace the proposal(s) with enthusiasm, while others will object to proposals and find ways to resist them. Since resistance is guaranteed, actions should be taken whenever possible to reduce the level of resistance, and to figure out how to best manage the resistance that does surface.

While there are no panaceas when it comes to managing resistance, there are some general principles that can be applied to the preparation and implementation of organizational change. The first group focuses on steps that can be taken in the planning phase. The second group focuses more sharply on actions and behaviors that should occur once implementation begins. But the advice applies equally to planning and implementation.[10]

Planning Phase Guidelines

- *Allow time for staff to acknowledge and celebrate past accomplishments—* Some staff need time and an opportunity to separate themselves from the present system because they feel a special attachment for the status quo. The prospect of change can provoke feelings of loss that are not totally different from experiencing a death in the family. These staff members may need time to mourn the old system or familiar way of doing things. It is during this period that one is likely to hear stories about the "good old days." I have overheard reference librarians reminiscing about the good old days of reference as remote reference services displace face-to-face reference service.

  It is also easier for some staff to accept a change if their past accomplishments are publicly acknowledged. For example, when libraries adopted OCLC cataloging, how many library directors went out of their way to celebrate the many contributions of their catalogers who had been responsible for most of the library's original cataloging? Very few, if any. Too many directors simply announced that the library was going to adopt OCLC cataloging in order to increase productivity and to reduce costs. Perfectly sensible from a managerial perspective, but that approach was not necessarily the best tactic for achieving a buy-in from the cataloging staff.

- *Draw a clear picture about the proposed changes*—The vision of what is to be achieved should be clearly drawn. It is important to identify the future the library wishes to achieve before even beginning a planning process. Staff members will want to know where they are headed and what will be different. It is very difficult to plan if one doesn't have clear picture of what is expected.[11]

- *Address unspoken issues*—No vision, no matter how exciting and challenging, will cause existing organizational baggage to disappear. For example, if staff feel that management plays favorites and that salaries are inequitable or that internal communications stink, a new vision will not cause such grievances to disappear. Metaphorically speaking, this baggage will have to be dragged into the future. If such unaddressed issues exist, they should be addressed as part of the planning process, particularly if there is a chance that their continued existence could jeopardize the proposed change effort.

- *Share information about the planned changes*—Everybody needs to be in the communications loop. It is often said that there is no such thing as bad information; what is bad is the absence of information. The goal should be to strive for an even playing field so that staff members at all levels are informed about decisions. We will be successful when staff members are able to share perspectives and are able to see their organization through the eyes of others.

- *Provide opportunities for staff to contribute their ideas*—It is often pointed out that "people do not resist change; people resist being changed." Staff members who are actively involved in the planning of a change are more likely to accept the change once implemented. It is equally true that staff members who are given a role in shaping the work environment are more likely to support and sustain the environment than those who are not involved.

- *Allow sufficient time to explore options, compare alternatives, and consider consequences*—If staff are really involved in the planning process, there should be opportunities to explore options and alternative approaches, and to consider possible consequences. If management favors a top-down approach, it is very likely that management had, but didn't share, its vision of the future with staff. In such instances there will be a temptation on the part of management to act too quickly without considering options, alternative approaches, or consequences.

- *Remember the real experts are your own staff*—It's best to keep in mind that the real experts are your own staff, not consultants who come and go. It is management's challenge and responsibility to find ways to tap into that knowledge.

- *Seek to avoid win-lose situations*—This might seem to be an obvious observation, but too often one finds that individuals or groups of staff are intentionally or unintentionally backed into a corner. For example, making a job assignment that management knows a staff member won't like, or giving the person a job he/she is really only marginally qualified to perform. Keep in mind that people who feel that they are being backed into a no-win situation can find ingenious ways to block or resist a change.

- *Be honest with staff*—If job reassignments or even layoffs are likely out-comes of a change process, affected staff members need to be told directly; they do not need to find out the unpleasant news through the grapevine. The rumor mill can quickly create a negative climate if the personnel changes are linked to a new service or workflow. One enlightened approach is to make every possible effort to create attractive alternative career paths for staff. If staff reductions are necessary, try to do it through attrition: resignations, transfers, and retirements, whenever possible.

- *Encourage staff and reinforce your belief in their success*—Management, as noted earlier, has a broader view of what the future holds because it has access to more information than does the front-line staff. Keep in mind that in the absence of information some staff will become discouraged and/or begin to feel overwhelmed. It is important for management to encourage staff and periodically reinforce to them the belief that they will be success-ful. Management would be wise to engage occasionally in old-fashioned cheerleading and, figuratively speaking, handholding.

Implementation Phase Guidelines

- *Leaders need to be clear about their own commitment*—Leaders through-out the organization must clearly stake out and relentlessly make clear what they want the organization to become. If a leader lacks the courage to live the change, how can he/she expect others to follow?

- *Break down the "big" changes into a series of smaller steps*—There is a tendency to take on too much when we plan for changes. For many staff mem-bers a more effective approach is to break down "big" changes into a series of smaller changes in order to make the path ahead seem less daunting. A series of smaller changes can often produce the big change that is desired.

- *Increase staff involvement*—Continually strive to increase the number of staff members who are directly involved with and responsible for new activi-ties. The goal is to create a "we" attitude and a cohesive group. The sooner staff members are directly involved in the process, the sooner they are likely to get on board.

- *Give advance warning of new job requirements; avoid unpleasant last-minute surprises*—It should become pretty clear early in the change process which jobs will be affected. In most cases, staff members who are directly involved with the change process will be in a better position to know what behavioral changes and skills will be required in the new environment. This information needs to be widely shared with staff so that they can begin to think about what will be expected of them in the new working environment.

- ***Tell staff how their roles and jobs contribute to the goals of the organization***—There is nothing more frustrating for a staff member than not understanding how his/her job will be affected by the changes, and/or how it will contribute to the organization's goals and objectives. Every person wants to feel that his or her work contributes to the overall picture. If one can't explain how a job contributes, then the person involved is likely to ask the question: "Why should I go through the agony of learning new behaviors and skills if I'm not making a meaningful contribution to the organization?" Or maybe an even more pointed question is in order: "Why is this job being done at all?"

- ***Provide staff with the tools they will need ahead of time***—Make sure that staff have the information and training they will require before they are asked to perform new jobs. They also need to know the job requirements and the organization's expectations. Again, no surprises. It is rare for someone to do poor work deliberately, but it is common for a person to perform a job inefficiently without realizing it. Whenever this occurs, a principal share of the burden should fall not on the staff worker, but on the person(s) responsible for the job's design and for training. Poor training that leads to poor performance is bound to make the staff workers involved feel ill at ease; no amount of assurances to the contrary is going to assuage completely a staff worker's basic insecurity.

- ***Collaboration entails special challenges***—Mastering new skills and behaviors that depend on collaboration with other staff workers in a unit is more difficult to achieve than when people are able to rely solely on themselves. Moreover, collaborative projects that extend across unit or organizational boundaries are more difficult to achieve than collaborations within such boundaries. Mastering new skills and behaviors with staff one has not worked with or barely knows can prove particularly challenging. And, if the organizational cultures of the two units or organizations are different, problems are likely to arise. For example, a collaborative reference project in which one library's staff believes that questions must be answered by professionals, trying to work with a second library that believes support staff can be used in the reference process.

- ***Focus on the work staff do and not on the decision-making authority***—What is most important is the work that needs to be done. Informed and trained staff workers will often be motivated to take responsibility for change. If attention gets diverted to debates about decision-making authority, the focus on work can get lost in the shuffle as key staff jockey for power.

- ***Extrinsic or intrinsic rewards are important***—Be sure to reward the innovators and pioneers and be sure that people feel compensated for the extra time and efforts that are required. Most workers will decide to go along with the changes, some will drag their feet, but a few staff are likely to make special efforts to help achieve the goals, so it is important to find ways to acknowledge their contributions. It is also worthwhile noting that a change effort is likely to identify the next generation of staff leaders. I've seen this happen time and time again. What happens is that a staff member who has been considered just another member of the staff steps forward when the opportunity arises and excels beyond anyone's expectations.

- ***Celebrate "first steps" or milestones of progress along the way***—Design the implementation process so that there will be some early successes to celebrate. It is important for a number of reasons to celebrate progress. Progress helps to create credibility for management, and helps to generate momentum for the new activities being introduced. Many staff will not be directly involved with the actual change-related initiatives, so they might not know what is happening. Staff members will want to know what progress is being made, particularly if they were involved with the planning for the changes.

Final Thoughts

As has been pointed out, individuals and groups react differently when confronted with the prospect of change. As most readers have already discovered, some staff workers are reluctant to participate in any form of time, motion, or cost studies simply because they do not wish to be placed under close scrutiny. They would prefer to be at the eyepiece rather than the objective end of the microscope. However, that doesn't mean their reluctance to engage in studies necessarily portends that they as individuals will resist changes. I believe the goal of every manager should be to give each person in the organization an opportunity to contribute and to come aboard "the new train as it leaves the station." And, if management has made every effort to explain what is being done and has provided opportunities for staff to contribute ideas, most employees will board the train and be willing to accept, if not embrace, the new system, workflow, or even a new service.

Notes

1. Sara Fine, "Change and Resistance: The Cost/Benefit Factor," *The Bottom Line* 5, no. 1 (Spring 1991): 18-23.

2. A stakeholder is defined as anyone, whether an individual or an organization, who feels he/she/it have/has a stake in the outcome of the change.

3. Ironically the volumes were never moved back to the open shelves because we all forgot about the issue as we were suddenly confronted with a nasty budget crisis that required us to prune our list of periodical subscriptions. A faculty friend asked me about the transferred periodicals about six months later, and I told him I assumed that they had been transferred. Much to my chagrin, I learned that nothing had happened because all hands had been involved with the periodical cutbacks. When I told my faculty friend the situation, he smiled and went about his way. Nothing more was ever said.

4. Katherine D. Myers and Linda K. Kirby, *Introduction to Type ® Dynamics and Development; Exploring the Next Level of Type* (Palo Alto, Calif.: Consulting Psychologists Press, 1994).

5. There have been several articles that have addressed the use of MBTI® techniques in libraries. To gain a flavor of the technique, I suggest consulting Mary Jane Scherdin, "Vive la Différence: Exploring Librarian Personality Types Using the MBTI®," in *Discovering Librarians: Profiles of a Profession,* ed. Mary Jane Scherdin (Chicago: Association of College and Research Libraries, 1994): 125-58.

6. Sandra Krebs Hirsh, *MBTI® Team Building Program* (San Diego: Consulting Psychologists Press, 1992).

7. Maureen Sullivan, "Using the MBTI® for Team Building," in *Discovering Librarians: Profiles of a Profession*, ed. Mary Jane Scherdin (Chicago: Association of College and Research Libraries, 1994): 173-80.

8. Everett Rogers, *Diffusion of Innovations* (New York: Free Press, 2003), 344.

9. This chart is based on information from Everett Rogers, *Diffusion of Innovations*, 281.

10. The literature of organizational change is extremely diverse. At one end of the spectrum is the classic work of Rosabeth Moss Kanter, *The Change Masters: Innovations for Productivity in the American Corporation* (New York: Simon and Schuster, 1983). At the other end are those texts that provide practical advice on how to implement organizational changes. *See* Murray Dalziel, *Changing Ways: A Practical Tool for Implementing Change Within Organizations* (New York: American Management Association, 1988). There are also many books that focus on planning strategies for introducing large-scale organizational change. Two such volumes are: *The Change Handbook: Group Methods for Shaping the Future,* ed. Peggy Holman and Tom Devane (San Francisco: Berrett-Koehler Publishers, 1999), and Dannemiller Tyson Associates, *Whole-Scale Change: Unleashing the Magic in Organizations* (San Francisco: Berrett-Koehler, 2000).

11. One excellent way to identify the futures that libraries prefer is to engage in Preferred Futuring. This process can also be used as a first step in a strategic planning process. *See* Lawrence L. Lippitt, *Preferred Futuring: Envision the Future You Want and Unleash the Energy to Get There* (San Francisco: Berrett-Koehler, 1998).

Index

About the Author

Richard M. Dougherty is a former professor of Information and Director of Libraries at the University of Michigan. He also served as University Librarian at the University of California at Berkeley, in administrative positions in the libraries at the Universities of Colorado and North Carolina at Chapel Hill. Since the early 1990s he has served as a consultant to numerous libraries that were striving to introduce organizational change and conducted many workshops on change management (www.rmdassociates.com). Most recently Dougherty has worked with the College of DuPage's Instructional Technology Division to organize and co-host live teleconferences, "Library Challenges and Opportunities," which has kept him current with new developments.

Dougherty has also authored numerous monographs and articles. He served as editor of *College and Research Libraries* for 5 years and then, with considerable help from his wife and partner, Ann, founded, published, and edited *the Journal of Academic Librarianship* (1975) and *Library Issues: Briefings for Faculty and Administrators* (1980) for over 20 years. Today, Ann is still editor of *Library Issues*.

Dougherty currently resides in Ann Arbor, Michigan and has a quiet cottage in Mackinaw City where he does most of his writing while watching boats traverse the Great Lakes. During the summer months he spends a great deal of time on local golf courses. He is quick to admit that golf can be even more difficult than academic administration, but he persists in trying to hit fairways and greens.